MIGRATION, MINORITIES AND CITIZENSHIP

General Editors: Zig Layton-Henry, *Professor of Politics, University of Warwick*; and Danièle Joly, *Director, Centre for Research in Ethnic Relations, University of Warwick*

This series has been developed to promote books on a wide range of topics concerned with migration and settlement, immigration policy, refugees, the integration and engagement of minorities, dimensions of social exclusion, racism and xenophobia, ethnic mobilization, ethnicity and nationalism. The focus of the series is multidisciplinary and international. The series publishes both theoretical and empirical works based on original research. Priority is given to single-authored books but edited books of high quality are considered.

Titles include:

Muhammad Anwar, Patrick Roach and Ranjit Sondhi (*editors*)
FROM LEGISLATION TO INTEGRATION?
Twenty-two Years of the Race Relations Act 1976

Naomi Carmon (*editor*)
IMMIGRATION AND INTEGRATION IN POST-INDUSTRIAL SOCIETIES
Theoretical Analysis and Policy-Related Research

Adrian Favell
PHILOSOPHIES OF INTEGRATION
Immigration and the Idea of Citizenship in France and Britain

Simon Holdaway and Anne-Marie Barron
RESIGNERS? THE EXPERIENCE OF BLACK AND ASIAN POLICE OFFICERS

Danièle Joly
HAVEN OR HELL?
Asylum Policies and Refugees in Europe

SCAPEGOATS AND SOCIAL ACTORS
The Exclusion and Integration of Minorities in Western and Eastern Europe

Jørgen S. Nielsen
TOWARDS A EUROPEAN ISLAM

John Rex
ETHNIC MINORITIES IN THE MODERN NATION STATE
Working Papers in the Theory of Multiculturalism and Political
Integration

Carl-Ulrik Schierup (*editor*)
SCRAMBLE FOR THE BALKANS
Nationalism, Globalism and the Political Economy of Reconstruction

Steven Vertovec and Ceri Peach (*editors*)
ISLAM IN EUROPE
The Politics of Religion and Community

Östen Wahlbeck
KURDISH DIASPORAS
A Comparative Study of Kurdish Refugee Communities

John Wrench, Andrea Rea and Nouria Ouali (*editors*)
MIGRANTS, ETHNIC MINORITIES AND THE LABOUR MARKET
Integration and Exclusion in Europe

Migrants, Ethnic Minorities and the Labour Market

Integration and Exclusion in Europe

Edited by

John Wrench
Senior Researcher
Danish Centre for Migration and Ethnic Studies
University of Southern Denmark

Andrea Rea
Researcher
Centre de Sociologie Politique
Institut de Sociologie
Université Libre de Bruxelles

and

Nouria Ouali
Researcher
Centre de Sociologie du Travail, de l'Emploi et de la Formation
Institut de Sociologie
Université Libre de Bruxelles

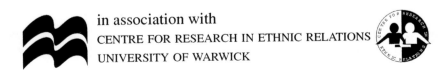

in association with
CENTRE FOR RESEARCH IN ETHNIC RELATIONS
UNIVERSITY OF WARWICK

First published in Great Britain 1999 by
MACMILLAN PRESS LTD
Houndmills, Basingstoke, Hampshire RG21 6XS and London
Companies and representatives throughout the world

A catalogue record for this book is available from the British Library.

ISBN 0–333–68279–3

First published in the United States of America 1999 by
ST. MARTIN'S PRESS, INC.,
Scholarly and Reference Division,
175 Fifth Avenue, New York, N.Y. 10010

ISBN 0–312–22187–8

Library of Congress Cataloging-in-Publication Data
Migrants, ethnic minorities and the labour market : integration and
exclusion in Europe / edited by John Wrench, Andrea Rea, Nouria
Ouali.
    p.   cm. — (Migration, minorities, and citizenship)
"In association with Centre for Research in Ethnic Relations,
University of Warwick."
Includes bibliographical references and index.
ISBN 0–312–22187–8 (cloth)
1. Alien labor—Europe, Western.   2. Discrimination in employment–
–Europe, Western.   3. Europe, Western—Emigration and immigration.
I. Wrench, John.   II. Rea, Andrea.   III. Ouali, Nouria.   IV. Series.
HD8378.5.A2M537   1999
331.13'3094—dc21   99–11215
                                                         CIP

Selection, editorial matter, Preface and Introduction © John Wrench, Andrea Rea and
Nouria Ouali 1999
Chapter 2 © Nouria Ouali and Andrea Rea 1999
Chapters 4 and 13 © John Wrench 1999
Chapters 3, 5–12 © Macmillan Press Ltd 1999

This book is printed on paper suitable for recycling and made from fully managed and
sustained forest sources.

10   9   8   7   6   5   4   3   2   1
08   07   06   05   04   03   02   01   00   99

Printed and bound in Great Britain by
Antony Rowe Ltd, Chippenham, Wiltshire

Contents

List of Tables and Figures   vii

Preface   viii

Notes on the Contributors   ix

1   Introduction: Discrimination and Diversity   1
     Andrea Rea, John Wrench and Nouria Ouali

I   Internal Processes

2   Young Migrants in the Belgian Labour Market:
     Integration, Discrimination and Exclusion   21
     Nouria Ouali and Andrea Rea

3   Workers of Migrant Origin in Germany:
     Forms of Discrimination in the Labour Market and
     at the Workplace   35
     Nora Räthzel

4   From School to the Labour Market in Britain:
     the Qualitative Exposure of Structures of Exclusion   54
     John Wrench, Edgar Hassan and Tarek Qureshi

5   Foreigners and Immigrants in the French Labour Market:
     Structural Inequality and Discrimination   72
     François Vourc'h, Véronique De Rudder and Maryse Tripier

6   Migrants and Ethnic Minorities in the Netherlands:
     Discrimination in Access to Employment   93
     Mitzi Gras and Frank Bovenkerk

7   The Labour Market for Immigrant Women in Sweden:
     Marginalised Women in Low-valued Jobs   108
     Wuokko Knocke

8   Young People of Foreign Origin Born in Switzerland:
     Between Invisibility and Diversity   132
     Francesca Poglia Mileti

II   New Flows

 9   Seasonal Work in Italy: Flexibility and Regularisation   155
     Giovanna Campani and Francesco Carchedi

10   Immigrants in Spain: From Institutional Discrimination
     to Labour Market Segmentation   174
     Lorenzo Cachón

11   Refugee Care in Sweden: the Problems of Unemployment
     and anti-Discrimination policies   195
     Maritta Soininen

III   Responses and Implications

12   Migratory Movements: the Position, the Outlook.
     Charting a Theory and Practice for Trade Unions   219
     Albert Martens

13   Employers and anti-Discrimination Measures in Europe:
     Good Practice and Bad Faith   229
     John Wrench

Bibliography   252

Subject Index   267

Name Index   272

List of Tables and Figures

Table 3.1	Number and percentage of migrant population in the workforce (Germany, 1993)	38
Table 3.2	Distribution of migrant population in different sectors of employment (West Germany)	39
Table 3.3	Job levels and professions	41
Table 7.1	Relative activity rates for women by age and citizenship, 1981	114
Table 7.2	Unemployment by age and citizenship	118
Table 7.3	Relative unemployment figures by citizenship	118
Table 7.4	The ten most common occupations among foreign-born and Swedish women	120
Table 10.1	Origin of legal foreign residents in Spain (1983 and 1993)	176
Table 10.2	Estimated number of non-EU immigrant workers for the three segments proposed (1993)	188
Table 10.3	The 15 branches of productive activities with a larger relative number of non-EU, 'settled' and 'precarious' immigrant workers	190
Figure 12.1	Overview of union strategies and their appearance in time	226

Preface

The genesis of this book lies in the European Union's COST (A2) Migration initiative. Most of the contributors to this volume are specialists in the field of migration and the labour market in Europe who were brought together as members of the network 'The Labour Market, Ethnic Minorities and Citizenship' (1994–95), which operated under this particular EU initiative.

An edited volume of international papers, many of which were first written in languages other than English, takes time to process, and we are aware that some of the detail in a few of the papers in this volume may have been superseded by, for example, developments in legislation since they were first collected together. Nevertheless, we feel that the broad principles and conclusions which characterise this discussion remain as valid as they ever were.

The editors would like to thank the Danish Centre for Migration and Ethnic Studies for the allocation of time and resources which made it possible for this volume to be produced. Grateful thanks are also due to Sheila Kirby of Esbjerg and Jacqueline Cliquet of the Université Libre de Bruxelles.

John Wrench, Andrea Rea, Nouria Ouali

Notes on the Contributors

Frank Bovenkerk is Professor of Criminology at the Willem Pompe Institute for Criminal Sciences, University of Utrecht. He has a long-standing record of research and publication on migration, discrimination and ethnic studies. At present his main research focus is on organised crime, and on ethnicity and delinquency. He has recently co-authored *The Nature of Organised Crime in the Netherlands* (1998) and *De Maffia van Turkije* (forthcoming, with Yucel Yesilgoz).

Lorenzo Cachón is Professor of Sociology at the Universidad Complutense de Madrid. He has researched and published on aspects of immigration, local development and other labour market problems, as well as on employment and training policies. Publications include: *Social Mobility or Trajectories of Class?* (1989), *Preventing Racism at the Workplace: Spain* (1995), *Policies for Inserting Young People into EU Labour Markets* (1997) and *New Sources of Employment in Spain* (1998).

Giovanna Campani works at the Dipartimento di Scienze dell'Educazione, Università degli Studi di Firenze. Her research interests include immigrant women in the labour market, family networks and racism. Recent publications include *Immigration and Racism in Italy* (*Ethnic and Racial Studies*, 1993), *Preventing Racism at the Workplace – Italy* (1995, with F. Carchedi, G. Mottura and E. Pugliese) and *Migranti, rifugiati e nomadi dai Balcani* (Migrants, Refugees and Gypsies from the Balkans) (edited with F. Carchedi and G. Mottura).

Francesco Carchedi is the President of PARSEC (Research and Social Intervention) in Rome. He has published extensively on immigration in Italy, with particular reference to work, patterns of settlement, and utilisation of social services and training. Recent publications include *Migranti, rifugiati e nomadi dai Balcani* (Migrants, Refugees and Gypsies from the Balkans) (edited with G. Campani and G. Mottura) and 'The Chinese Presence in Italy: Dimensions and Structural characteristics' (with M. Ferri) in G. Benton and F. Pieke *The Chinese in Europe* (1998).

Véronique De Rudder is a CNRS researcher attached to URMIS (Unité de Recherche: Migrations et Société). She has recently researched and published on the subject of immigrants in the French labour market for two international projects coordinated by the European Foundation for the Improvement of Living and Working Conditions. She is a member of the editorial committee of 'Vocabulaire historique et critique des relations inter-ethniques' and Director of the Research Group 'Migrations internationales et relations inter-ethniques' of the CNRS.

Mitzi Gras studied cultural anthropology and medical biology at the University of Utrecht, and then worked at the Willem Pompe Institute for Criminal Sciences in Utrecht, where she researched discrimination against ethnic minorities in the Dutch labour market, within a programme of the International Labour Organisation. She is currently affiliated to the Municipal Health Service in Amsterdam as a researcher on HIV/AIDS and sexual behaviour among ethnic groups in the Netherlands.

Edgar Hassan is a researcher with the School of Education at the Open University, Milton Keynes, and an Associate Fellow of the Centre for Research in Ethnic Relations, University of Warwick. His research has focused primarily on aspects of youth, and he is a founder member and activist in a multicultural youth centre. Publications include *Ambition and Marginalisation: a Qualitative Study of Under-achieving Young Men of Afro-Caribbean Origin* (1996, with John Wrench).

Wuokko Knocke is a sociologist and senior researcher at the National Institute for Working Life, Stockholm. Her research has principally focused on the work life and labour market situation of immigrants, with particular reference to issues related to gender, class and ethnicity, and the analysis of the mechanisms and processes of marginalisation. Recent publications include *Gender, Ethnicity and Technological Change* (1994) and *Migrant and Ethnic Minority Women: the Effects of Gender Neutral Legislation in the European Union* (1997).

Albert Martens is Professor in the Sociology of Industrial Relations at the University of Leuven. He has researched and published on aspects of migrant workers, equal opportunities and housing problems. Recent publications include *Case Studies of Good Practice for the Prevention of Racial Discrimination and Xenophobia and the Promotion of Equal Treatment at the Workplace – Belgium* (1997, with K. Sette) and *La polarisation sociale des villes européenes* (1997, with M. Vervaeke).

Nouria Ouali is a sociologist and researcher at the Centre de Sociologie du Travail, de l'Emploi et de la Formation at the Université Libre de

Bruxelles. She is member of the Study Group on Ethnicity, Racism, Migration and Exclusion. Her research interests include immigrant women in the labour market and immigration and media. Recent publications include *Les télévisions francophones et l'image des femmes immigrées* (*Annuaire de l'Afrique du Nord*, 1995), *Télévision et immigration: un enjeu pour l'intégration et la lutte contre le racisme* (*Migration Sociétés*, 1997) and 'Emploi: de la discrimination à l'égalité de traitement?', in *La Belgique et ses étrangers. Les politiques manquées*, 1997).

Francesca Poglia Mileti is an assistant at the Institute of Sociology, University of Neuchâtel. Her research interests are in aspects of identity, migration and ethnic relations in an international perspective. Publications include *Pratiques, stratégies et représentations de jeunes Italiens, Espagnols et Portugais au chômage vivant dans le canton de Neuchâtel* (1995) and *Le concept d'immigré: référent identitaire et enjeu social, perception des notions d'immigré et d'immigré de deuxième génération par une population migrante* (in press).

Tareq Qureshi is Policy Officer with the Centre for Policy on Ageing, London. He was previously employed as a research fellow at the Centre for Research in Ethnic Relations, University of Warwick, and before that worked on several research projects covering the areas of East London, including a study on the effectiveness of anti-harassment procedures in combating racial violence on council housing estates. Recent publications include *Higher Horizons: a Qualitative Study of Young Men of Bangladeshi Origin* (1996, with John Wrench).

Andrea Rea is a researcher at the Centre de Sociologie Politique, and coordinator of the Study Group on Ethicity, Racism, Migration and Exclusion, at the Université Libre de Bruxelles. He has researched and published for many years on questions of the labour market, education and citizenship with regard to the immigrant population in Belgium. He is author of *La Société en Miettes: Epreuves et enjeux de l'exclusion* (1997), editor of *Immigration et Racisme en Europe* (1998) and co-editor (with Pascal Delwit and Jean-Michel De Waele) of *L'extrême droite en France et en Belgique* (1998).

Nora Räthzel is a researcher at the Institute for Social Sciences, University of Bremen. Her main fields of research are racism, gender and ethnic relations in relation to questions of the nation, and youth. Publications include *Nationale Identitaeten durch Konstruktionen des Anderen* (1997) and

Die Schwierigkeit, nicht rassistisch zu sein (1994, with Annita Kalpaka). She is a member of the editorial board of the journals *Das Argument* and *Social Identities*.

Maritta Soininen is a lecturer at the Department of Political Science, University of Stockholm. Her main research interests have been in the area of immigrant and refugee questions, including an examination of the political and administrative aspects of the Swedish Refugee Reception Programme in terms of local policy implementation. She has also focused on the political participation of immigrants and is co-author of 'Immigrants in the Political Process' in *Scandinavian Political Studies* (1998, No. 1).

Maryse Tripier is Professor of Sociology at the University of Paris 7, Denis Diderot. She is the present director of URMIS (Unité de Recherche: Migrations et Société), linked to the CNRS. She has researched and published on the general theme of immigrants in the French working class and the attitudes of trade unions. Recent publications include *The Prevention of Racism at the Workplace in France* (1995, with V. De Rudder and F. Vourc'h) and *Jeunes Issus de l'Immigration de l'École à l'Emploi* (1997, with F. Aubert and F. Vourc'h).

François Vourc'h is a sociologist and CNRS researcher attached to URMIS (Unité de Recherche: Migrations et Société – Universités Paris 7 and Paris 8). He has recently researched and published on the subject of immigrants in the French labour market for two EU projects. Recent publications include *Case Studies of Good Practice for the Prevention of Racial Discrimination and Xenophobia and the Promotion of Equal Treatment at the Workplace – France* (1997, with V. De Rudder and C. Poiret) and *Jeunes Issus de l'Immigration de l'École à l'Emploi* (1997, with F. Aubert and M. Tripier).

John Wrench is Senior Researcher at the Danish Centre for Migration and Ethnic Studies, University of Southern Denmark, and an Associate Fellow of the Centre for Research in Ethnic Relations, University of Warwick. He has researched and published widely on aspects of racism and the labour market, equal opportunities and employment, and trade unions. Recent publications include *Racism and Migration in Western Europe* (1993, edited with J. Solomos) and *Preventing Racism at the Workplace: A Report on 16 European Countries* (1996).

1 Introduction: Discrimination and Diversity

Andrea Rea, John Wrench and Nouria Ouali

During the past decade European countries have registered important changes in immigration experiences and in national migration policies which have had various consequences for the labour market. Five major developments have occurred. First, in countries where the first large-scale, postwar migrations took place (Germany, the Netherlands, Belgium and France), policies to encourage foreign residents to return to their country of origin were abandoned in the 1980s. Second, except for Ireland where the migration balance is still negative, all EU member states are now immigration countries, with the southern European countries experiencing migratory flows from Africa and Asia. Third, the number of asylum-seekers and refugees, notably from the former Yugoslavia, Africa and Asia, increased dramatically over this period (Salt 1992). Fourth, the collapse of the communist regimes, the conclusion of cooperation agreements between EU countries and some countries of Central Europe (Poland, Hungary, the Czech and Slovak Republics) and their future membership of the European Union have induced forms of 'pendulum migration' (De Wenden and Tanguy 1995). Fifth, the European states confronted with the new migration flows have attempted to control them according to an increasingly repressive 'law and order' or '*sécuritaire*' logic (Bigo 1996).

In the early 1970s the organised postwar recruitment of immigrant, largely manual workers, by European countries came to an end. Such workers became increasingly difficult to see as temporary guestworkers, even though politicians in some countries still prefer to see them as such. Immigrant groups have been transformed into settled ethnic minority communities. The existence of something called 'the second generation' is now recognised in countries that had not planned for such a phenomenon. The context they face is unsympathetic in new ways. For example, European countries have been facing major social and economic restructuring processes, especially in the industrial sector, as well as massive unemployment, limitations on workers' rights and, consequently, contraction of the social citizenship previously guaranteed by these states. At the same time, despite the closing of their borders in the early 1970s by countries with long traditions of immigration, new migration flows into Europe started again during the 1980s, largely as a result of family reunions, an increase in asylum-seekers and the arrival of undocumented workers from Eastern and Southern countries. Partly because of the pressure on the labour market induced by new immigrants, the original migrants and their descendants are encountering increasing ethnic discrimination as a new reality.

This book examines issues of discrimination and exclusion in the labour market in Western Europe, in relation to both types of migration: first, the settled ethnic minority communities whose existence results from a previous generation of migrants, including their children who were born and educated in a European country; and second, the 'new' migrants who continue to enter despite high levels of unemployment in the receiving countries. There are important implications for the labour market with regard to both these groups.

In Part I we focus on the experiences of the more established second, and third, generations of postwar migrant descent, and issues relevant to them. As many essays in this volume show, there are similarities in this new generation across many European countries. In terms of aspirations, they do not want to be restricted to the same limited fields of employment as were their parents; in terms of experience, they are facing unemployment, or insecure, unstable employment. The problems they face are seen to stem from several different sources. In some countries there is an ideological problem, namely that important sectors of opinion persist in the assumption that these people remain a transient community with their sights set on a return to their 'homeland'. Such a view fails to allow that they have the employment rights and expectations of citizens. Another ideological problem is the refusal to acknowledge the existence of racial or ethnic discrimination and its implications for whole sections of people in their society. Some essays in the first part of this volume address these ideological issues; others in various ways demonstrate the operation of processes of exclusion and their implications for young ethnic minorities and people of migrant descent in different countries. In Part II we look at issues relating to 'new' migrants, including seasonal and undocumented workers in countries of Southern Europe, and refugees in the North. In the final part we address some of the implications of issues raised in the first two parts for trade unions and employers in Europe.

PROBLEMS OF COMPARISON IN DIFFERENT
EUROPEAN COUNTRIES

When looking at these issues across different national boundaries in Europe we must be aware of the important differences that exist both in the concepts and terminology used to describe the circumstances of migrants and ethnic minorities and in the history of major policy responses to immigration and ethnic diversity (Castles 1995; Wrench 1996). The first issue to clarify is that of terminology. For example, in the UK the words 'migrant' or 'immigrant' are rarely used. Common usage employs the term 'ethnic minorities', and sometimes 'black' is employed to cover all non-white minorities. In the UK most ethnic minority residents are full British citizens; therefore, to talk of them as 'foreigners' is incorrect. In the Netherlands the concept 'ethnic minorities', as used in government documents, refers to ethnic groups that are target groups of the Dutch minorities policy, and includes non-nationals as well as nationals. Another term used in the Netherlands is that of 'allochtones' (non-indigenous); this refers to people of a different socio-cultural origin coming from a foreign country, whatever their current nationality.

Although the term 'ethnic minorities' is used in the UK and the Netherlands, in many other countries the use of this term would be inappropriate. In Greece, Spain, Italy and Portugal, the more recent groups of migrant workers are generally referred to as 'immigrants' or 'foreign workers', along with more specific national usages such as 'extracommunautari' in Italy or more generally extra-European Union. In Scandinavia the word 'immigrant' is commonly used. Sweden has traditionally attempted to avoid the creation of 'ethnic minorities', which have been seen as contrary to the aims and spirit of the country's integration policy, and the Danish definition of an ethnic minority is a group of people indigenous to Denmark but with close cultural and linguistic links to another nation. For the German government Turks and other immigrant groups are not recognised as constituting an 'ethnic minority'; official German usage is likely to employ the term 'foreigner' (Ausländer). Furthermore, the use of 'ethnic minority' is inappropriate in Germany, not only because of its very specific official usage, but, more importantly, because populations of migrant origin in Germany do not define themselves as 'ethnic minorities'. Whenever they voice their demands in public, most of their organisations stress their members' status as immigrants (Einwanderer). This has to be understood as a conscious reaction against the government's position that Germany is not a country of immigration (Räthzel 1995). It is likely that, in the future, the term 'migrant', which is increasingly used by social scientists and also in public discourse, will replace the term 'Ausländer', as blanket use of the term 'Ausländer' becomes discredited.

Another contrast in terminology usage between the UK and Germany is the idiosyncratic British use of the word 'race' or 'racial' minorities. 'Race' is usually used in the UK as a social construct, with no correspondence to any biological reality. Many British writers prefer to use the term in inverted commas to emphasise this point. However, whereas in the UK and US it is largely accepted that 'races' are a social construction and not a biological fact, this qualification would still not legitimate its use in Germany, where 'race' has a clear biological meaning and is therefore hardly ever used (except by self-confessed racists). In France the term 'immigrant' (immigré) is the category most favoured by popular usage. Both French nationals and foreigners who may never have actually migrated, including children of 'immigrants', who are themselves French nationals, are routinely classed as 'immigrants'. The concept of 'ethnic minority' is very little used, reflecting the French universalist, republican tradition which does not easily allow for ethnic difference, in contrast with some other Northern European countries (see Vourc'h et al. in this volume). In Belgium, as in France, the term 'immigré' is conventionally used, and is generally restricted to migrant workers from the Maghreb and Turkey. Another term sometimes used in Belgium is 'allochtones' (non-indigenous), which is used in the Netherlands and, by extension, in the Flemish-speaking part of Belgium.

Although there are qualitative differences between the communities described by different terms in different countries, what they have in common in terms of this book is their potential for experiencing exclusion through ethnic or 'racial' discrimination. Each country uses its own appropriate teminology regarding the making of the state as an 'imagined community' (Anderson 1983) to identify the 'Other' and to designate 'outsiders'. Moreover, the construction of a 'European identity' inevitably involves a pattern of exclusion of the 'Other', whether they be 'blacks', 'immigrés' or 'Ausländer' (Miles 1993). There are also national differences in the usage and understanding of concepts of discrimination and equal opportunities. In some countries the acceptance of a broad definition of 'discrimination' allows for measures that tackle indirect, institutional or unintentional discrimination. In others, avoiding discrimination is seen more narrowly as simply paying equal wages for equal work. In countries of Southern Europe, tackling discrimination is likely to be seen as including measures to alleviate the conditions of migrants who are deliberately included in highly exploitative or illegal work, such as campaigns for the regularisation of illegal workers. (For examples of each, see Wrench et al., Räthzel, and Cachón in this volume.) There are similarly different assumptions about what 'equal opportunities' means in different countries; sometimes these differences are related to differences in the legal status of the groups who form the concern of this volume, as shown in Wrench's concluding essay.

MIGRANTS, NEW GENERATIONS AND DISCRIMINATION

There is now an increasing cohort of 'second-generation' migrants, born and educated in Europe, speaking a European language as a native and often becoming new nationals after naturalisation, for instance. The problems facing this generation are of a different order from those faced by their parents. Often the inferior employment conditions experienced by the first generation was because they migrated precisely to fill these jobs. In some countries, access to jobs may have been restricted in law. This is less likely for second and third generations, who more usually have similar rights to indigenous white workers. However, in many countries, citizenship is still not easy to obtain and many jobs – such as those in the public sector – are not open to foreigners. Even when the 'second generation' are not faced by legal exclusion, they can face exclusion by forces of direct and indirect discrimination. The exclusion experienced by young ethnic minorities reflects a 'paradox of integration'. Whereas their parents often remained relatively 'invisible', separated out in sectors of work where few indigenous people worked, these young people put themselves forward to a much broader range of occupations, thereby putting themselves in positions where they are more likely to encounter racism and discrimination.

The evidence quoted in many of the chapters in this volume makes it clear that young ethnic minorities and second-generation migrants in Europe are disproportionately concentrated amongst the unemployed and those with only a tenuous hold on regular employment. The conventional 'human capital' approach is inadequate in explaining the labour market exclusion of young migrants. For example, as Räthzel argues in this volume, if the population of migrant origin born and raised in the country has a lower level of qualification than the indigenous population, this in itself could reflect discrimination in the resources made available to that population. Furthermore, it is not necessarily the case that the greater unemployment levels found in one social group reflect simply and directly the lack of human capital skills achieved through education. There is plenty of evidence quoted in this volume that equal qualifications do not lead to equal opportunities for the population of migrant descent. It also works the other way round – a perception of poor opportunities and a lack of fairness in the labour market for ethnic minorities can reduce educational motivation and performance and the desire for vocational training after school.

Evidence on the labour market exclusion of young people of migrant descent has led to speculation as to the long-term social implications of persistent unemployment over two or perhaps three generations, and whether this will lead to something like an 'underclass' in Europe. The concept of underclass signifies a segment of people at the bottom of or beneath the class structure, permanently excluded from the labour market, with no power or stake in the economic system. However, the concept of underclass, as used in the US to represent the black urban poor, is inappropriate in this European context. As Heisler argues, immigrants in advanced industrial European countries, even though they do occupy low socioeconomic positions, come from a tradition of above-average participation in the labour market, and they are not completely disconnected from mainstream social institutions, often creating their own social and political organisations (Heisler 1991). Nevertheless, in the context of shrinking European welfare states and the increasing concentrations of poverty and long-term unemployment, the growing racialisation or ethnicisation of poverty and exclusion will have major implications across most EU member states.

NEW MIGRATION AND THE ILLEGAL LABOUR MARKET

In contrast to the earlier phases of postwar migration, which was largely in response to labour demand at a time of full employment, the new migration continues despite high unemployment. Of course, the demand for 'new' migration is linked to broader structural economic transformation. Sassen (1996: 25) writes:

> the formation of transnational economic processes has itself contributed to a restructuring of labour markets in the advanced receiving economies which in turn has contributed to an expanded demand of immigrant workers. Deregulation and the search for flexibility and low costs have led to a growing casualisation of the employment relation. Through these institutional developments immigrants are being constituted as a low-cost flexible labour supply.

Even after the official cessation of labour migration to countries of the European Union in the mid-1970s, a study of nine EU countries found that all had admitted foreign workers from outside the EU during the 1980s and 1990s (Groenendijk and Hampsink 1996). Admission of foreigners for temporary labour is thus an exception to the restrictive immigration policies in EU countries. Temporary labour migration includes those in seasonal work, asylum-seekers, au pairs, trainees and students (as well as those higher-status cases where someone is subcontracted by his or her company to work abroad). Two major sources of migrant labour are new immigrants admitted for family reunification, and asylum-seekers. Refugees and asylum-seekers can be particularly vulnerable to exploitation on the fringes of legal work. Soininen (this volume) describes the particular problems of refugees in the Swedish labour market, and sets out the reasons for the failure to integrate refugees into employment, including the rather late (1994) introduction of legislation against ethnic discrimination. This she sees as a result of the special corporate character of the Swedish state, where employers' organisations and trade unions are responsible for labour market policy.

In general, the borders between many types of temporary work and illegal work are often vague. The main problem of illegal labour remains in Southern European countries such as Spain, where many migrants are found in 'precarious' work, with low wages and bad working conditions. Cachón (this volume) shows how immigration policies in Spain have helped to create three categories of migrant: settled, precarious and illegal. The last group are employed without a contract or social security benefits, where employers pay lower wages than those stipulated, and where working conditions are worse than those of the corresponding nationals – all practices that violate regulations and union contracts. Campani and Carchedi (this volume) describe the new flows of seasonal workers in Italy who work in the peripheral sectors of the labour market characterised by high exploitation, low wages, high insecurity and extreme 'flexibility' in the use of labour. They also point to the complexity of the picture – although seasonal work is characteristically insecure work at the periphery of the labour market, not all seasonal work is illegal and not all illegal work in Italy is poorly paid or highly exploitative.

However, the issue of the illegal labour market is not restricted to the countries of Southern Europe. Agreement has been reached between EU and four Eastern European neighbours that their nationals no longer need visas to enter relevant member states. Currently, in Germany and Belgium, for example, there is a question of Poles who enter as tourists for short periods and work illegally, and who have the freedom to move (and continue working illegally) in other European countries. This gives them an advantage compared to other established migrant workers who do not have the freedom to move to other countries and to work on (Rea 1995). Furthermore, Campani and Carchedi's chapter shows how citizens of Eastern European countries can be more attractive to employers for (legal) seasonal work in Italy than those from North Africa, because they require less paperwork.

RACIAL AND ETHNIC DISCRIMINATION

In Europe, unlike the experience of the United States, in Canada or in Australia, the social and vocational advancement of migrants has remained rather weak. In many European countries, migrants and their descendants still occupy social and occupational positions similar to those they achieved at their arrival (Zegers de Beijl 1990). The high proportion of migrants and of their descendants working in the manufacturing and industrial sector make them even more vulnerable to economic restructuring and to plant closures. This is one of the reasons why, in Europe, migrants and their descendants are more frequently hit by unemployment. Moreover, in countries characterised by highly restrictive legislation on naturalisation (Germany, Belgium, France, Austria), the status of 'foreigner' given to nationals from non-EU countries excludes them from employment in the public sector. Last but not least, different forms of ethnic discrimination are routinely practised in most European countries. However, the factor of discrimination is often neglected in public discussions on issues such as the high unemployment rate of young people of migrant descent. Whilst factors such as educational and language problems, regional disparities in employment and structural decline in old industries are recognised and accepted as playing their part in social exclusion, there is still a tendency to underplay the routine processes of exclusion of migrants and ethnic minorities through acts of discrimination in daily life (Gras and Bovenkerk, this volume).

The international convention whose object is to prevent racism and racial discrimination is the International Convention on the Elimination of All Forms of Racial Discrimination (ICERD), which was adopted by the UN Assembly on 19 December 1965. Racial discrimination is defined in part one:

> The term 'racial discrimination' shall mean any distinction, exclusion, restriction or preference based on race, colour, descent or national or ethnic origin, which has the purpose or effect of nullifying or impairing the recognition, enjoyment or exercise, on an equal footing, of human rights and fundamental freedoms in the political, economic, social, cultural or any other field of public life. (Banton 1994: 39)

More narrowly, discrimination in employment can be said to occur when migrants or ethnic minorities are accorded inferior treatment in the labour market or in the workplace relative to nationals or whites, despite being comparably qualified in terms of education, experience or other relevant criteria.

EVIDENCE FOR DISCRIMINATION

There are a number of ways that we can gain evidence for the operation of discrimination in the labour market. Some of this evidence is only indirect.

For example, in the US, comparisons of the earnings of black and white men who are equal in terms of education, experience and other relevant factors, show that black men earn about 85–90 per cent of the earnings of their white peers. The gap is assumed to be attributable to discrimination (Burstein 1992: 906). Similar indirect evidence can be found in European countries. Gras and Bovenkerk, and Wrench et al. (this volume) cite research from the Netherlands and the UK indicating that after holding constant other variables, such as education, age, sex and region, discrepancies still exist between the unemployment rates of ethnic minorities and those of native Dutch and British. Soininen, who writes in this volume on the discrimination faced by refugees in Sweden, notes elsewhere that, after other things are held constant, refugees from Eastern Europe and Latin America are found to do better in Sweden than refugees from Iran, Iraq, Africa, the Far East and the Middle East (Soininen and Graham 1995). Ouali and Rea (this volume) use a longitudinal study of young Belgians and descendants of migrant workers in order to show the exclusion that affects ethnic minorities in the context of high unemployment. The study suggests that third country nationals suffer more discrimination than EU nationals, and shows that many of these young people of migrant descent are worse off than their parents were when they first emigrated.

It is also possible to get *direct* evidence of racial discrimination through 'discrimination testing'. This method utilises two or more testers, one belonging to a majority group and the others to minority ethnic groups, all of whom apply for the same jobs. The testers are matched for all the criteria which should normally be taken into account by an employer, such as age, qualifications, experience and schooling. If over a period of repeated testing the applicant from the majority background is systematically preferred to the others, then this points to the operation of discrimination according to ethnic background (see Bovenkerk 1992). Gras and Bovenkerk (this volume) describe how tests that they themselves carried out in the Netherlands demonstrate the operation of ethnic discrimination in recruitment, with the implication that this must go some way to explaining the disadvantaged position of ethnic minorities in the Dutch labour market.

The method of discrimination testing is one of the most important and effective means of demonstrating the existence of the problem area in the face of those who deny that discrimination occurs. Under the ILO programme 'Combating discrimination against (im)migrant workers and ethnic minorities in the world of work' similar research has been promoted in a number of EU countries, including Germany, Spain, Belgium and Denmark. Initial findings show that net discrimination rates of around 35 per cent are not uncommon (see Goldberg et al. 1995; Angel de Prada et al.

1996; Hjarnø and Jensen 1997). Unfortunately, although the method has been used Canada and the US for example, it has still not been widely applied in other EU countries. In some countries – Sweden, for example – the method has been deemed to be in breach of research ethics guidelines (see Banton 1997).

Qualitative research can give an insight into what lies behind the direct labour market exclusion revealed in discrimination testing, and many of the chapters in this volume give examples of this. Sometimes such research can discover open prejudice, directly expressed, despite the fact that employers and personnel managers are unlikely to be completely candid and open to researchers about their actions (Wrench et al.; Gras and Bovenkerk). Others show how managers interviewed say they give preference to 'white' native applicants over migrants and ethnic minorities in the case of equally qualified applicants (Gras and Bovenkerk; Räthzel). Some French employers systematically refused to recruit applicants from North Africa and Africa generally (Vourc'h et al.). Some of these would argue that their actions are determined not by their own prejudices but by the prejudices of others (as did British employers; see Wrench et al.). The subtle strategies used in recruitment procedures in France to avoid 'undesirable' and 'coloured' candidates persist despite the French model of integration which ostensibly forbids the practical recognition of ethnic categories.

Many of these practices of exclusion come under the heading of *indirect* discrimination: this exists with job requirements or recruitment practices which, although applied equally to all, in practice treat members of one ethnic group more favourably than another. Perhaps the most common practice, described by many authors in this volume, is the failure to advertise vacanices and instead rely for recruitment in significant part on the family members of existing employees. Thus, in a largely white workforce, migrants and ethnic minorities are excluded. Recruitment through the family and friends of the company's own personnel was found to lead to indirect discrimination in the Netherlands, France and the UK, as shown in the chapters in this volume by Gras and Bovenkerk, Vourc'h et al., and Wrench et al. This phenomenon has also been reported in Portugal (Carlos and Borges 1995), Denmark (Hjarnø 1995), Germany (Schaub 1993), Finland (Ekholm and Pitkänen 1995) and Sweden (AMS 1991; Paulson 1991). Thus immigrants are at a clear disadvantage if their principal means of finding work is through the employment services.

Although discrimination is unseen by many of its victims, interviews carried out by the researchers in the volume have shown that some are well aware of the extra hurdles they must face in the labour market. Thirty per cent of young foreigners in the Belgian study believed that they had been refused jobs because they are foreign; ethnic minority young people in Britain described how their awareness of discrimination affected their job-seeking behaviour, and immigrants in Germany talked of daily abuses at the workplace, which others failed to take seriously (Ouali and Rea, Wrench et al., and Räthzel, this volume).

Immigrant women have often suffered both 'racial' and gender subordination, and, more than other groups, their problems have remained 'invisible', masked by a combination of cultural and gender stereotypes. Knocke (this volume) shows how immigrant women in Sweden often remain confined to the monotonous and repetitive work in 'male' industrial sectors which they had originally taken on as immigrants many years ago, whilst others had moved on. Räthzel comes to similar conclusions regarding immigrant women in Germany. Although these 'disagreeable' jobs were those for which immigrant women were recruited in the first place, after 30 or 40 years they could have been expected to have moved on. Hence, she concludes, migration theory needs to take more account of racism and discrimination.

The continuing psychological importance of work, and the destructive effects of being excluded from it, are shown in Poglia Mileti's study of second-generation immigrants in Switzerland. The young unemployed Italian, Spanish and Portuguese immigrants she interviewed were less 'racialised' than the non-white immigrants in other European countries. Nevertheless, in common with young immigrants elsewhere, their rate of unemployment was more than twice that of their indigenous peers. Contrary to the views of some contemporary sociologists, who see work as less central to an individual's social identity and self-esteem at a time of 'normal' structural unemployment, these second-generation immigrants increasingly valued work as necessary and central to their lives. Also significant was the fact that for an alleged 'gastarbeiter' community, mainly without naturalisation, they had no intention of 'returning' to the countries of origin of their parents to find employment (Poglia Mileti, this volume).

THE RESPONSE TO DISCRIMINATION:
EQUAL OPPORTUNITY POLICIES

Within the chapters of this volume there is therefore a great deal of convincing evidence of differential treatment, exclusion, discrimination and abuse affecting migrant workers in Europe, and their descendants. However, as Soininen argues in her chapter, more attention needs to be paid to the policies – or the absence of policies – which allow ethnic and 'racial' discrimination in the labour market to arise and persist, rather than simply stocktaking the frequency of discrimination and the immigrants' experience of it. The sort of evidence described in this book on the operation of discrimination at work has led to legislation against its practice in many EU countries. There has been much recent academic and policy-related scrutiny of such national measures within different European countries (Zegers de Beijl 1991; Forbes and Mead 1992; CEC 1993; MacEwen 1995, 1997). The unanimous conclusion is that legislation needs to be improved, something echoed by many of the contributors to this volume. For example, the absence of proper anti-discrimination legislation in Germany seriously impedes those who wish to challenge discrimination in that country (Räthzel). In France, the nature of the anti-discrimination legislation means that actions against discrimination in law are very rare indeed (Vourc'h et al.), and the way that the Swedish 1994 law is formulated makes it very difficult for a case of discrimination to reach a tribunal (Soininen).

However, legislation in itself is not enough. Laws against discrimination need the support of equal opportunity policies implemented at an organisational level. Such policies first emerged in the United States; later, employers in the UK copied many aspects of US practice and now the UK has a relatively long record of equal opportunity initiatives. More recently, in other European countries a greater interest is being taken in the sorts of policies which could be applied to their own contexts. Equal opportunity policies are designed to facilitate equal treatment in recruitment and selection, work allocation and promotion, training and development, and dismissal and redundancies, as well as dealing with discrimination, and showing respect for cultural and religious differences. There is a great deal of variety in the approaches of employers to equal treatment measures in Europe, as described by Wrench in the concluding chapter in this volume. In some European countries such policies are already in operation, most commonly in the public sector. Initiatives of various sorts are noted in the Netherlands, in Sweden and in France, though the latter are expressed not in terms of 'anti-discrimination' or 'anti-racism' policies for migrants, but as egalitarian approaches guided by a universalistic ideology. In Germany, it seems the most common policies by employers are the supporting of social or education policies against racial prejudice, xenophobia and right extremism, and training in cultural awareness. However, as Wrench's essay describes, in most countries the development of equal treatment measures at the level of individual organisations has been very patchy, poorly directed and often working from questionable assumptions. In some European countries there seem to be no examples at all.

In countries of Southern Europe, initiatives to tackle racism and discrimination are more likely to be considered at the level of trade unions or employers' organisations, or alternatively at sectoral level, rather than within individual organisations. The specific situation of new migration and illegal work in these countries has implications for equal opportunities practices. Anti-discrimination law and equal opportunities measures do not touch the large numbers of workers who are outside the formal labour market in highly exploitative illegal work. For people with insecure employment status, including undocumented workers and asylum-seekers, anti-discrimination law is almost irrelevant. This partly explains the lack of concern with equal opportunities and anti-discrimination measures of the 'UK type' in countries of Southern Europe. Equal opportunities measures were traditionally conceived as applying to settled ethnic minorities within the formal labour market. Recent changes both in the character of migration and in the labour market throw up major questions about such policies. The deregulation of the labour market and expansion of insecure and 'illegal' work means that people are often not in a position to claim the protection of anti-discrimination legislation.

> In the absence of a high general standard of employment protection, the existence of such laws merely accentuates the hierarchy of employment. Only those people with secure, permanent jobs and the protection of a strong trade union may be in a position to insist on their rights. Those at the bottom of the hierarchy – who are most vulnerable and disadvantaged and so most in need of legal protection – are precisely the groups who have the least access to the law. This is leading to a greater polarisation, whereby an ever increasing proportion of people find themselves in a twilight zone of temporary casualised, unregulated work. (Sales and Gregory 1995: 5)

Some of the seasonal work in Italy, as described in this volume, lies at the extreme, 'peripheral' end of employment, with low wages, no security and a high degree of exploitation. Campani and Carchedi argue that the worst excesses of this could be contained by regulation, but this, at the time of writing, had not materialised. Similarly in Spain, Cachón portrays the extreme exploitation suffered by immigrants in the precarious and illegal sectors. Being non-EU foreigners, it is Spanish law which helps to confine them to these areas of work.

In these circumstances, the first stages of anti-discrimination work are more likely to be seen as measures to increase the personal power of people to resist exploitation, and this could include measures such as organising and campaigning for the regularisation of people in illegal work, or even increasing people's language skills. The specific and important role of trade unions in fighting for the equal treatment of such migrant workers is stressed by Martens in the penultimate chapter of this volume.

ANTI-DISCRIMINATION MEASURES IN AN UNSYMPATHETIC CONTEXT

Over the past three decades there has been structural transformation in European economies, with a decline in traditional manufacturing and the growth in some service sectors, which have had direct implications for the employment of migrants and ethnic minorities, particularly since migrants have been disproportionately represented in those industries and jobs suffering the greatest attrition. There has been a growth in subcontracting by companies, and at the same time an expansion of the sweatshop sector and the 'informal' economy, creating a greater number of vulnerable workers who by the nature of their employment remain untouched by equal opportunities measures. Along with these transformations there have been shifts in business practices and economic decision-making – particularly in the UK – which may well have direct and negative consequences for the adoption of or successful implementation of equal opportunities policies.

There are a number of specific developments which may produce negative effects for anti-discrimination activities and equal opportunities policies, over and above the 'normal' resistance such policies have always engendered on the part of employers and trade unionists. One is the persistence of long-term structural unemployment. When companies are shedding workers rather than recruiting, policies to remove racist barriers to recruitment will not produce much overall change. Furthermore, indigenous workers may well be more resistant to the introduction of such measures in times of high unemployment. Another development is the drive for flexibility of labour and changing work practices. In countries such as the UK there has been a movement away from relatively stable working conditions, characterised by institutionalised wage agreements and strong trade unions and secure, full-time employment. There has been a corresponding growth in temporary part-time and contract work, greater 'flexibility' of labour and a weakening of workers rights (Hutton 1995).

The equal opportunities implications of many of the recent changes are clear. When workers' general employment rights are undermined, when their protective organisations are disempowered, and when they work in a permanent state of extreme insecurity, equal opportunities protection becomes a lower priority. Other changes can also undermine equal opportunities progress. Many industries have seen the increasing spread of team working, including multi-skilling. It has been argued that this stimulates informal 'acceptability' criteria in recruitment – the more subjectively judged characteristics on which recruiters form judgements as to whether someone will 'fit in' to the organisation. It is precisely the criteria of 'acceptability' where negative racial and ethnic stereotypes come in to play. The articles in this volume by Wrench et al., Gras and Bovenkerk, and Vourc'h et al. describe evidence for this practice in the UK, the Netherlands and France. Socially normative criteria, such as the motivation and reliability of the applicant and 'fitting into the team', appear to be becoming increasingly important factors in the selection of personnel. In Sweden, Soininen and Graham (1995) describe the expansion of new types of job which require communication skills, especially a good command of Swedish, and a high level of education, as well as 'social competence'. Some authorities saw this as an understandable justification for not employing immigrants. Thus, one 'new context' for this book is the structural changes which have occurred in Western European economies which have a direct effect on the employment of migrants, and the related changes in business and organisational practices which undermine equal opportunities practices.

POLITICAL DEVELOPMENTS IN EUROPE

The disappearance of what essentially characterised the old migration waves towards Europe has led to a change in migration policies as well as in rules and provisions for granting rights. The old migrations were often organised through bilateral agreements (mainly for Benelux, Germany and France) that specified not only the migratory flows but also some practical aspects such as settlement requirements or housing and working conditions for immigrants. These agreements could also provide specific social and civil rights. Nowadays, the migratory flows towards the European Union are no longer ruled by bilateral agreements. They are based on two new trends: individualisation on the one hand, and coordination on the other. In Southern Europe especially, migration is more individual. Evidence of this is the great diversity of national origins among the new immigrants. In the past, migration flows were organised to fit the mutual interests of the receiving state, of the state of origin and of the relevant industry. The present immigration is more attuned to the interests of migrants themselves and a number of specific economic sectors. The continuing arrival of new immigrants despite high levels of unemployment confirms that immigration and unemployment are not necessarily linked in a simple and direct way. This might be explained by the fact that divergent interests – of the migrant, of the industry and of the state – are at play in the migration process. If, from the migrant's point of view, getting a job without any social protection does improve his/her situation, it represents additional costs for the state, in terms of medical care, schooling, if the migrant has children, and political risks associated with the growth of racism and the influence of extreme right parties. Migrants offer industry new opportunities for increasing job competition and lowering wages and reinforcing flexibility on the labour market. The presence of undocumented workers tends to undermine regular employment protection, at least in some labour sectors.

Coordination is the second major trend. The European states are concluding supranational agreements in preference to bilateral ones: the EU (or, more precisely, the Council of Ministers) decides on migration control policies and concludes cooperation agreements with third countries that include specific clauses regarding immigration. During the 1980s, the European states, while encouraging the so-called brain drain, adopted measures aimed at preventing and repressing the entrance of irregular immigration. Under the increasing coordination of the EU, measures currently defining conditions and provisions for granting citizenship rights have been incorporated into the Schengen Agreements, the Maastricht Treaty, the Dublin Convention and the Treaty of Amsterdam. With this Treaty signed in October 1997, and in order to establish in Europe an area of freedom, security and justice, common action on issues such as asylum, visas, immigration and controls at external borders has been brought under Community rules and procedures – a situation that justifies the name 'Fortress Europe'.

There is another discourse taking place at EU level on the social and business costs of social exclusion. However, there are questions as to whether there exists the political will to implement the sorts of social, employment and anti-discrimination policies which could hope to tackle it. There has been an apparently growing awareness of the importance of discrimination, exclusion and its negative social consequences within European institutions. The EU's July 1994 White Paper (European Social Policy: A Way Forward for the Union) recognises that the marginalisation of major social groups is a challenge to the social cohesion of the Union: 'This is not just a question of social justice: the Union simply cannot afford to lose the contribution of marginalised groups to society as a whole' (p. 49). At the EU conference in Copenhagen on 'Combating Social Exclusion' Jacques Delors warned that the foundations and democratic processes of Europe could be threatened by the rupture of social links and lack of solidarity. The future of the EU could be jeopardised if member states cannot reconcile competitiveness, cooperation and equality of opportunity. Alongside the discourse on the negative effects of increasing social exclusion runs a parallel debate on the business advantages of diversity and equal opportunity initiatives, as discussed in the concluding chapter to this volume. Some employers have already recognised the market advantages which can accrue from such policies and have embraced them with enthusiasm, although these are clearly the exception rather than the rule. Räthzel (this volume) argues that in an era of globalisation, workers with intercultural competence, who have a command of two or more languages and an active knowledge of different cultures, must be seen to have rather desirable qualifications. Business organisations must develop the flexibility to recognise and use these talents, rather than assuming that such workers are in some way deficient. It is not only employers who are often slow to realise the need for change. Trade unions are also slow to recognise that polices to promote the equal treatment of migrant workers are in fact in the interests of the unions themselves (Martens, this volume).

Thus the labour market exclusion of migrants and their descendants in the EU could be seen to be both a waste of resources and a factor which undermines social cohesion. There are also arguments that anti-discrimination measures can reduce barriers to mobility. Racism and xenophobia can in practice act as obstacles to the freedom of movement of people within the Union. The European Commission wishes to press for specific powers to combat racial discrimination to be included in the Treaty, and the committee of experts appointed after the EU Corfu summit in June 1994 recommended the amendment of the Maastricht Treaty to provide explicitly for EU competence on discrimination against migrants and ethnic minorities. The 1994 White Paper also stated the Commission's intention to consult the social partners at European level on the possible adoption of a code of good employment practice against racial discrimination. In the interim, in the absence of an agreement on this code of practice, the social partners adopted in 1995 a 'Joint Declaration on the Prevention of Racial Discrimination and Xenophobia and the Promotion of Equal Treatment at the Workplace'. Its aim was to raise awareness of the problem and provide guidance on the prevention and elimination of racism at work, as well as promoting the idea that it is in the interests of business to implement equal opportunity policies. The 1997 Treaty of Amsterdam did, for the first time, specifically authorise action against racism within the EU, although without making it mandatory with a timetable for legislation. Furthermore, in 1997 it was also agreed to set up the European Monitoring Centre on

Racism and Xenophobia in Vienna, whose remit includes providing comparable data at a European level on racism, and helping member states of the EU to formulate action against it.

This book does not exhaust all the issues relating to ethnic and 'racial' discrimination at work in Western Europe. It presents an overview of discrimination in various European countries, and shows the complexity and subtlety of the forms it takes. It confronts the denial of the issue, the continuing 'no problem here' ideology found in many national contexts, and demonstrates the necessity for research and investigation to bring to the surface something which is frequently hidden, even to its victims. The book aims to be a contribution to stimulate the public and political debates necessary to raise up both legal and voluntary measures to oppose discrimination in employment.

I
Internal Processes

2 Young Migrants in the Belgian Labour Market: Integration, Discrimination and Exclusion

Nouria Ouali and Andrea Rea

It is not always possible to compare the situations of young migrants or young people from ethnic minorities in the labour markets of different European states. Such comparative analysis is difficult, basically because of the multiplicity of legal definitions of foreigner and of the terminology of nationality, which cover situations on grounds that differ enormously from one state to another. The same difficulty arises with the analysis of the labour market: the relationship between the education and production systems is so dependent on the type of structure and formation of nation-states that the international comparison of the job situations of young people, for example, is extremely complex. Such a comparison requires an initial step involving adjustment of the perception of how national realities come about. If a subject for study such as an international comparison of discrimination against foreigners in the labour market is to be established, it must necessarily involve the reconstitution of the structural elements of the labour market and of the composition of the populations within it. What might, in fact, look like a difference attributable to the characteristics of individuals – for example, young people have a lower unemployment rate in Germany than in France – may simply be a manifestation of a structural difference in the way the transition from school to work is organised.

Both the definitive settling of immigrants and their children and the economic crisis have caused noticeable changes in the immigrant population's situation in the labour market. In this essay we shall attempt to highlight the situation of young people from ethnic minorities in the Belgian labour market and to describe the discrimination that puts that population, for whom Belgian nationality is not easy to obtain, on a legally inferior footing. We shall then show that those young people, like young Belgians of modest social origins, do not all occupy the same social positions. Finally, we shall consider the effects on the employment of those young people of massive unemployment through the new, selective mechanisms of racial discrimination and social exclusion.

ESTABLISHED DISCRIMINATION

Originally, the purpose of importing foreign workers was to balance a labour market which had a short-term shortage of supply (Martens 1976). That policy, which had basically been contemplated as a short-term remedy, then took the form of a systematic absorption of immigrant workers by the Belgian production system. Since 1974, the Belgian labour market has undergone enormous changes which have led both to increased unemployment in certain sectors of production and to a destabilising of the ways in which young people join the labour market. The restructuring of employment caused by the recession was accompanied by the strengthening of certain selective mechanisms, some of which specifically affected young people, women and immigrants. But by virtue of their very status as foreigners,[1] immigrants suffer legal discrimination in the labour market, and there is even a hierarchy of discrimination based on national origin. The history of immigration in Belgium provides an explanation for that discrimination, the fundamental cause of which is the late appearance of a policy of integration. Accordingly, it was not until after 1985 that measures were taken to enable children born in Belgium of foreign parents to acquire Belgian nationality more easily in certain circumstances.

A foreign worker does not have free access to the labour market: both the employer who wants to employ a foreigner and the foreign worker who wants to work in Belgium have to obtain authorisation, the former to take on foreign labour and the latter to take paid employment (Nys and Beauchesne 1992). The rules on work permits[2] apply to all foreigners who want to take paid employment and their employers, with the exception of EU nationals.

The Belgian labour market distinguishes between three categories of workers: private sector employees, public sector employees and the self-employed. *Public sector* posts are legally reserved for Belgians and, in certain cases, for EU nationals under Articles 7 and 48 of the Treaty of Rome.[3] Such posts account for more than 20 per cent of all the jobs from which immigrant workers are automatically excluded. Access to *private sector* jobs is conditional, in the case of non-EU workers, on the possession of authorisation of access to the labour market (a work permit) issued by the regional Minister for Employment. Such authorisation may be of limited duration but valid for all employment sectors ('A' permit) and issued once only, or it may be limited to a specific sector, with a specified duration ('B' permit) or a specific trade ('C' permit) for one or more specified employers and is issued to each employer. To practise a *self-employed* activity a non-EU national must have a professional card issued, once only, at the commencement of the activity, by the Minister for Economic Affairs. This card is granted on the basis of the residence permit, the personal status of the applicant (criminal record, previous bankruptcies, and so on) and the type of activity contemplated (restricted or not), its economic importance from the point of view of investment or the jobs it creates, its duration or its degree of specialisation.

Since the government's decision to stop immigration in 1974 the work permit most frequently issued has been an 'A' permit without immigration. Above all, it concerns the children of immigrant workers. The requirement for young non-EU nationals to obtain an 'A' work permit to gain access to the labour market is a first level of discrimination. That situation results from the lack of consistency between the rules governing employment and those governing the right of establishment of foreign workers. A second form of discrimination affects non-EU foreigners who have unlimited residence permits and want to establish themselves as self-employed workers. They have to obtain professional cards to carry on their activities. The requirement for these two documents[4] is not a fundamental obstacle to access to the labour market for young foreigners in that both work permits and professional cards are issued almost automatically. Although they are no longer the means of effective control that they were first intended to be, they are certainly a means of classifying foreigners, symbolic manifestations that distinguish between foreign populations. In addition, their incorporation into law maintains the precarious nature of the foreigner's status[5] since, for example, young people who are not nationals of an EU member state, but who have been authorised to reside regularly within Belgian territory, do not automatically have guaranteed free access to the labour market. The law on residence permits and that on work permits must be merged if greater equality of opportunity and professional mobility are to be ensured.

The third way in which the law discriminates against young people from ethnic minorities is that it makes it impossible to obtain employment in the public sector. Foreigners are thus barred from 20 per cent of all the jobs available. Young foreigners are not all equal before the jobs available and the openings offered to them are fewer in number than those offered to Belgians. That restriction leads to exclusion from the benefits of certain measures, intended to help insert young people in public institutions, therefore conflicting with the expressed intention of politicians to encourage the occupational integration of young people from ethnic minorities.

In the field of unemployment legislation, young Moroccans and Tunisians have recently been eligible for provisional benefits on the basis of their academic records.[6] The new legislation has not, however, done away with the nationality condition; it has merely added two nationalities to the list of those eligible. The law still discriminates. Foreigners are also victims of a form of discrimination that affects their access to the basic social security benefit called the 'minimex'. The law requires the classification of minimex recipients on the basis of their nationality. Belgians are entitled to the minimex, as are EU nationals since 1992, but other foreigners do not have entitlement. That legislation highlights the fundamental contradiction in present immigrant policy as it shows that a person who has unrestricted right of residence is not entitled to basic social security benefits. This discriminatory measure excludes young foreigners from certain integration measures proposed by local authority social assistance bodies (the CPAS) for young people receiving the minimex.

FOREIGNERS IN THE LABOUR MARKET

One way of analysing the situation of foreigners in the labour market is to study the situation on the basis of work permits issued. This approach still involves a major bias as it does not include EU foreigners who do not need work permits to practise a trade. The Second Report by the Royal Commissioners on Immigrant Policy (CRPI 1990) identifies three phenomena in the employment field since the cessation of immigration in 1974:

- a major reduction in immigration by manual workers from Mediterranean countries, who would have taken low-skilled work;
- a new wave of immigration of highly qualified people and executives from industrialised countries such as the United States and Japan;
- a major 'induced' flow of young immigrants, the children of immigrants long established in Belgium.

These three phenomena emerge clearly from the allocation of work permits issued since 1974. The largest category of work permit is 'A' (without immigration) (90,181), issued mainly to the children of immigrants. The 'B' permits issued to immigrants principally concern US and Japanese citizens. Permits issued to citizens of countries that have traditionally provided Belgium with manual workers are few in number.

Albert Martens shows that 'until 1974 employment was therefore the reason and the cause of immigration. Social integration was achieved by passing the factory gate' (Martens 1990). In fact, the same author has shown elsewhere (1976) that economic policy, driven by necessity, has regulated the flow of migrants to and fro, exploiting that potential reserve of labour as a means of effecting short-term adjustments in the labour market.

However, the economic crisis, the halt of immigration and above all the permanent establishment of that population in Belgium have made it necessary to rethink what is still, for lack of a better term, called 'immigration'.

As regards the change in the share of the labour market occupied by foreigners (of all ages), Martens notes that between 1970 and 1977 the total employment of foreigners increased in both relative and absolute terms. On the other hand, between 1977 and 1981 employment fell. During that period male employment dropped by a proportion comparable to that of all Belgians, but female employment fell while female Belgian employment rose. According to the 1981 general census the foreign population included 250,000 economically active persons consisting of 68 per cent manual workers, 19 per cent non-manual workers and 10 per cent self-employed people. That distribution confirms the subordinate function of immigrant labour.

An analysis of changes in employment reveals an increase in skilled rather than unskilled jobs for women in the tertiary sector. For men, the proportion of jobs in the 'industrial' and 'tertiary' categories, unskilled and skilled, has remained the same, which justified the statement made at the time that 'it is difficult to forecast the future employment of foreign workers' (CRPI 1990). With the decline in industrial employment and jobs traditionally occupied by foreigners the number of the self-employed has increased remarkably. According to the 1988 Institut National de Statistiques survey, of those aged 45 and 46, 19.7 per cent of EU foreigners were self-employed as against 13.6 per cent of non-EU foreigners. The stabilisation of that foreign population is perhaps contributing to a phenomenon observed in the United States: the development of ethnic business, which certain studies have attempted to demonstrate (Vanhoren and Bracke 1992).

THE EMPLOYMENT OF YOUNG PEOPLE FROM ETHNIC MINORITIES

Integration through work as encapsulated in the 'passing the factory gate = integration' equation has become less of a certainty for young people. The terminology used to refer to them signifies the changes that have occurred: the first generation is usually referred to as 'immigrant workers' and their children are the 'second generation'. Between the two generations the 'work' qualification has completely disappeared.

The little scientific research that has been carried out in Belgium into the occupational integration of young people from ethnic minorities generally proposes three types of interpretation of this process. The first interpretation, on the basis of studies specifically focusing on young people (Bastenier and Dassetto 1981, 1985, 1986), argues for the reproduction of the social positions acquired from parents and their tendency to be underqualified. Although they have been to school, the young people are poorly qualified and have jobs similar to those of their parents. According to the same interpretation, young migrants or young people from ethnic minorities are characterised by their failure to establish themselves within the working class and, instead, form an underclass. On the conclusion of the first investigation of young people and the labour market Bastenier and Dassetto detected a tendency for underqualification and concluded that 'the male population of the second generation of immigrants occupies a position in the labour market similar to that of the first generation' (Bastenier and Dassetto 1981: 26). This conclusion also emerged from a study on the second generation of Italian immigrants in Belgium. The same authors confirmed that finding in an article on the occupational integration of young Moroccans and Turks, in which they claimed that those young people are becoming a new underclass (Bastenier and Dassetto 1987).

On the basis of a study on the short-term labour adjustment function of immigration the second argument seeks to show that as well as the dualism of the labour market there is an ethno-stratification of jobs (Martens 1990). Within the secondary labour market, it is argued that there are employment sectors entirely occupied by workers of foreign extraction. The area occupied by foreign workers within the labour market (subordinate functions, low-skilled jobs, limited training, arduous working conditions, and so on) is dominant in the secondary sectors according to Martens. That author argues that the competitiveness of undertakings assumes 'the sidelining of the weakest, including immigrants'. Accordingly, 'on the polarisation and dualisation of the labour market will be superimposed an ethno-stratification of jobs' (Martens 1990: 154). In a study of two local labour markets Martens tries to demonstrate the theory of ethno-stratification which would be accompanied by the process of generational reproduction, young people from ethnic minorities not automatically achieving higher social positions than their parents (Rosvelds et al. 1993).

Finally, a third interpretation (Manco and Manco 1990) would show, on the basis of a survey of young people living in francophone Belgium, 'hierarchisation' in occupational integration on the basis of foreigners' nationalities, with EU member state nationals achieving better social and economic integration than so-called 'Muslim' foreigners (Moroccans and Turks). Italians[7] and foreigners who have obtained Belgian nationality are said to occupy the most highly qualified jobs and the Moroccans and Turks, less highly trained, are recruited for less qualified and less well-paid jobs. This analysis also shows a change in the status of young people compared with that of their parents, the former being manual workers less often. This analysis, which covered foreigners only, avoids any comparison with young Belgians. It does, however, show the importance of the impact of time as a factor. The longer the period of residence and establishment in Belgium, the greater the degree of occupational integration.

Because of the very construction of their study subjects, these three interpretations neglect the time aspect of the process of occupational integration. In fact, the study of occupational integration requires an analysis that includes changes in the labour market, the timing of waves of migration, since not all foreigners arrived at the same time, and the emergence of a 'youth' occupational integration problem. In addition, the question that must be asked in a period of recession is no longer only whether young people have a different status from their parents but, more specifically, whether they have access to employment in this period of massive unemployment and whether they are subject to indirect discrimination.

The vocational insertion of young migrants or young people from ethnic minorities can no longer be reduced to one factor; simple reproduction is being replaced more and more by differentiation of the social positions occupied, which in turn depends on a number of factors only one of which is nationality. When the question is about discrimination in the labour market, however, it must be determined how a reference to young people's national origin can be an obstacle to entry to, and stabilisation in, the labour market.

Various statistics and surveys demonstrate the differentiation of social positions occupied today. One of the statistical references that remains is the 1981 census, which shows that young immigrants – like their parents – are predominantly manual workers and the proportion of them that are manual workers is much higher than for Belgians. Amongst foreigners, two out of three young people in the active population are manual workers. A breakdown by sex shows that 75 per cent of young men are manual workers and only 10 per cent are non-manual workers. Amongst young women the division is less striking as 48 per cent are manual workers and 34 per cent are non-manual workers.

More recent data on the employment of those young people is provided by the INS 1988 survey of the labour force. Presented in the report by the Royal Commission on Immigrant Policy, they give interesting details of the places occupied by young migrants or young people from ethnic minorities in the labour market. It would appear that most young immigrants (aged 14 to 24) – both EU and non-EU foreigners – enter the labour market as manual workers. That is the case for 76.9 per cent of the non-EU nationals, 61.9 per cent of the EU nationals and 46.4 per cent of Belgians. The EU nationals account for most of the non-manual positions (29.1 per cent), the non-EU nationals 15.0 per cent and Belgians 30.0 per cent. Comparison of the distribution of their status with that of their parents would appear to show a tendency for status to move from manual worker to non-manual. That change of status is, however, more frequent in EU young people than among non-EU young people. That led the members of the Royal Commission to conclude that foreigners were still to a very large extent employed as manual workers.

A recent study of young Italians in Brussels (CASI 1990) used a small sample, but usefully highlighted a process of vocational mobility amongst young Italians. The authors noted that, compared with their parents, 'young Italians were more highly qualified, and that was demonstrated by two major movements: from unskilled to skilled work on the one hand, and from blue-collar to white-collar work (non-manual workers, managers or technicians) on the other' (CASI 1990: 27). According to another study (CEFA-UO 1989), that tendency can also be detected amongst Spaniards.

By way of information we should note the development of the situation in France. On this subject, Lebon notes in particular the feminisation of the economically active foreign population, the young women being more likely to work than their mothers. That process is accompanied by a movement towards the tertiary sector. He concludes that there is 'a certain reproduction of the foreign labour force that is more marked amongst young male workers than among economically active females less than 25 years old, who are proportionally more numerous than older women in carrying on an activity and have different employment patterns' (Lebon 1986: 76). That analysis has been confirmed for young Spanish women in Brussels at least.

Even if social and vocational mobility does not necessarily assume concrete form, at least at present, it is part of such young people's hopes. These children of immigrant workers say they do not want to do the same work as their parents. The young display new socio-vocational behaviour, they want to escape from the subordinate positions their parents occupied and they demand general acceptance. Unlike their parents, whose lives and identities were rooted elsewhere, the young people want to be considered as full individuals, rather than just as workers, in the host country. Derriche (1992) shows that aspirations for autonomy or independence on the part of young Moroccan and Turkish women who have undertaken vocational training lead to feelings of guilt and are never grounded in prospects of professional work. This would appear to differ from the case of young women who have followed a general education. Work is considered solely from the point of view of additional income. Here the difference is not between nationalities; it is determined by the academic course 'chosen', which is itself a function of the lifestyle and/or job chosen.

The change of status from manual to non-manual worker does not necessarily mean that young people will achieve higher social positions than their elders. For that to be true, account would have to be taken of the changes that have taken place in the structure of jobs and in particular of the effects of the movement of translation (Bourdieu 1979). While many young foreigners are more highly qualified than their parents, those from more favoured social backgrounds have, at the same time, also increased their level of qualification. The pyramid of academic qualifications has moved upwards without producing any essential change within the hierarchy. The disappearance of industrial employment has inevitably reduced the number of jobs for manual workers. The proportion of this group in the workforce has consequently dropped, but it does not automatically follow that the jobs held by certain young people, even with non-manual status, are not today low-skilled jobs.

In addition, a straightforward comparison of the social positions of the parents and children is inherently biased. In fact, studies on social and vocational mobility have shown the inherent limitations of comparisons, at a precise point in time, between the positions occupied by different generations when assessing the impact of mobility. They show that whatever his nationality, a child at the beginning of his working life occupies a position nearer to that occupied by his father or mother at the beginning of their careers, rather than the point where the son enters the labour market. In other words, between the position occupied by a child on first starting work and the position his father occupied at the same stage, there is a whole vocational history. Finally, the many studies on young people starting work tend to show that despite a general raising of the training level of younger generations, they encounter a lot of problems on entering and becoming stable in a scarce jobs market and the struggle between the age groups for employment is also one of the reasons why the employment of young people is precarious.

DISCRIMINATION, RACISM AND EXCLUSION

In order better to assess occupational integration, one must consider time as a factor and regard insertion not as a temporary, short-term mechanism,

but as a process. One way of avoiding short-term and unchanging interpretations is to adopt a dynamic interpretation of the concept of occupational
integration as an institutional process crossed by selective movements.
This approach is attracting increasing attention from social science
researchers, in particular, due to the study of occupational integration
histories, and has governed the research we have carried out, based on a
longitudinal survey of young Belgians and foreigners resident in the
Brussels region (Ouali and Rea 1993).

The methodological approach consisted in stressing both the 'youth'
problem of occupational integration and highlighting the differences
and the similarities of the insertion routes of Belgians and foreigners, taking into account the effects of nationality at study level, social differentiation and sex. On the basis of a longitudinal study of a group of young
people completing their general, technical and vocational secondary education, this survey has made it possible to highlight certain processes of
discrimination operating in the local employment market and in integration arrangements, principally on the basis of two factors: sex and
nationality.

Those differences are already identifiable in the school and vocational
aspirations expressed by school-leavers. The differentiation of integration
projects by sex shows that at study levels equivalent to those of young
men, young women are more likely to pursue further studies and less
likely to enter the labour market. Another important distinction emerges
through the nationality of origin variable. While young Belgians may form
plans relatively close to the average for young people, EU and non-EU
foreigners form relatively different plans. The former basically want to
enter the labour market, while the latter choose to continue their studies.
This difference essentially divides young Italians from young Moroccans
and in a certain fashion, echoes the opposition recorded in a French survey
of young Algerians and Portuguese. For the latter group, social promotion
is, above all, a matter of economic success while Algerians prefer academic success (Abou Sada and Zeroulou 1993). Paradoxically, when these
two groups, young women and non-EU foreigners, are in the labour market, they are the ones that, comparatively, have the greatest difficulty in
achieving stability, suffer the most from selectivity in the labour market
and are most affected by discrimination. While academic investment may
be considered a strategy to ensure better integration in the labour market it
can also be an avoidance tactic, because of the fear of being confronted
with discrimination and unemployment.

In the labour market, 24 months after leaving school, the difference in
patterns by nationality is marked. The dominant pattern amongst Belgians is

rapid integration and stabilisation in conventional employment (long-term contracts). The same is true of EU foreigners, amongst whom this pattern is even more frequently exhibited. On the other hand, the dominant pattern amongst non-EU foreigners is, very generally, unemployment. The later entry into employment of non-EU foreigners compared with Belgians and EU foreigners, does not make up for the shortage of temporary jobs (jobs of fixed duration) or conventional jobs (long-term jobs) that they have accumulated from the start. Those whose career structures resemble those of Belgians and EU foreigners are only a minority. Access to a first job is achieved with much more difficulty. The more Belgians' careers seem to be aimed at integration in employment, the more those of non-EU foreigners seem to have difficulty in pulling out of unemployment. The careers of EU foreigners, however, are characterised by two opposing features: conventional employment and permanent unemployment.

For young women and non-EU foreigners the main problem is not achieving stability in employment but getting a first job. In addition, changes in status are proportionally more disadvantageous for them. Thus, they lose conventional jobs and find themselves looking for work more often. They hardly ever find themselves in an intermediate situation such as having a temporary job, either moving onto a more stable situation or avoiding unemployment. Stabilisation by stages is more a characteristic of young Belgian men, who also benefit from greater mobility in unemployment. The process of occupational integration for young women and non-EU foreigners involves, then, finding a first job and not losing it.

All young non-EU foreigners do not find themselves in the same situation. It is the young women who end up in the most precarious situations; young men take much longer to find their first jobs than young Belgians and EU foreigners, but they do find them. A large majority of young non-EU women, on the other hand, do not find their first job during the two years after leaving school.

In employment, there is a phenomenon of ethno-stratification: young foreigners, both young women and young men, are more often manual than non-manual workers and the sectors of activity are often different. In low-skilled jobs, for instance, which is what jobs for young people are, Belgians more often work in the retail sector while foreigners work in cleaning services and industry, the former less frequently manual workers than the latter group.

The academic level shows that the sex and nationality variables operate at certain levels as a source of discrimination. Young people with low-level diplomas, whatever their sex or nationality, are more often unemployed than in work; in general, it is then the qualifications that discriminate.

In the case of higher qualifications, however, young Belgians have more stable careers than foreigners.

Military service, which constitutes a special handicap for Belgians and young naturalised foreigners, cannot be compared to the obstacle of being foreign or a woman since those two groups have the greatest difficulty in obtaining first jobs and achieving stability in them. The differences between the careers of young men and young women and between nationalities have not diminished with time. On the contrary, getting bogged down in unemployment is a major difficulty in getting a job after a certain stage. Interrupting long-term unemployment, then, becomes a priority for any employment policy.

This precariousness and discrimination affect young women more than young men and non-EU foreigners more than Belgians and EU foreigners. They must not, however, be allowed to conceal the fact that young people in both categories, even if only a minority, succeed in achieving stability in the labour market. In fact, there is no simple polarity such as: the Belgians are in work and the non-EU foreigners are unemployed; the multiplicity of integration patterns show that the selectivity of the labour market does not produce a random distribution.

Discrimination is not perceived solely through place in the labour market but also through views that young people have about their situation as foreigners. A majority of young people believe that access to employment is an identical experience for all. Young non-EU foreigners, however, feel more often than other young people that foreign nationality makes integration in the labour market more difficult. That feeling is shared more often by young people who have kept their nationalities of origin than by those who have acquired Belgian nationality. In the same way, it is more prevalent amongst young men than amongst young women. Thus, 30 per cent of young non-EU foreigners claim that they have been refused jobs because they are foreign.

Comparison of the occupational integration patterns, taken from a cohort of young migrants or from ethnic minorities on completing full-time education, casts a new light on their situation in the labour market. The first aspect refers to the recruitment and selection mechanisms operating in a labour market characterised more and more by scarcity of jobs and increased competition between workers. Young foreigners, like other young people, find themselves in a new situation unknown to their parents: the question is not to determine in which sector they will be recruited and at what wage but, more seriously, whether they will obtain their first jobs easily and whether they will quickly achieve stability in the labour market.

The various forms of discrimination to which they are subject are as much matters of their foreign status and legal distinctions, as of the more recent, indirect forms of discrimination, which are linked to a negative image that the media and political rhetoric have combined to produce since the employment crisis began. Thus, for example, unlike Belgians and EU nationals, young non-EU nationals suffer doubly from the employment crisis: there is the difficult experience of unemployment and socio-economic exclusion, and from the challenge to their presence in Belgium on the grounds that they are no longer able to perform what they (they and their parents) were recruited to do in their countries of origin; namely, work (Costa-Lascoux 1991). And yet the first demand made by those young people is to work. During the urban riots of 1991 many young people of North African origin expressed their distress at not being able to work: 'I want to pay taxes... work and pay taxes like everyone else.' Costa-Lascoux writes:

> The symbolic force of those words was to invert the logic of the derogatory stereotypes. The demand for dignity and identity through work, for recognition by virtue of contribution to national solidarity, operated against policies of assistance and against the paternalism used in speeches and actions for the benefit of immigrants. (Costa-Lascoux 1991)

Confronted by vulnerability resulting from foreign nationality, many young people have taken Belgian nationality (40 per cent of the young Moroccans in our sample). A change of identity card is not yet, however, sufficient to guarantee employment or to afford protection against those less formal forms of discrimination that still operate against and handicap those young people in their attempts to obtain employment. The negative and perverse effect of the generalisation of the criminal stigma on the image of all young people from ethnic minorities, Moroccans in particular, has already been fully demonstrated and would appear to characterise relations at the moment of employment. Not employing a Moroccan is, for certain employers, one way of avoiding anticipated problems. Such a discriminatory attitude is enormously prejudicial to the integration of those young people, who interpret and treat all refusals addressed to them as racist acts or thoughts.

With the onset of massive unemployment, certain young people find themselves in a particular situation that is almost worse than their parents experienced when they immigrated. The question that they face is not how to improve their social status, but how to obtain one. Immigration was justified by work and it was by means of work that foreigners integrated. Now that cultural integration has been achieved, social disintegration is destroying the migratory instinct and undermining the future of younger generations. While not all young migrants or those from ethnic minorities are in precarious situations, and some have been able to improve their social status vis-à-vis that of their parents, others are suffering racial discrimination, a new selective factor because of increased competition in the labour market, and are finding themselves relegated to social exclusion.

NOTES

1. On 1 January 1993 foreigners accounted for 9 per cent of the total population of Belgium, being mainly immigrants who had settled more than 30 years earlier and whose children were born in the country.
2. These matters are regulated by the Royal Decree of 20 July 1967 on the employment of foreign labour and the Royal Decree of 6 November 1967 on the conditions governing the granting and the withdrawal of authorisations for occupations and work permits.
3. It should, however, be noted that Articles 7 and 48(2) of the Treaty of Rome provide that the criterion of Belgian nationality for the recruitment of EU nationals into the public service or bodies dependent on central government is valid only for functions that involve participation in the exercise of public power and for functions whose purpose is the protection of the general interests of the state or of other official authorities.
4. The Royal Commission on Immigrant Policy has proposed that the government abolish those papers for young people who were born in Belgium or arrived there when very small. That has not yet been done. CRPI, *L'intégration: une politique de longue haleine*, three volumes, Brussels, INBEL, 1989.
5. It should be noted that the acquisition of a professional card is subject, for young, non-EU foreigners, to examination of the applicant's criminal record and it may be refused on account of the content of that record. That procedure is not applied to any other category of foreigner. See F. Brion, 'Extranéité, stigmate pénal et exclusion du marché du travail. L'exemple de la carte professionnelle', *Critique Régionale*, No. 21, 1994, Brussels, Institut de Sociologie, Cahiers de Sociologie et d'Économie Régionales.
6. These are unemployment benefits that school leavers receive when looking for work.
7. The Italians are still the most numerous national grouping amongst foreigners (26.7 per cent). The other nationalities present in large numbers are Moroccans (15.7 per cent), French (10.4 per cent) and Turks (9.4 per cent).

3 Workers of Migrant Origin in Germany: Forms of Discrimination in the Labour Market and at the Workplace

Nora Räthzel

The first section of this chapter explains what is meant by the term 'workers of migrant origin'. The second section gives an overview of the situation of migrant workers in the labour market and the third describes some of the forms of discrimination that workers of migrant origin face in German enterprises. The last section summarises results from a pilot study that was undertaken in Hamburg by the author and Ülkü Sarica.

MIGRATION AND DEFINITIONS OF MIGRANTS IN GERMANY

To understand the concepts used in Germany for ethnic minorities it is necessary to understand the self-image of the German nation. German nationality was first defined at national level in 1917. According to the legislation concerning nationality (Staatsangehörigkeitsgesetz), which – although often amended – is still in force today, one is German if born of German parents. But, according to the law of 1917, one could also become a German national by living for a certain time on German soil, or by working for five years as a civil servant. During the Weimar Republic, the Constitution (para. 113) provided the right to a mother tongue for the non-German parts of the 'Volk' (the people). That is, although German nationality was defined mainly by descent, the connection between descent and nationality was not exclusive. It was only in 1934, under fascism, that German nationality was defined exclusively by descent, as it still is today.

The first migration process into postwar West Germany[1] consisted of Germans expelled from former German territory in the East, including the territory of East Germany and other Eastern European countries. These migrations brought about 12 million people into West Germany. The integration of these populations is, today, often quoted as an example of the possibility of good integration, as long as the immigrants are 'culturally

35

close' to the population of the host country. However, if one reads newspapers from that period, discussions about the numbers, dangers and barbarism of the immigrants sound very familiar, in that they remind one of recent discussions concerning asylum-seekers (see Harzig 1994). That, in retrospect, they are regarded as being so readily assimilable is due to the fact that they are defined as Germans. As a result, the vast majority of accounts of migration into postwar Germany start with the recruitment of the so-called 'guest workers'. The first contract was between Germany and Italy in 1955, a time where additional and cheap labour was badly needed by expanding German industry. The next contracts were with Spain, Portugal, Tunisia, Morocco and Turkey, until labour migration was legally stopped in 1973. Throughout this time (particularly until the Berlin Wall was built in 1961) large numbers of immigrants came from East Germany (1.8 million), where the West German employment bureau was busily trying to recruit highly skilled workers. In addition, many fled to West Germany from the repression of the regime of state socialism. They were never counted or regarded as migrant workers, nor as asylum-seekers. Because West German nationality included East Germans, they were entitled to a passport and the same rights as West German citizens from the moment they set foot on West German soil. Between 1989 and 1992, about 1 million East Germans came to live in West Germany.

The same is true up to the present time for the so-called 'ethnic Germans' (Aussiedler). These are populations from Eastern European countries, mainly from Russia and other areas of the former Soviet Union and Poland, whose ancestors left for the East some 400 to 800 years ago. Although a German nation-state did not exist at that time, they are seen and see themselves as Germans. They are entitled to German citizenship, as long as they can prove their German descent and their belonging to a 'German culture'. These migrants are not counted as migrants either. Their number increased considerably (300,000–400,000 per annum in 1989 and 1990) after the relaxation of laws in Eastern European countries. Meanwhile, there are quotas restricting entry to only 200,000 persons per annum.

Between 1989 and 1991, about 3 million people migrated into West Germany: 1 million were ethnic Germans, 1 million came from East Germany and 1 million were non-German immigrants. Only the latter were subject to public discussion about a 'full boat' and the conflicts arising from immigration. If we examine accounts concerning migration, in terms of the group that is mentioned, discussed, seen as posing a problem, as needing integration, and so on, we discover that mainly workers from the former countries of recruitment, and asylum-seekers, attract the attention of politicians and social scientists. In other words, it is mainly those migrants who are not thought of as Germans who are regarded as posing a problem to German society. This explains the name given to migrant workers in Germany: 'Ausländer' (foreigners or aliens). Strictly speaking, the concept is legally correct, as the overwhelming majority of migrants who are not entitled to German nationality due to ancestry do not have German nationality.

Why this should be the case is often discussed. Why is it that the degree of naturalisation in Germany is one of the lowest in Europe?[2] One reason is that naturalisation used to be very difficult in Germany. With the 'aliens' law' (Ausländergesetz) of 1991, this has become easier for certain groups of migrants: for young people who have attended a German school for at least six years, and for people who have lived in Germany for at least 15 years. However, the population having Turkish origin in particular has had a very low incidence of naturalisation (0.1 per cent in 1988; see Fleischer 1991). It has been argued that this is due to the fact that dual nationality is not possible in Germany and that Turks, in general, are unlikely to adopt another nationality because they are proud of being Turkish or because this would disadvantage them in Turkey. But the rate of naturalisation for the Turkish population is much higher in other countries (e.g. 15 times as high in Sweden). This leads to the assumption that the rate of naturalisation may also have something to do with the general acceptance of a migrant population by the host country.

As I have pointed out, legally speaking, the term 'Ausländer', for those who are defined as migrants in Germany, is correct. Nevertheless, the term seems inappropriate. A majority of 'Ausländer' have lived in West Germany for more than ten years and two-thirds of the young people were born in Germany (see Bericht der Beauftragten der Bundesregierung für die Belange der Ausländer 1993: 16). If German legislation were to include at least elements of *ius soli*, it would be possible for the majority of those young 'Ausländer' to be German nationals. There is another reason for avoiding the term migrant in official, that is, political, discourse. To this day, the German government does not regard Germany as a country of immigration – despite the facts which are that those who came as 'guestworkers' have largely remained here, established families and become part of the population. Because the term 'Ausländer' ignores the social reality of a settled population of migrant origin, I will be using the term 'migrant workers'. As a matter of fact, though, this term has its own problems: first, the majority of the population of which I am going to speak migrated to Germany but are no longer migrants; they have become settlers. In addition, their children and grandchildren have not migrated at all; they were born in Germany and have lived there ever since. The term 'settler' would be more appropriate, but as it is very unusual in this context I will not use it.

Secondly, using the term 'migrants' or, more accurately, 'population of migrant origin', poses the problem of whom to include. If one were to be precise, that is, if one wants to avoid reproducing the restriction of the term 'migrant' to migrants who are not defined as German nationals, the article would have to include 'Aussiedler' and migrants from East Germany. The problem with this is that they do not appear as a separate category in statistics about work. It is therefore not possible to gather the same kind of statistical information about their situation in the workplace. Because of this difficulty these migrant populations are omitted from this essay.

WORKERS OF MIGRANT ORIGIN IN THE LABOUR MARKET

In the following section, I want to present some data regarding the structure of the migrant population in paid employment. The raw figures were provided by the Federal Office of Statistics, and are partly the results of the Microcensus of April 1993 in Germany as a whole and partly general statistics for West Germany only.

The unemployment rate of the migrant population has risen since April 1993. According to the National Employment Bureau, it was 16 per cent for West Germany in November 1994. The overall unemployment rate in West Germany at this time was 8.8 per cent and in East Germany, 13.8 per cent. There is no special rate for migrant unemployment in East Germany because the number of migrants there is too small. The unemployment rate

Table 3.1   Number and percentage of migrant population in the
workforce (Germany, 1993)

Population	Nos.	%
Population in total	81,338,930	
Migrant population in total	6,763,000	8.3
Migrant workforce	3,548,000	52.5
Employed	2,989,000	84.2
Self-employed	227,000	6.4
Unemployed	413,256	11.6
Migrant women in total	2,988,000	44.2
Migrant women workforce	983,000	32.2
Unemployed migrant women	197,000	20.0

is calculated on the basis of all 'dependently employed civilians': (the self-employed and armed services are not taken into account).

Table 3.2 shows that migrant workers are concentrated in manual work and highly under-represented in areas where non-manual work and more qualified white-collar work is the norm. The fact that migrant workers are also slightly over-represented in the service sector is due to their

Table 3.2 Distribution of migrant population in different sectors of employment (West Germany)

	Men	Women	%
1. Distribution of employed migrant workers in relation to the total workforce			
Number of employed workers in general	20,595.100	9,024.600	43.8
Number of employed migrant workers	2,127.100	731.200	34.4
Percentage of employed migrant workers in relation to workers in total	9.4%	8.1%	

Trades	All Workers	Migrants	%
2. Distribution of migrant workers in different sectors			
Production trades	9,677.315	1,113.916	11.5
Energy, hydraulic engineering, mining	405.897	26.284	6.5
Manufacturing Trades	7,721.865	885.093	11.5
Chemical industry, Mineral oil/petroleum processing	583.737	47.076	8.0
Plastic, synthetic, rubber and asbestos processing	384.427	63.443	16.5
Ferrous-metal ore Foundry and steel-casting procedure	541.603	89.619	16.5
Steel tool-machine and vehicle construction	2,390.889	247.280	10.3
Electrical engineering and precision mechanics	1,604.858	189.943	11.82
Leather, textile and clothing	388.204	54.958	14.2
Provisions and semi-luxuries (e.g. tobacco)	701.321	76.548	10.9
Building trades	1,549.553	202.539	13.0
Commerce	3,289.476	220.218	6.7
Signal communication traffic and transmission of communications	1,157.653	101.752	8.8
Credit institutions and Insurance branch	974.355	22.754	2.3
Service sector	5,385.942	557.518	10.4
Catering and accommodation branch	918.758	193.277	21.0
Science, Education, Art and Publishing	1,005.186	61.888	6.2
Health and Veterinary practice	1,540.612	109.290	37.0
Cleaning and personal hygiene	388.202	91.210	23.5
Regional administrative bodies and Social services	1,452.311	53.953	3.7

Note: No information about migrant women was available here.

over-representation in cleaning and catering. These are the sectors with the highest percentage of migrant work. Both sectors are among those with the lowest pay, insecure jobs (often seasonal work) and hardly any opportunity for promotion. Another sector with a comparatively high rate of migrant labour is the textile industry. As we shall see in Table 3.3, this is mainly due to migrant women's work in this sector. Although the situation of migrant workers slightly improved in the 1980s, Tables 3.2 and 3.3 show that migrant workers are still predominantly found in those sectors of the labour market where manual work is hard, and/or the prospects of promotion or even the future of the whole industry are poor. This is true for mining and energy, and the steel, construction and textile industries.

Table 3.3 shows more precisely than Table 3.2 how migrant workers are over-represented in jobs in the metal industry and in unqualified jobs within the service sector. It shows also very clearly the domains of women's work like simple electrical assembly work, cleaning and health-care, as well as catering and the social professions. Whereas there is no difference between indigenous women and migrant women concerning their over-representation in social professions and healthcare, indigenous women are less likely to be found in the cleaning sector and especially not in semi-or unskilled jobs in the production sphere. For instance, 0.8 per cent of indigenous and 2.9 per cent of migrant women work as electrical appliance assemblers, 4.9 per cent of indigenous women but 14.4 per cent of migrant women work in the cleaning sector (own calculation based on figures taken from the 'Statistisches Bundesamt'). As migrant men are employed to do work that indigenous men have abandoned for better jobs and better pay, migrant women are employed for the most disagreeable, dangerous (e.g. chemicals) and low-paid jobs that were previously done by indigenous women. One could argue that this is the fate of the migrant population, indeed, that this was the reason for their recruitment. But after 40 years of migration, the structure of migrant employment could have improved. As this has happened only to a small extent (see below), research into the causes of the position of migrant workers needs to become a main focus of migration theory and of research on racism and discrimination. Such research on migrant workers is scant. What research there is, however, has always found indications of the existence of discrimination (see Fijalkowski et al. 1940; Köhler and Preisendörfer 1988).

In Table 3.3, though, we do find some remarkable figures that do not fit into the general picture of migrant work. Although these findings are based on a small number of employees, they seem worth commenting on. Migrant women are not only highly over-represented in a number of unskilled and semi-skilled jobs, they are also slightly over-represented in

Table 3.3 Job levels and professions

Professions	Men	%	Women	%
Distribution of migrant workers according to groups of professions				
Miners	14.800	23.5		
Chemical workers	47.300	18.4	9.200	19.5
Synthetic-material processors	41.700	24.8	12.100	29.0
Metal producers, Rollers	11.800	24.8	200	
Moulders/Casters	17.600	37.4	1.100	
Metal moulders	22.600	25.1	5.900	
Metal-workers	13.800	28.1	1.500	
Metal assemblers	25.300	28.2	2.600	
Welders	21.600	28.3	400	
Fitters	64.600	9.1	1.600	
Mechanics (incl. vehicle mechanics)	36.200	8.2	1.400	
Electricians	48.500	7.3	6.600	13.6
Riggers and workers in metalwork trades	119.000	25.7	50.300	42.3
Electrical apparatus and part assemblers	28.600	22.9	20.900	73.0
Workers in spinning trades	8.400	40.8	3.000	35.7
Textile preparers	6.600	20.6	2.100	31.8
Textile finishers	5.000	29.4	0.900	18.0
Food preparers,	94.500	29.1	45.000	47.6
other workers in nutrition	13.800	23.2	5.700	41.3
Building labourers	47.900	26.0	300	
Casual labourers	66.700	23.9	29.100	43.6
Service sector occupations:				
Salespersons	67.600	5.7	46.400	68.6
Motor-vehicle drivers	44.600	7.1	700	
Inventory clerks, Storage and transport workers	103.300	14.4	14.300	13.8
Artists, Publishers, Interpreters, Librarians	11.800	10.4	4.100	34.7
Doctors/Chemists	8.600	5.8	3.100	36.0
Health service occupations (excluding doctors and chemists)	78.500	6.2	68.300	87.0
Workers in catering supervision	66.100	24.0	29.800	45.0
Cleaning professions	152.600	21.7	105.200	68.9
Clerical and auxiliary office workers	105.900	3.0	76.200	71.9
Technicians	25.900	3.2	2.800	10.8
Tracers	6.000	3.7	2.500	41.7
Bank employees and insurance-salespersons	13.900	1.8	7.700	55.4
Entrepreneurs/contractors, chartered accountants	19.200	3.8	4.200	21.9
Members of Parliament, administrative decision-makers	2.100	3.0	600	28.6
Accountants, Electronic data-processers	21.500	3.8	10.000	46.5
Workers in social care/and welfare professions	19.700	3.4	15.500	78.7
Kindergarten teachers, Kindergarten nurse/carers	6.100	2.5	5.800	95.0

highly skilled jobs: artists, journalists, interpreters and librarians, surgeons and pharmacists, accountants and computer specialists. Regarding the two first groups, the proportion of the indigenous population and the proportion of the migrant population working in those professions does not greatly differ: 0.5 per cent of the indigenous and 0.6 per cent of the migrant population work as artists, journalists, and so on. Concerning surgeons and pharmacists, the rates are 0.6 and 0.4 per cent, respectively. One would have to look more closely at these groups in order to find out if they are the children of migrant workers, or if their presence is due to the 'brain drain'.

Upward Mobility of Migrant Workers

The following section summarises an account by Wolfgang Seifert on migrant workers' mobility between 1984 and 1989. The raw data were taken by the author from the results of the socio-economic panel questionnaire (SOEP). It is based on representative questionnaires sent to 12,000 individuals and 6,000 households. Migrants are over-represented; they are described separately from the following five countries: Turkey, former Yugoslavia, Italy, Greece and Spain. The questionnaire was translated into five languages and special questionnaires were sent to migrants.

Developments in the Situation of Migrant Workers between 1984 and 1989

The majority of migrant workers were recruited for industrial work. In 1989, two-thirds of the migrant population worked as unskilled or semi-skilled workers. The number has slightly decreased, as in 1984 the percentage was 70 per cent. While every second German was a white-collar worker in 1989, this was true for only one in ten migrant workers (Seifert 1994). The low percentage of self-employed migrants (4 per cent) had not changed in 1989. This percentage was three times higher in the German population.

Migrant women and men, and women of Turkish origin, are over-represented in unskilled work. Three-quarters of migrant women work in unskilled jobs, while 15 per cent of them are white-collar workers. The percentage of German women is 61 per cent. To analyse this upward mobility, Seifert looked at the development of work positions between 1984 and 1989. For second-generation workers, it is difficult to stay in skilled positions. Only 59 per cent of those who worked as white-collar workers in 1984 held the same position in 1989. The rate in the German group was 82 per cent. Of the skilled workers of 1984, 61 per cent are still in those positions, while 28 per cent were working as semi-skilled workers in 1989. Seventy-six per cent of German skilled workers kept their jobs and only 6 per cent worked as semi-skilled workers.

The greatest mobility lies with second-generation unskilled workers. Only 28 per cent of those who worked as unskilled workers in 1984 were doing the same in 1989. The majority occupy semi-skilled jobs, but 17 per cent have managed to become skilled workers. German unskilled workers of the same group show a higher mobility rate. Only 16 per cent stay in unskilled jobs and only 6 per cent become skilled workers, but 15 per cent become white-collar workers. Mobility amongst second-generation semi-skilled workers is also high. Thirty-six per cent of the semi-skilled workers in 1984 defined themselves as skilled workers in 1989. This points to the fact that migrant workers have the opportunity of obtaining higher positions, while it is almost impossible for them to get positions as white-collar workers. Once achieved, positions as qualified or white-collar workers are much less stable than are the positions of German workers.

Concerning migrant women, one-third of those who worked as skilled workers in 1984 had lost their positions by 1989, and worked as unskilled or semi-skilled workers. Only 8 per cent of employed migrant women obtained positions as white-collar workers. Turkish workers have the lowest mobility rate. Half of the unskilled workers stayed in their positions and only 2 per cent were working as skilled workers in 1989. Two-thirds of the semi-skilled workers stayed in their positions, but a quarter became unskilled workers.

Generally, Seifert concludes, migrant and indigenous employees showed different mobility patterns. While indigenous employees become white-collar workers and stay in these positions, mobility for migrant workers occurs mainly within blue-collar positions, and a substantial number of white-collar workers in 1984 are working as blue-collar workers, mainly in semi-skilled positions, in 1989. Second-generation workers show a slightly greater mobility rate, although only within blue-collar positions. Turkish workers have the lowest mobility rate (Seifert 1994: 19–24).

Seifert (1994) also compares second-generation migrant workers with the respective groups of German workers. He defines 'second generation' as those having attended a German school, his sample being young people between 16 and 25 years. Of these, more than half work as unskilled or semi-skilled workers. Only 17 per cent of Germans of the same age work in these positions. One fourth of the second generation were able to establish themselves as skilled workers in production. The percentage is higher than the one in the respective German group. This is due to the fact that almost half of them are white-collar workers, which is true for only 20 per cent of the migrant group.

Mobility Regarding Branches and Sectors

There were hardly any differences between 1984 and 1989 concerning the branches and sectors in which migrant workers worked; 64 per cent worked in the production branch, 14 per cent in the sector of construction. Less than a quarter worked in the service sector and, if so, mostly in unattractive and low-paid jobs. The higher qualified positions in banking and insurance are not open to migrants.

The risk of becoming unemployed is especially high (as compared to their German counterparts) for migrant workers in better positions, or for those who are self-employed. The second generation experiences great problems integrating in the labour market. Almost half of them experience unemployment, while this is true for only one-third of the indigenous population of the same age. Turkish workers, and especially Turkish women, are more exposed to unemployment than the average migrant worker (Seifert 1994: 26).

Concerning income, Seifert's analysis finds that migrant workers generally earn the same as German workers. There is a mobility of income amongst them, in both directions, though on the whole there are more losers than winners. Migrant women in particular are losers. The second generation – the winners, at least according to their income – was able to move out of the lowest income bracket. This analysis is based on gross income (Seifert 1994: 32). A different picture emerges if one looks at the net income per capita of households. Here, Seifert states that the financial situation of migrant households has worsened in relation to German households. Migrant workers had barely increased their income and, in particular, the financial situation of Turkish households had clearly deteriorated (Seifert 1994: 44).

In most empirical studies on the segmentation of labour markets, migrant workers have not been taken into account. Seifert used a panel study to answer the question of whether segmented labour markets exist for migrant workers. He comes to the conclusion that segmentation of labour markets exists for them, although this does not mean that the boundaries between the segments are impermeable.

Seifert divides the labour market into three segments: (1) the unstructured market segment: these are jobs requiring few qualifications and generally offering no possibility for promotion within an enterprise; (2) the job- or profession-specific segment: this is a segment where high qualifications are demanded in enterprises with more than 200 employees. The qualifications have universal recognition and workers are relatively free to choose jobs within the branch; (3) the enterprise-specific segment: here, high qualifications are necessary, especially enterprise-specific knowledge and qualifications, both of which are the basis for promotion. This segment is particularly important for the analysis of migrant workers' upward mobility.

In analysing the positions of migrant workers within these labour market segments, Seifert came to the following conclusions: while the enterprise-specific segment is the most stable one for indigenous workers, almost half of the migrants working in this segment in 1984 lost their jobs. Thirty per cent of them returned to work in the unstructured segment. The relatively small proportion of German workers in the unstructured segment had a good chance of upward mobility and almost half of them were able to change to the job-specific or enterprise-specific segment. There is hardly any difference between migrant and indigenous workers in the job-specific labour market, where migrant workers tend to have stable positions to the same degree as indigenous workers. It seems as if migrant workers with job-specific qualifications have fewer problems staying in qualified jobs than those who have enterprise-specific qualifications.

This seems to contradict the segmentation theory, as it is generally the case that employers in companies tend to keep fluctuation to a minimum. However, considering the findings of other authors (Gillmeister, Kurthen and Fijalkowski 1989), who found out that employers prefer to recruit indigenous workers, and fire migrant workers first (see also Köhler and Grüner 1988; Köhler and Preisendörfer 1988), the instability of migrant workers in the enterprise-specific market segment becomes explicable. Seifert sees this as an indication of discrimination against migrant workers in the qualified sector of the labour market (Seifert 1994: 59).

The most common argument explaining the disadvantaged position of migrant workers in the labour market is their lack of qualifications and, especially, their difficulties with the German language. It is certainly true that the average migrant worker is less qualified than the average German worker. But this does not imply that higher qualifications improve the position of migrant workers. Already in 1980 representative studies about the social position of migrant workers demonstrated that a higher qualification did not necessarily improve their job status. A good qualification together with 'perfect knowledge of German', as the authors called it, did have a positive effect on a migrant worker's mobility, especially when the qualification was acquired in Germany. But more than 50 per cent of those migrants questioned in the study (75 per cent of the Italians and 69 per cent of the

Turks) could not improve their status in spite of a German qualification (Kremer und Spangenberg 1980: 73). Nine years later, Biller (1989) came to a similar conclusion. He conducted an in-depth study in a large German car company and found that qualifications improved the chances of only Italians and workers from the former Yugoslavia but not those of Turks and Greeks. Even the qualified ones occupied mainly jobs requiring no qualifications.

In spite of such findings there is no recent thorough or representative research into the situation of migrant workers at the workplace. No research has been published about recruiting practices, except an enquiry amongst entrepreneurs done in Berlin in 1988. There, the authors found that half of these would recruit German workers, in preference to migrants, if both had the same qualification (Gillmeister et al. 1989). Those managers who had better, white-collar jobs to offer preferred German workers, while those with unattractive jobs said they would employ migrants. One might guess that this has something to do with the difficulties of finding German workers for those types of jobs.

FORMS OF DISCRIMINATION IN ENTERPRISES

The following section summarises some findings made in a pilot study in Hamburg carried out in 1991 and 1992 by the author and Ülkü Sarica. We visited 18 enterprises which employed over 26,000 workers, almost 7,000 of whom were migrant workers (26 per cent). We spoke to 61 migrant workers, some being members of the 'workers council', the representative body of workers in an enterprise, and some being ordinary workers. Twenty-three of our informants were of German origin, mainly members of workers councils or persons who worked for the trade unions. With two exceptions the interviews were conducted in the mother-tongue of the informants. The enterprises visited belonged to the following sectors: the chemical industry, the cleaning, catering and accommodation sector, the steel, tool-machine and vehicle construction sector, the public transport and public health sector. We also interviewed school teachers and visited a 'multicultural kindergarten'.

The aim of the pilot study was to explore the field, looking at different sites where discrimination could take place: the labour office, the recruitment system, the workers' councils, everyday relations at the workplace, and finally, the school for apprentices. In the following summary I shall not use any figures because, given the nature of the study, they could not offer conclusive proof. However, we have found that our findings were confirmed when presented to trade unionists or to other migrant workers.

This demonstrates that more in-depth, but also representative research, into these issues is needed.

The Concept of Discrimination

The term discrimination is certainly a contested one. In Germany some authors believe that one can only talk about discrimination when migrant workers are paid less in the same job as an indigenous worker or when special jobs are assigned to them, that indigenous workers do not occupy at all (see Baker and Lenhardt 1991). With such a definition, one could find only little discrimination. The trade unions do make sure that people doing the same job get the same rate of pay for it – most of the time. The problem, as we see it, is rather one of the distribution of workers in a given work hierarchy. We speak of discrimination whenever a group of people is over-represented in lower, and under-represented in higher, job positions.

This does not mean that in every case there must be an intention to discriminate, for instance, on the part of the recruitment manager. The reason for a disadvantaged position in the workplace can also be a result of so-called 'institutional discrimination'. In the German case, this means migrant workers are suffering institutional discrimination because they do not have German nationality in the first place. Besides, the social institutions, for instance schools, are not designed according to the needs of a multilingual community. As a result, the special qualifications of migrant populations (biculturalism, bilingualism) are not noted as being of value. In many workplaces, perfect knowledge of the German language is seen as indispensable by employers, although the work does not require such fluency. In short, German society as a whole is still largely organised as a homogeneous society. The reality of a multicultural society is not taken into account. This is, itself, a form of discrimination against the ethnic minorities living in the country.

If it is true, then, that the population of migrant origin born and raised in the country does have in general a lower degree of qualification than the indigenous population, this cannot be seen as a *cause* of their disadvantaged position. Rather, this must be analysed as a symptom, indicating the lack of resources available to that population. In other words, this is already a *result* of discrimination, be it direct or institutional.

In our study we distinguished four different forms of discrimination: (1) discrimination within the existing work hierarchy, (2) discrimination outside the work hierarchy, (3) discrimination through equal treatment, and (4) discrimination in everyday work relations.

Discrimination within the Work Hierarchy

If we look at existing hierarchies in the workplace, non-discriminatory policies would result in a more or less equal distribution of different social groups within this hierarchy. As shown in the statistics above, this is not true for migrant workers. The same result was found in our study. In all enterprises we visited, the least attractive, most dangerous and worst paid jobs with a greater risk to health were occupied, to a large extent, by workers of migrant origin, especially women. That is, if migrant workers were employed at all. Some of the enterprises we visited had not been recruiting migrant workers for the past ten years. In one case, the workers' council went to court, trying to use the Industrial Relations Act (Betriebsverfassungsgesetz), the only law against discrimination on the grounds of nationality. As expected, the workers' council lost the case, because they could not prove that management had rejected the migrants who applied for jobs on the grounds of nationality. Instead, they argued that they had been unqualified. When their counterparts could prove that, in two cases, the applicants had even had two formal qualifications, they replied that these had been 'overqualified'. This points to the necessity for anti-discrimination legislation in Germany, which still does not exist today.

Discrimination outside the Work Hierarchy

Another form of discrimination we called discrimination 'outside the work hierarchy'. By this, we mean practices that are applied only to migrant workers, thus putting them outside the work hierarchy – to their disadvantage. One such practice was the recruitment of migrant workers on short-term contracts, despite their interest in a permanent job. In one hospital, for instance, the recruiting manager filled out the application form for the applicants as if they wanted a fixed-term job. By doing this, the hospital could avoid the vetoing of such job appointments by the workers' council, whose consent is required for all appointments. A fixed-term contract has some advantages for the employer: they can put pressure on the worker to work longer without extra pay or to do work that is not part of their contract. This will usually be done by the worker, because s/he is afraid not to get her/his contract extended. Every work contract in Germany can be terminated by either party without further explanation during the first six months. By giving workers a time-limited contract first, and an unlimited contract later, the employer can extend the period of time during which s/he can end the contract easily.

Concerning the work process itself, migrant workers in lower positions are made to work during breaks and clean their work area and that of their colleagues – work that indigenous workers do not have to do. This practice was reported to us by all migrant workers and is also mentioned in another study (Toksöz 1990). The fact that indigenous workers do not do this kind of extra work ('We would tell the overseer to do it himself', was one answer we got), but do not protect migrant workers from having to do it, points to a lack of solidarity.

Discrimination through Equal Treatment

For an English-speaking readership the term 'discrimination through equal treatment' must sound especially controversial, as 'equal treatment' and 'equal opportunities' are key terms in anti-discrimination policies. In general, the same is true for Germany. 'Equal treatment' is equated with just treatment. When asking employers and trade unionists about the situation of migrant workers, the most common answer was that their situation was no different from that of German workers as they were 'treated equally'.

According to a constitutional court ruling, equal treatment, guaranteed in Art.3, Abs.1 GG (Basic Law), means that 'substantial equals ought not to be treated arbitrarily unequally, nor ought substantial unequals be treated equally' (BVerfGE 1, 13 (52); 1, 208 (247); 4,144 (155); 51, 1 (23)). This interpretation is often used against migrant workers, for instance, in claiming that migrant workers have limited access to jobs, not because they are migrants, but because they lack the necessary qualifications. But it could also be used in their favour. For discrimination is, in fact, often the result of not taking into account differences, or special needs of migrant workers.

One point that can amount to a major conflict in enterprises is, for example, the duration of vacations. In Germany, workers usually have six weeks' vacation per year. As many migrant workers have a long journey home and usually have to organise things during their stay in their country of origin, this time is too short for them. In some enterprises, managers have fired workers because they returned too late to work after their vacations. This is one example where, due to different conditions, a different regulation would be needed. The same is true for information in the respective languages, as well as education/training courses in different mother tongues, or space and time for religious practices as well as regulations about religious holidays. While it is normally seen as self-evident that workers who are Muslims can do shift work during Christmas, there is no self-evidence concerning special regulations during Ramadan, for instance.

One might argue that the modern industrial process is defined by levelling the differences between workers of different social or ethnic backgrounds. But on the other hand, especially with hi-tech production, there is much talk about flexibility concerning working hours, duration of work and the constant change of qualifications and work requirements, to which workers have to adjust. By the same token, one could argue for flexibility on the side of the employers. Such flexibility and an adjustment to the different needs of migrant workers would certainly improve their productivity. At a time when international relations are becoming the norm, workers with intercultural competence who have command of two or more languages and knowledge of different cultures must be seen as having special qualifications. It is a rather shortsighted view to see them as deficient and lacking qualities that indigenous workers have. We have seen one enterprise beginning to acknowledge the advantage of biculturalism and bilingualism. They have designed training courses for apprentices of Turkish origin in both Turkish and German.

Discrimination in Everyday Work Relations

This form of discrimination is perhaps the most distressing one. Discrimination concerning recruitment, job opportunities and upward mobility is bad enough. But living in a market society, where enterprises must make a profit in order to survive, these forms of discrimination can be expected. They are part of the strategies enterprises use in order to secure extra profit. Trade unions have been founded to resist those strategies by creating solidarity amongst workers. Therefore, it is particularly disappointing to see how solidarity seems to stop when workers belong to another 'ethnic group'. Of course, this is nothing new and similar processes of competitive behaviour can be observed in relation to women and unskilled workers. Yet, we did not expect to find such a degree of animosity at the workplace combined with so much ignorance and indifference towards it on the part of indigenous workers and trade unionists.

We asked all our informants if they had heard of any 'conflicts at the workplace' between migrant and indigenous workers. We used this phrase because it was the most neutral one. Had we mentioned 'discrimination' or 'racism', the answers might have been mostly in the negative. It was interesting to see that there was strong disagreement between migrant and indigenous informants concerning this point. While all reported conflicts, they assessed them differently. The indigenous informants tended to see them as merely 'incidents of teasing' between colleagues. They described as teasing, addressing a worker by saying, 'Hey nigger, what do you want again?' or calling someone 'Kanacke' – a similar derogatory term used for people from Turkey, Greece, Italy, or others identified as non-Germans by features such as darker hair. 'Of course', we were told, 'there are graffiti in the toilets saying "Turks out" or worse expressions wishing Turkish workers the same fate as the one the Jews suffered in Germany. But usually this is not meant seriously, or those people are a minority.' While only four of our 23 indigenous informants took such incidents seriously, all informants of migrant origin did. Two members of a workers' council explained the higher rate of illness amongst migrant workers by the daily abuses they have to endure at the workplace. Every now and then they are called 'Kanacke' or insulted in some other way. Colleagues bump into them, pretending it was by accident. Sometimes, therefore, workers stay at home just to have a break from these daily insults.

One account, especially, of women who worked as cleaners in a hospital owned by the Protestant Church, made clear how extensive daily discrimination can be. When we started our conversation, my colleague with the Turkish women, and myself with the Italian and Portuguese women, we were told that they had no problems with German colleagues; that they got on fine, really. Only after we gave some examples about problems we had seen in other enterprises did they gain confidence to talk. For over an hour we were then told of the daily incidents that made life hard for them: they are not greeted by their German colleagues, they are constantly criticised for doing the wrong kind of work and accused of not understanding enough German (most women had been cleaning at the hospital for more than ten years), they are not properly informed about the dangers of certain cleansing agents, they do not get the necessary protective gloves, the overseers complain about them to the higher ranks, without having talked to them beforehand. 'The problem is not the criticism', one woman said, 'but the disrespectful way in which the criticism is voiced.' From those conflicts at the workplace, the women turned to the problems their children have at school and the disrespect with which they are treated as parents by the school. 'These are only small things', one women said at the end, 'but they happen daily and we have to swallow them daily. By the time they hurt you, they hurt inside.'

PERSPECTIVES FOR CHANGE

Given this picture at the workplace it is more easy to understand, although not to legitimate, why trade unions are so hesitant to take up the issue of discrimination in the labour market and in the workplace. As we were told by several trade unionists and members of workers' councils who try to set the issue on the agenda, most trade unionists fear that they will lose their German members if they engage too much in anti-discrimination politics. Since the amount of racist violence against refugees and people of migrant origin made this into a public issue, there have been several campaigns, launched by trade unions and employers, against racism. But all these campaigns have concentrated on distancing themselves from violent forms of racism ascribed to a right-wing extremist minority. There is a remarkable silence about daily and 'normal' forms of racism and discrimination, and about the disadvantaged position of migrant workers in the labour market. One reason for this lies in the arguments used in those campaigns against 'hostility against foreigners' as it is known. The main argument being that it is wrong to say migrant workers are taking the jobs of German workers, because they mostly occupy positions German workers would not like to do. This 'argument against racism' depends on the disadvantaged position of migrant workers. It would be a contradiction in itself if the trade unions started to campaign against these disadvantages. They would then discredit their own argument why racism is 'wrong'.

If the German trade unions are not very likely to put the issue of discrimination on their agenda, one would expect migrant's organisations to do so. As a matter of fact, this is not happening. First of all, those organisations are not very prominent in public discussions. If they do raise their voices it is mostly in relation to legal rights, asking for dual nationality or for the right to German nationality by birth or condemning racist attacks and demanding security. The work situation is not a major issue. One of the reasons may lie in the fact that this is seen as a task of trade unions. However, it is only the metal workers' trade union which has granted migrant workers the right and opportunity to organise themselves as a special group. Another obstacle is the divisions existing between different groups of migrants from different countries. As they are subject to different legislation (for instance as EU or non-EU members) it is not easy to find common ground. One reason for this difficulty might also lie in history: whereas the majority of the migrant populations in Britain, France and the Netherlands share a common history with their host country, their country of origin having been colonised by it, this is not the case for migrant populations in Germany. They do not have anything in common apart from being discriminated against as 'foreign workers'. Finally, German legislation sets limits to the rights of non-Germans to find their own organisations. They are not encouraged to do this, in contrast to the case of Sweden, for example. Although this has led to an incorporation of migrant's organisations into the state system (see Ålund and Schierup 1991), at the same time it has made it easier for migrant populations to have their voices heard.

Given these circumstances, social scientists have a special obligation in Germany to investigate the situation of workers of migrant origin, in order to put this question on the agenda of public concern.

NOTES

1. The correct term would be 'the former territory of the Federal Republic of Germany' or 'the old Länder of the Federal Republic'. In order to avoid this long expression, I am going to speak about West Germany and East Germany respectively. This differentiation is still valid today, after unification, because the living and working conditions in each part of the country are quite different. Also, sometimes statistics exist only for West Germany or only separately for the two parts of unified Germany.
2. In 1986 0.5 per cent of the migrant population who lived more than 10 years in the country had German nationality. In 1987 it was 0.5 per cent, in 1988 0.6 per cent (see Fleischer 1991: 321).

4 From School to the Labour Market in Britain: the Qualitative Exposure of Structures of Exclusion

John Wrench, Edgar Hassan and
Tarek Qureshi

The number of 16–24 year olds in the UK labour force has been falling, and within this falling number an increasingly large proportion of new labour market entrants will come from ethnic minorities, young people who will have received all or most of their education in Britain. Research has shown that the descendants of Britain's postwar migrants – those who came from ex-colonies, primarily the Caribbean, India and Pakistan – are more likely than their equivalent white peers to be unemployed, or employed beneath their qualification level, even though they were born and educated in the UK (Drew et al. 1992).

The problem this chapter addresses is the issue of labour market discrimination in the post-school experiences of these young people. This is not to say that the persistence of inequality in the labour market for migrants and ethnic minorities in the UK is simply a result of racial discrimination. In societies like the UK, where most postwar migrants have citizenship and civil rights and face no legal barriers to employment opportunity, there is nevertheless a whole range of forces which could still conceivably lead to the perpetuation of inequality amongst migrant groups and ethnic minorities long after the first generations have become settled and consolidated. Perhaps the most influential of these have been developments in the economy and the labour market, with a loss in low-skilled jobs, a shift to the service sector and a polarisation between higher level jobs and low-skilled part-time work. The industries which have declined have been those which have traditionally employed migrants, and much employment has been relocated away from the urban areas and old industrial conurbations where migrants originally settled, to new greenfield sites and areas where ethnic minorities are few. There has been shown to be a clear relationship between unemployment and the industrial specialisation and location of an ethnic group. For example, Pakistanis have tended to be concentrated in major urban areas of the Midlands and northern England and to be employed in manufacturing industries and manual occupations. The severe employment contraction of these areas and sectors has led to particularly high unemployment amongst this ethnic group (Owen and Green 1992). The economic restructuring which has so severely affected the employment experiences and opportunities of postwar migrants and their descendants forms the context in which other factors such as discrimination make their effect felt.

EVIDENCE FOR RACISM AND DISCRIMINATION

There are various ways in which research has produced evidence of employment discrimination against ethnic minorities in Britain. One is at the level of broad surveys, using large, perhaps national, data-sets. Another is by discrimination testing, whether carried out by academic researchers, journalists or the Commission for Racial Equality (CRE). Third is research of a more qualitative nature, usually carried out by academic researchers, into the processes and experiences of labour market discrimination. In this essay, we shall briefly describe examples of each of these in turn, before focusing in more detail on research evidence at the qualitative level, with particular implications for *young* people from minority ethnic backgrounds.

Indirect Evidence at the Statistical Level

In Britain the existence of racial discrimination has been deduced from analyses of statistical data. For example, a nationally representative cohort of 28,000 young people who were first eligible to leave school in 1985 and 1986 had their subsequent progress tracked (Drew et al. 1992). It was clear from this study that even after taking account of factors such as attainment and local labour market conditions, young people from ethnic minorities were more likely to experience both higher rates and longer spells of unemployment. These findings strongly suggest, therefore, that racial discrimination remains a factor operating in the labour market for young people. Nevertheless, such statistics by themselves constitute only *indirect* evidence, and are no more than indications that discrimination is likely to lie behind the inequality. Direct evidence of this has come from other sources.

Discrimination Testing

Discrimination testing – or 'practice testing' – has an established history in the UK. The method utilises matched pairs of testers, one belonging to a majority group and the others to minority ethnic groups, all of whom apply for the same jobs, either in person, by letter or by telephone. One example of such testing was commissioned by the CRE to test labour market discrimination in those jobs for which 'second-generation' young minority ethnic people would be reasonably expected to apply. In the late 1970s researchers acting in the guise of equally matched young applicants from different ethnic backgrounds 'applied' by letter to non-manual jobs advertised in the local newspaper of one English city (Hubbuck and Carter 1980). Where all three candidates were called for an interview, this was seen by the researchers to be 'non-discrimination'. In fact in 48 per cent of the cases the Afro-Caribbean or Asian 'applicant' was refused an interview whilst the white applicant was called for interview, whereas in only 6 per cent of the cases did the reverse happen. The researchers concluded that this represented clear evidence of racial discrimination in employment recruitment. Fourteen years later the CRE commissioned a repeat of the study in the same town to see if things had changed (Simpson and Stevenson 1994). One difference from the previous study was that, after a decade of mass unemployment, job prospects were bleak for all the applicants, and in some of the job categories tested, the very low success rate for *any* candidate created methodological problems. Nevertheless, the test found that, as before, the white applicant's chance of getting an interview were twice as high as those of either the Asian or Afro-Caribbean applicant.

A more recent example focused on racial discrimination in the medical profession (Esmail and Everington 1993). The researchers developed a curriculum vitae for each of six equivalent applicants, three with Asian names and three with English names. All the 'applicants' were male, the same age, and educated and trained in Britain, with a similar length of experience of work in hospitals. All were applying for their first senior house officer post, and each CV was tailored to the particular post by including a short paragraph on why the candidate was applying for the job. The comparability of the CVs was confirmed by two consultants who were unaware of the purpose of the research and who were asked to rate the CVs after the names had been removed. Matched pairs of applications were sent for each post to see who would be called for interview, and when applicants were short-listed the researchers immediately cancelled any interviews. A total of 46 applications were sent to 23 advertised posts. The researchers found that NHS hospitals were twice as likely to shortlist candidates for medical jobs if they had Anglo-Saxon rather than Asian names. (The Asian candidate was never shortlisted unless the English-named candidate was also shortlisted.) Similarly, following a Law Society study in 1992 which suggested that it is at least three times more difficult for black students to become solicitors than for white students, students from minority ethnic backgrounds complained that the more 'foreign-sounding' their name was, the more likely they were to be turned down (*Migration News Sheet*, June 1992). Because of this syndrome, some Asian young people in Britain are even changing their names in their attempts to get job interviews. It was reported by the Council of Sikh Gurdwaras in Birmingham that Davinders were becoming David, Charanjits becoming Charlie and Surinders becoming Sarah, simply to get over the hurdle of employers' prejudices at the first stage (*Independent*, 31 August 1992).

Qualitative Research

Although discrimination testing is effective in demonstrating discrimination at the first stages of the recruitment process, it offers little insight into the processes and experiences of exclusion, and this has to be provided by more qualitative research. The major part of this chapter concerns evidence at this level, drawing on sequential programmes of research in which at least one of the authors was involved. These projects involved interviews with the three main 'actors' in the processes of the transition from school to work: employers who recruit school leavers, a national agency which counsels young people and helps them find work or training, and a sample of 'excluded' ethnic minority young people themselves.

The implications of the first two projects have been described elsewhere (Wrench and Solomos 1993; Wrench 1995) and will be summarised briefly here. One was a study of access to apprenticeships (Lee and Wrench 1983) focusing on employers who were connected with the apprenticeship recruitment of over 300 West Midlands firms, as well as monitoring the fifth-form school leavers of four Birmingham schools. Ethnic minority young people who applied for apprenticeships were found to be just as well qualified as their white peers. However, there were significant differences in success rates in gaining a craft apprenticeship: whites had a success rate of 44 per cent compared to only 15 per cent for Afro-Caribbeans and 13 per cent for Asians. Most employers offered the usual denial of racial discrimination, arguing 'we don't care what colour they are' and explaining the absence of ethnic minority apprentices by saying 'they don't apply' or 'they don't get the qualifications'. In fact, well-qualified black young people were applying, and a programme of qualitative interviews with employers revealed a number of factors which helped to explain the lower success rate. For example, some employers had stereotyped perceptions: they labelled West Indians as 'lethargic', or thought Asians were 'weak in mechanical design'. Some employers described 'No go areas' in their firms, where white workers refused to work with a black: these tended to be skilled areas of work, such as craft, toolroom, sheet metal working, maintenance and supervision. Many firms relied for recruitment in significant part on the family members of existing employees, and trade unions would often support this policy. Thus, in a largely white workforce, this excluded ethnic minorities. This factor was compounded by the fact that many firms didn't advertise their vacancies for apprenticeships. They relied on word-of-mouth recruitment, with the result that ethnic minorities would be less likely to hear of vacancies than white school leavers who had contacts within a firm. Finally, many employers restricted their recruitment to a local catchment area when faced with a large number of applicants. As the largest employers were located in white outer suburbs of cities this excluded ethnic minority applicants from the beginning.

Many of these factors fall under the heading of *indirect* discrimination. Indirect discrimination exists with job requirements or recruitment practices which, although applied equally to all, in practice treat members of one ethnic group more favourably than another. The intention by an employer to discriminate *directly* would be unlikely to be admitted to a researcher during the interviews. However, employers do make their preferences quite clear to those agencies which are in the business of sending them recruits. One such national agency is the careers service, where careers officers give vocational advice to school leavers and put them in touch with suitable local employers or training schemes. The second study fills in more of the picture of labour market discrimination by another programme of qualitative interviews, finding out from careers officers themselves what employers say to them (Cross et al. 1990; Cross and Wrench 1990).

Careers staff were able to recount many examples of direct racial discrimination by employers, encountered when they were trying to place young people in schemes or jobs. Officers told of stories of employers who provided work experience for training schemes refusing to interview Asian youngsters on hearing their name, and of supervisors on schemes collaborating with such employers who specified 'We want a white youngster'. One careers officer reported, 'We rang up to submit someone to a vacancy, and everything seemed to be all right, until we mentioned the name, and then it suddenly changed – "Oh, I'm sorry, the vacancy's been filled".' Another described an employer who refused to take an Asian girl for a vacancy in an electrical shop because 'they don't dress smartly enough'.

Although according to the 1976 Race Relations Act an instruction to submit only white candidates amounts to unlawful pressure to discriminate, the interviews revealed that many careers staff were unwilling or afraid to challenge them and were reluctant to report a case of infringement of the Race Relations Act to the Commission for Racial Equality (CRE). Many careers staff seemed fatalistic, feeling that the Service was powerless when jobs were scarce and 'proof' of discrimination was difficult. Careers officers argue that they have very little power – that if they refuse to action a vacancy the employer can simply fill it elsewhere.

Therefore, instead of confronting racist employers, many careers officers would engage in 'protective channelling', directing ethnic minority young people away from firms and schemes where they anticipate they will be rejected. For example, it would become apparent which training schemes were willing to take on ethnic minorities, and the young people would be sent to these in the knowledge that they would be accepted. Their stated aim was to protect the young person from negative and disappointing experiences. However, the effect of this practice, no matter how well intentioned, was to collude with and perpetuate processes of exclusion and inequality without a specific racist act of rejection needing to take place each time.

Furthermore, it was clear that these processes were encouraged by the economic and political environment in which careers officers worked. New political pressures on the Service in the 1980s directed the emphasis of the Service away from counselling and guidance work with young people towards servicing the needs of employers (Wrench 1990: 430). Subsequent developments in the direction of the privatisation of the Service put it in competition with other agencies for clients, and in this climate there are pressures to avoid the potential loss of time and customers which may result from the confrontation of racist practices in the labour market.

INTERVIEWS WITH YOUNG PEOPLE

Whilst these first two qualitative pieces of research demonstrated how the interlocking practices of gatekeepers reduced the opportunities of ethnic minority young people, the third programme of research completed more of the picture of labour market discrimination processes by interviewing young minority ethnic people themselves (Wrench and Hassan 1996; Wrench and Qureshi 1996). Amongst the aims of this last exercise were a desire to see if a group of (often unemployed) young people were aware of the operation of racism and discrimination in their lives, and whether their own labour market behaviour reflects or compounds the discrimination.

Interviews were tape-recorded with 50 Afro-Caribbean and 50 Bangladeshi young men. They young men were aged 16–24, deliberately selected from the least qualified end of the attainment spectrum, and the interviews covered their educational and employment experiences and aspirations. The Afro-Caribbean respondents were split equally between Coventry and Birmingham, and of the 50 Bangladeshi young men, 20 came from Birmingham and 30 from Tower Hamlets in East London. Tower Hamlets is the area of largest Bangladeshi population in Britain, and is also – according to social indicators of poverty, over-crowded accommodation and unemployment – one of the most deprived urban areas in England.

There are particular reasons for focusing on these two groups of young men. In 1994 the Fourth National Survey of Ethnic Minorities was undertaken in Britain by the Policy Studies Institute (PSI) and Social and Community Planning Research (Modood et al. 1997). Since the 1970s the discourse on 'racial' and ethnic discrimination in Britain has usually worked from the assumption that discrimination operates along a simple white/non-white distinction. However, this latest PSI survey suggests a more complex picture of ethnic diversity and works from a slightly different assumption: 'that the various aspects of social life that we investigate are structured by racial exclusion and inequalities past and present, but that these do not necessarily operate uniformly on all groups or result in uniform outcomes' (Modood et al. 1997: 9). The survey reveals considerable diversity between minority groups in Britain: whilst some are clearly over-represented amongst those experiencing low wages, unemployment, poor housing, ill-health and general poverty, others have rates of success closer to whites than non-whites (Modood et al. 1997: 84). The diversity which exists between groups can be seen quite clearly with regard to unemployment rates. For example, for white and Indian men under retirement age the unemployment rate was 15 per cent and 19 per cent respectively, whilst the rate for Caribbean men was 31 per cent and for Bangladeshi men 42 per cent (Modood et al. 1997: 89). Unemployment rates are generally higher for young people in most labour markets, and here again the survey showed that young Caribbeans and Pakistanis/Bangladeshis had much higher rates of unemployment than other groups.

Therefore, if we are interested in subjective experiences of discrimination, disadvantage and exclusion it is important to look at two groups of people who are amongst the most severely affected: young Afro-Caribbeans and Bangladeshis. Furthermore, it is the males (rather than the females) of both these groups who are seen in public consciousness to be a 'problem' group. Afro-Caribbean young men have since the 1970s had the status of a 'folk devil' in the British tabloid press, synonymous with crime and muggings (Hall et al. 1978). In recent years, after some street disturbances in the East End of London, young Bangladeshi men have joined them as victims of negative stereotyping, and have also begun to be defined as a 'law and order problem' (Keith 1995).

The tape-recorded interviews were carried out by two researchers, one of Bangladeshi and one of Afro-Caribbean origin.[1] Young people were first contacted through youth and community organisations, followed by 'snowballing' to get to other friends and acquaintances. Interviews took place in community organisations, snooker halls, hostels for the homeless, in cars and in university offices.

Although we were primarily interested in the young people's employment-related experiences, it was clear that the young men themselves were aware of factors in their educational years which negatively affected their later chances of labour market success. For the Bangladeshi young men there were seen to be three particular barriers to educational achievement. One was the lack of English language amongst their parents which meant that they could not give practical guidance with homework, and led to serious problems of liaison with schools. Second, serious overcrowding in the home could make it difficult for young people to do their homework. Third, relative poverty meant that there was pressure on some of the sample to leave school and start working as soon as they could in order to help with the family's financial problems.

These factors relating to their families' recent migration, poor housing conditions and relative poverty were then compounded by experiences of racism. One third of the Bangladeshi sample reported experiencing racial harassment at school by other pupils, particularly when Bangladeshis were in a real minority at school. Whilst some pupils were able to ride above this, many others clearly had their school years blighted and their educational achievement severely undermined by this factor. One 17-year-old said:

> School could be dangerous place, especially if you're Bengali. Nothing happened to me but some of my friends used to get picked on by the older white kids. Racial abuse was like an everyday thing, they were always calling you names, 'Paki, go back to where you came from.' But you learn to deal with it. It wasn't always like that. Once you were in the fourth year and a bit older they [whites] were scared and left you alone. ... Anyway I just stayed out of trouble and tried to concentrate on passing the exams. But some of the Bangladeshi kids let all the harassment get to them. I don't blame them, it really fucked them up. Some of them just left in the fifth year without doing their exams.

Racial harassment was one reason for the fact that respondents preferred to be in groups of their peers, both in school and when walking the streets.

They did this for protection and sociability, and did not see themselves as being in 'gangs', although they were conscious that others tended to see them as such.

In contrast to the school experiences of Bangladeshis, the Afro-Caribbean respondents had relatively little to say about racism and harassment from other pupils. However, they complained a great deal about the problems they encountered in their relationships with teachers. Respondents remembered their school days in terms of great unfairness and injustice. Criticisms included suspicions of stereotyping and its effect on subject and examination choices, arbitrary physical and verbal abuse, periods of temporary exclusion, and finally permanent expulsion, mostly interpreted by respondents as being unjustified. A common theme among respondents was how, when they gained the confidence to begin to resist what they perceived as unfair treatment, this often brought them further problems, in a vicious circle of resistance and reaction with the teaching staff. It was felt that many black youths went through the same experience: as one put it: 'All it takes is the first bit of conflict you have with a teacher, and then you get labelled, and throughout all of the school you are seen as a troublemaker.'

These conflicts would frequently escalate into exclusion from school. Twenty out of 50 of these low-achieving respondents – 40 per cent of the sample – had been excluded from school at some time, and 11 of these – 22 per cent of the sample – had been permanently excluded. Although some admitted that their exclusion had been deserved, far more were adamant that they had suffered injustice, and had a strong sense of grievance. An 18-year-old who had been excluded from his school felt that the teachers had formed an incorrect impression of him as someone with a 'chip on his shoulder'. He felt that he had a reputation for fighting, so that he would get the blame for other people's fights. 'Like, teachers would grab me and if I said it weren't me, they didn't believe me, and like the more I went mad at them, the more they wouldn't believe me.' He described one incident which led to his exclusion for a week:

> The first one was, one of my mates was smoking. A teacher come down, he give my mate a lot of aggro about it and then I went into the lesson – I had him for the next lesson, and he said to me 'I don't want no trouble from you this lesson.' Like I hadn't even done nothing, I'd just walked through the door, so I go 'What you on about?' He goes, 'You just don't give me no trouble' so like I was going mad at him because I hadn't even done nothing. I hate being accused of something I ain't even done. Like he come up to me and he pushed me, so I hit him. Then like he sent me to the head teacher and I got suspended – for a week.

He had last been excluded six months before his exams. Since then he had been out of school two years, with no job.

The exclusion phenomenon needs to be located in a broader context. Bridges (1994) sees this problem exacerbated by recent educational reforms in Britain. As schools are made to compete with one another in the new educational marketplace, those pupils who are seen as troublesome or expensive to deal with are more likely to be expelled. This includes black children with their perceived 'behavioural problems' or 'learning difficulties'. In British schools today, the head teacher's role has been transformed into that of manager, making them all the more conscious of the budgetary and other consequences of retaining difficult or disruptive pupils. For Bridges, racism, both as reflected in teachers' stereotypical assumptions and attitudes towards black children, and as institutionalised in policies that disproportionately identify black children as educationally backward or as having behavioural problems, has a hand in the exclusions process. Educational reforms have exacerbated the syndrome. Teachers have come under increased pressure due to the introduction of the National Curriculum and its additional paperwork. With fewer reserves of energy to deal with disruptive children there is a more frequent resort to in-school disciplinary measures. In many schools these measures come in the form of penalties which quickly escalate into a series of fixed-term exclusions, leading to indefinite or permanent exclusion. Furthermore, the system of checks and balances of formal review procedures for appealing against exclusions has been undermined (Bridges 1994).

Many of those who were interviewed in our research were of the view that their expulsions had disastrous effects on their education, and subsequent employment prospects. In contrast to the satisfaction generally expressed by the minority of the Afro-Caribbean sample who were in work, those in the sample who were unemployed were more likely to be disillusioned, and to feel that their self-respect had been undermined. Unemployment could lead to difficulties mixing with friends who have jobs, and to increased social isolation. Out of the 34 in the sample who were unemployed, 28 were actively seeking work. Nevertheless, they had a strong sense of pride and a desire for respect, and would therefore choose to remain unemployed rather than tolerate racist practices or demeaning work.

Perceptions of Racism and Discrimination

Interviews on a respondent's subjective experiences of racism and discrimination in recruitment are likely to be a somewhat unreliable source of information. A victim may perceive discrimination where it does not exist; conversely, research has demonstrated that ethnic minorities can under-estimate the discrimination they are in reality exposed to (Smith 1977). As we have seen, processes of discrimination can operate quite invisibly. Nevertheless, Afro-Caribbean respondents did talk about their suspicions of racism and how it made their life harder. When asked what they felt hindered them in finding work, several replied simply 'racism' or 'my skin colour'. A Coventry respondent working full-time stated:

> How do I see it? … I see that a black guy gotta basically be twice as good as like a white compatriot – for like certain, like what virtually everything, thing that he does. … When you know of black guys with seven O levels and a white guy's got five … like the white guy's got the job. … I actually seen it in the past … .

Racism was seen to manifest itself at different stages in the employment process. One respondent described how it prevented him getting to the interview stage. This Birmingham man, unemployed for five years since leaving school, told of encountering discrimination when he applied for his first job:

> I mean as soon as I left school, I applied for this job, I went to the [local] careers office and I applied for this job at this firm, and the next thing you know, they [the careers office] phoned me back and said could I come up to the office to have a chat with them. They have had this phone call saying that 'They cannot accept people like yourself' and I was thinking like 'What?', and the staff goes 'because of your colour' and that was the first thing that really hit me.

His parents urged him to fight it and get compensation, but he refused: 'I won't bother, because I know at the end of the day, because of my colour, I will lose out.'

Other respondents told of their impressions at the interview stage that things were unfair – for example, when someone was wanted 'urgently', and yet after the interview they still were not offered the job. Other times the evidence of unfair treatment was more tangible. One Birmingham respondent, unemployed for six years since leaving school, felt that the interviewer had made his mind up already to reject him:

> Just by the way he was carrying on and, you know, if you are going to interview someone, you don't make them stand up in a middle of a shop and you serve customers at the same time. You tend to give them all your attention.

A Birmingham man, unemployed for three years, got an interview with the assistance of the Careers Service but found the experience 'unfair':

> I went there for an interview to work at a timber yard. I went there and the man's asking me questions. The man's asking me do I have qualifications and that madness, but on the card it said 'qualifications are not needed'. So the man is chatting shit in my head now and at the end of the day I find out the man says 'No' just because I got no qualifications. And the card just said you don't need none.

A Coventry respondent, unemployed for two years after losing his job, recounted:

> The last thing – I tell you – the last interview I had, it was for a maintenance trainee and I went and sat down, and a lady goes to me 'He will personally interview you in a minute' … and he looked at me and, like a look of shock on his face like 'Oh my god he's black' … and for the whole interview he was just talking to me like 'Yeah, I don't really want you, but I am just going through the process'.

A Coventry young man, currently working part-time, related bad experiences when going for a job in person: 'It's like you go for a job, and you know that they're not interested, its like body language.'

> Me and C——went for enough of them, when West Orchards [a shopping centre] first opened up we went looking for jobs around the shops, it was a case of, they looked at us, they thought, 'Two black guys, no.' And like a white girl would walk in, they would take an application form out in front of us and would say, 'There you go, bring it back tomorrow.' And we'd be like, where's ours? and they'd be like, 'Well you're not really suited for this job.'

Of the Bangladeshi sample, one third were in work, and roughly half of these worked in the catering trade. Furthermore, of those who were still in full-time education, about half were also working part-time in restaurants. This work is low-paid, insecure and casualised, with long hours and often cash-in-hand payment. The industry was seen to represent a valuable option for members of a new and relatively poor community of migrant origin, offering work in the locality amongst people of the same linguistic and cultural background, and enabling people without qualifications or without knowledge of the English language to gain paid work. However, it was also recognised that if a young man spent too much time in this type of employment it then became harder to move on into more mainstream employment.

Like the Afro-Caribbean young men, the Bangladeshi respondents saw racism as one of the factors which constrain their employment options. Indeed, one stated reason for getting employment in restaurants is that they won't experience racism there. The research sample remained disproportionately employed within the geographical locality of the Bangladeshi community itself, and respondents were well aware that some local 'white' areas are closed to them because of the likelihood of racist attack. Although the young men in the sample had very little experience in working within white businesses, the attitude persists that they will have extra difficulties in the mainstream labour market. Some local white-collar employment in surrounding areas they saw to be effectively closed to them, in the sense that they feel that they are not expected to apply.

The sample interviewed in London saw the adjoining Isle of Dogs and Docklands area to be a highly racialised place. Despite developments and the inward investment that has been made into the Docklands area in recent years, and the employment opportunities that have arisen, Bangladeshis were on the whole not willing to take jobs in this area, even if offered.

I would work anywhere in London except of the Isle of Dogs, simply because I wouldn't feel safe travelling in that part of East London. It is a racist area, you only have to go there and the white people give you funny looks. One of my cousins got attacked there, he was walking down the road when he got jumped by these whites. They beat him up badly, he was in hospital for a month. (London respondent, aged 21)

I don't mind getting a job locally [East London] as long as it isn't too far … the Isle of Dogs is definitely a no-go area for Bangladeshis. The place is full of racist whites, no way would I go there if for a job. The developments with Docklands isn't really for us, it's for people from the City. (London respondent, aged 18)

Similar views were expressed by the Bangladeshi sample in Birmingham about the white-dominated suburbs of the city.

There are some areas around here that's not for Bangladeshi people. Where we are now [Saltley, Birmingham] used to be a white area, then Asians started to move into Saltley and the whites moved out. Now we don't go into their area and they don't come into ours…. If somebody was to give me a job in one of these white areas I would have to think very hard whether or not to take it. The white areas are racist, Asians that live in those areas get a hard time. I would prefer to work around here, in my own area. (Birmingham respondent, aged 16)

It is true that some parts of Birmingham are dangerous for Bangladeshis and that is a reason the community sticks together and defends itself. Most of the Asians and Bangladeshis work and live in this part of the city. Certain places are out of bounds, I mean you can go there, but you wouldn't feel safe. I feel safe amongst my own people. Although sometimes you get trouble with the Pakistanis and Blacks, we know how to handle them. If any white kids come down here looking for trouble they wouldn't get very far … I used to work in a restaurant that my uncles owned in one of the white areas. It wasn't a nice place at all. Every night you got in fights with the locals, they would come into the restaurant and treat you like dirt. That's why most of the Asians stick to Asian areas, they can go without the hassle. (Birmingham respondent, aged 17)

The racialisation of areas into black/Asian spaces and white spaces undeniably affects the employment patterns of different communities. The fear of racial attack has led to the indirect segregation of different communities in terms of residence and employment opportunities. However, the over-representation of Bangladeshi employment within their own community does not mean that they are an immobile workforce. The young men were highly motivated to find work, and many of those in the London sample were travelling to take jobs in Kent, Birmingham and Swansea. Significantly, however, in these far-away places they were still working within the Bangladeshi communities.

Afro-Caribbean respondents were also asked 'Are there any parts of the city or parts of the country you would prefer not to take work in?' As with the Bangladeshi sample, the reason for avoiding certain areas was voiced in terms of the fact that in these areas black people were not welcome. For one unemployed Birmingham respondent, these were the affluent white areas beyond the suburbs:

I just don't think I would fit in somewhere like Solihull, Knowle and those kind of places. I just don't think I would fit in. I mean OK, I can make a statement of my being there and showing that as a black man I could be – I mean – 'I'm not as rich as you, but I can still work here'. But I would feel out of place, you know what I'm saying? … Because I'm not from that class and that setting, it just wouldn't feel right, I wouldn't feel happy there. I wouldn't feel at home. I have to be somewhere where I feel comfortable.

A Birmingham respondent in part-time work, referring to a nearby white area in the city, stated, 'I wouldn't like to work in Kingstanding. … I've had experiences there before. Also Erdington. There is just a vibe there which I detest.' Three other Birmingham respondents specifically mentioned Kingstanding, seen as an area of white working-class racism.

> It's racist … I've seen it – I've been down there. … I've seen skinheads look at me and call me, you know. I've been down there with my brethren … and like these white boys come over and these skinheads, and start taking out knives, and saying 'Come on, you nigger' … and all that do my head in.

Another described the same area:

> It totally puts you off because you know the area is, like, I would say it is a fairly racist area. There are groups that live in that area and they influence some of the other residents as well, so, like no, I wouldn't work there.

This avoidance of certain geographical areas is another factor which can be added to those which exclude young black men from opportunities. This was shown previously by researchers in Liverpool, who found that a majority of the sample of black young people felt unsafe during the day outside their own area of Liverpool 8, due to racial tension or fear of racial harassment or attack (Roberts, Connolly and Parsell 1992). Some felt unwilling to travel alone elsewhere in Liverpool. The authors concluded that as a result of this, their training, education and employment opportunities were severely restricted.

CONCLUSION

The research described in this essay shows the operation of processes of discrimination in practice, at various levels, and involving different groups of actors. The Youth Cohort Study showed that ethnic minority school leavers across Britain were having less success than whites even when other factors, such as educational attainment, were held constant. The discrimination tests showed that young people could be rejected at the first stage of application simply by having an Asian name. The apprenticeship study showed how some employers operated to ethnic stereotypes and prejudices, and sometimes took account of the racist preferences of their white workforce. Most of this happened quietly, but was revealed in the instructions given by employers to external agencies such as the Careers Service when seeking recruits. The apprenticeship study also showed how employers used recruitment practices which severely reduce the chances of success of ethnic minority young people by indirect discrimination. The Careers Service research shows that the extent of the problem is not identified by how often it breaks the surface. For example, the 'protective channelling' and the anticipatory avoidance of apparently racist employers lessens the likelihood that an act of racial discrimination by an employer will need to occur. The tape-recorded interviews with Afro-Caribbean and Bangladeshi young men provided further, more subjective, detail on processes of exclusion. Some of them encountered experiences at school which blighted their later chances of success, and most of them were conscious of the extra difficulties they faced or were likely to face when putting themselves forward for opportunities. This awareness constrained and restricted their job-seeking behaviour, so that again, the very anticipation of rejection on racial or ethnic grounds meant that, over time, processes of exclusion continued to operate without individual acts of direct discrimination taking place. Finally, we have also seen how the particular economic and political context of some of these processes of exclusion can work to increase their likelihood of occurrence or intensify their effects. The political decisions which have exposed British schools and the Careers Service to market forces have meant that such institutions can be faced by financial penalties for operating 'good practice' in the reduction of racial and ethnic inequalities.

The evidence above with regard to racism and discrimination in employment confirms the adage that 'If you don't look for it you won't find it', thereby demonstrating the importance of research investigation to help keep the issue on the public agenda. However, the picture as revealed by research in Britain is not totally negative. It is true that the 1994 PSI study found increasing reporting of experiences of racial discrimination in employment by ethnic minority respondents. This does not necessarily mean, however, that the real level of employment discrimination in Britain has been increasing. Indeed, the authors argue that 'increases in reports of discrimination are compatible with stable or even declining levels of discrimination' (Modood et al. 1997: 132). They argue that the fact that these reports have increased in a period when the position of minorities has generally improved – and that the ethnic groups in which these reports have increased the most are those which have made the most progress – suggest that such reports are related to factors such as the awareness of the issue and the perception of the receptivity of the climate of opinion.

A climate in which equal opportunities issues are being addressed may, at least initially, increase complaints of discrimination and perceptions about the prevalence of discrimination. (Modood et al. 1997: 132)

Since the late 1960s Britain has had anti-discrimination legislation in the sphere of employment, including since 1976 legislation which covers *indirect* discrimination. One positive consequence of the long-established existence of the Race Relations Acts in Britain is that they have helped to foster a public climate which denies the legitimacy of acts of racial discrimination. Similarly, the media attention paid to industrial tribunal discrimination cases and the formal investigations of the CRE over nearly 20 years have presented to aggrieved employees models and precedents for action. Many specific cases of racism and discrimination which would otherwise remain hidden come to the surface through the actions of concerned individuals or the anger of aggrieved parties, and it is likely that many of these would not have been exposed but for the existence of the Race Relations legislation and the availability of legal measures of redress for victims of discrimination.

An increase in the reporting of experiences of racial discrimination may also reflect an improved state of upward social mobility in that 'as ethnic minorities become more effective competitors for more prized jobs and professions, the salience of the issue of discrimination may, ironically, increase' (Modood et al. 1997: 132). This is not inconsistent with the fact that the findings from one of our studies, quoted earlier, proved different to those of previous studies. Earlier research had found a relatively high degree of job satisfaction among Bangladeshi workers, and little experience of discrimination, mainly because they worked for Bangladeshi employers. The generation represented in our sample, whilst still over-represented in the same limited occupational areas, were not generally 'satisfied' with their employment. They recognised that their work was temporary, insecure and poorly paid, with no promotion structure. The young men in this sample were far more concerned about racism and discrimination, precisely because many did not intend to keep their horizons low, as the previous generation had done.

Furthermore, the legislation in Britain has provisions which enable employers to take measures to help people from ethnic minorities to compete for jobs on a more equal footing in the labour market. This is an important socio-legal context which encourages action on this issue in Britain. Unlike in many other European countries, 'racial' inequality is an accepted part of equal opportunities issues. 'Most large companies' policies address the issue of racial equality, and considerable expertise in this matter has been developed in Britain (Virdee 1997). These may be part of the reason why, as shown in the PSI study, there is evidence in Britain of a long-term reduction in the differences in job levels achieved by people from different ethnic minority backgrounds.

There are therefore both positive and negative elements within the British experience, as revealed by research over recent years. There is a growing recognition and awareness of the issue of employment discrimination, and much progress has been made in developing policies to counter it. Nevertheless, there remains an 'ethnic penalty' to be paid by non-white people in Britain. In other words, ethnic minorities are steadily getting better jobs but are still doing so to a lesser extent than white people with the same qualifications (Heath and McMahon 1995, cited in Modood et al. 1997: 84). The research described in this chapter on the processes and structures of ethnic and racial discrimination experienced in the transition from school to the labour market form part of the explanation as to how this ethnic penalty is paid.

NOTE

1. The fieldwork for the Afro-Caribbean study was carried out by Edgar Hassan and for the Bangladeshi study by Tarek Qureshi.

5 Foreigners and Immigrants in the French Labour Market: Structural Inequality and Discrimination

François Vourc'h, Véronique De Rudder and Maryse Tripier

All international comparative studies are rendered questionable by the heterogeneity of the nomenclatures upon which national census, enumerations and indicators are based. Socio-economic or professional activity categories, for instance, generally present methodological problems for the comparative analysis of employment issues. These difficulties are also often theoretical and epistemological in nature. Such is the case, particularly for immigrant populations and their descendants on the one hand, and for cultural or so-called 'racial' minorities on the other hand. One of the characteristics of French official statistics is the almost total elimination of any 'ethnic' or 'racial' classification: the gathering of such data is virtually prohibited by law and analyses concerning these populations are extremely difficult to undertake. Consequently, international comparisons are almost impossible. The press, the body politic and the man in the street refer to these populations using terms that have widely varying definitions and which often reveal themselves as contradictory, mixing together judicial and geographical, linguistic and religious concepts. These issues nevertheless give rise to highly controversial debates that are much more political in nature than a detached scientific approach.

It is difficult, and not necessarily relevant, to analyse the realities of a society using categories inherited from different historical and social contexts. One cannot wish that ethnic and *a fortiori* 'racial' categories were adopted in French official statistics, and perhaps in census research as well, just because it would offer data 'comparable' to those of other countries. (In fact, how could we be sure that they would in reality – and not just formally – be comparable?) But neither can it simply be rejected in the name of 'French exceptionality' and the 'republican model' with which it claims kinship.

72

For us, the main issue seems to be of a different nature. It lies in the increasingly problematic ambiguity of this 'French model'.

OFFICIAL FRENCH STATISTICAL SOURCES AND THEIR LIMITATIONS

Laws in France forbid the recording or taking into consideration of ethnic or 'racial' categories, in order to prevent discrimination between citizens, who are declared equal in front of the *État de droit*. From this point of view, French law provides a textbook model of a socio-national integration political project and this project is partly a success in the sense that social and political life is not permanently constrained through such categorisation.

This equality principle, nevertheless, takes on a rather formal character. Despite a certain number of legislative precautions,[1] this interdiction is regularly evaded. In fact, many administrations' practices fall far short of ignoring origin or of being 'colour-blind' as the rule of 'common law' would want them to be. Barely legal and hidden classifications are made, not only by private sector firms or by individuals, but also by quasi-public institutions or corporations (Simon 1993). In other words, this principle rebounds on those whom it is supposed to protect, when officially illegitimate classifications in reality permeate institutional actions and daily life.

The standard and long-used practice in French official statistics is to make a distinction between foreigners and the French. If this dichotomy is based upon a simple criterion, its definition is, in fact, far from being as straightforward and exclusive as its apparent 'legal purity' would make it appear.

- Within the French category, statistics distinguish between those who are native French and those having acquired French nationality: French by acquisition.[2]
- Within the foreigner category, statistics register their nationality and then creates groups that variously cover geographical, cultural or political entities.

Some official statistical publications regularly make a distinction between 'European Union immigrants' and 'outside EU immigrants'. Others (survey institutes, media, and so on) make a distinction between 'non-European immigrants' and those coming from European countries, the former group being considered 'more immigrant'. Only very recently has there begun a redefinition of terms used in statistics (Tribalat 1989). Two official surveys – the 1990 census and an *Institut National d'Etudes Démographiques* survey entitled 'Geographic mobility and social integration' (Tribalat and Simon 1993) – have used the category 'immigrant' as well as that of 'foreigner', defining it as 'foreigner' or 'French-by-acquisition', born outside Metropolitan France.[3]

Thus, it is by crossing a certain number of criteria, such as place of birth or nationality of parents, that these new distinctions enable the subdivision of French or foreigners into different categories: originating from the DOM-TOM (that is, French departments and territories outside the EU), from the European Union, from North Africa. These categories only imperfectly answer the researchers' needs but do offer a few indications on the socio-economic evolution of populations who have come to France since the 1960s and who are currently called 'immigrants'.[4]

The distinction between being French and foreign in practice becomes more inadequate every day. Many authors stress the fact that due to the lack of reliable quantitative data in France on the evolution of foreign populations and particularly due to the lack of longitudinal statistics,[5] there is no really reliable general overview (Tribalat 1991). The statistics record the effects of the Nationality Code which gives 'second-generation' immigrants French nationality. It is thus impossible to 'follow' the evolution of populations of foreign origin inside the different sectors of social life (for example, employment, housing, social and political participation) since they 'disappear', statistically, as soon as they become French and especially as soon as the children of foreigners become 'native French'.[6] Michèle Tribalat (1991) estimates that '80 per cent of the children and grand-children of foreigners having come to France within the last hundred years are French since their birth', which corresponds to an extremely important demographic contribution:

'On January 1st 1986, there were just under 4 million immigrants of foreign origin living in France and almost 30 per cent of them are of French nationality. Their children are five millions, amongst which 80,000 are still foreigners. Their grand-children are between 4.4 and 5.3 millions and are all French. All in all, 14 million people are either immigrants or children or grand-children of immigrants and amongst them more than ten million are already French.

Regular updated surveys reveal an inter-generational upward social mobility: 'The majority of the immigrants' children born in France become employers or managers' (Borkowski 1990).[7] This social mobility does not, however, compensate for the development of 'blocked' opportunities, or the aggravation of already difficult socio-economic conditions (leaving school before graduation or without training, unemployment, and so on). But these facts also concern a large part of the population whose French origin goes back many generations. Here again, comparison is strongly impeded because of the way in which data are recorded.

This same weakness in the statistical sources makes it difficult to observe and analyse processes, and particularly that of discrimination phenomena. Concerning this subject, we are almost reduced to collecting 'anecdotes' such as they are reported by those directly concerned, gathered by anti-racist or immigrants' associations, mentioned by the media. Lawsuits involving discrimination during job interviews or at work are scarce and too insufficient to constitute an adequate source of information and data. What is more, as we shall see, the subject of ethnic or 'racial' discrimination is itself, in fact, in France, almost taboo.

GENERAL DATA

Immigration and Naturalisation

The relative percentages of foreigners and French by acquisition within the entire population have not really varied since 1946. Between 1946 and 1990 the entire population increased by 42.17 per cent. Native French people make up 83.5 per cent of this increase, French by acquisition make up 5.7 per cent, and foreigners 11.2 per cent. The number of French nationality acquisitions has considerably increased during the last inter-census period (1982–90). The number of foreigners, conversely, has fallen for the first time since 1946. These evolutions can be explained by the fact that many foreigners have been living in France for a very long time and that the rules and regulations regulating the entry and residence of foreigners have been modified, especially those concerning natives of non-European Union countries.

According to S. Hessel, the net immigration rate in the general population increase is 14.4 per cent (Commissariat Général au Plan, 1988).

Structural Modifications of Immigration

Since the 1950s, and particularly since the 1970s, the number of foreigners coming from European countries has been decreasing. This is due mostly to an important decrease in the number of foreigners coming from countries belonging to the European Union. Conversely, the number of foreigners coming from other parts of the world has increased. For example, the numbers of those originating from North Africa have regularly increased during the two previous inter-census periods, but remained stable since 1982, at about 38 per cent. New immigrations, some of which directly related to wider political events (Vietnam, Cambodia) have appeared. Others originate, at least partly, from restrictions imposed by their traditional host countries. Thus, the natives of Asian countries have increased by a total of 135,000, with more than half of them represented by Turks.

EMPLOYMENT AND UNEMPLOYMENT

The reduction from 12 to 9 per cent between 1975 and 1990 on the part of foreigners amongst the totality of workers stands in the context of a global diminution in the jobs of unskilled workers but also in the transfer, by subcontracting, of these jobs to the tertiary sector.

> Foreigners are less and less numerous in industry (−25 per cent compared to −9 per cent for the whole of industrial workers) and with more and more in the tertiary sector (+22 per cent as against +16 per cent). After having been workers in the large industrial firms where employment is stable and the division of labour very advanced, foreigners are becoming the labour force on which small artisan entrepreneurs, businesses and services depend. (Echardour and Maurin 1993)

In these firms employees do not have necessarily better qualifications, a higher status or better conditions than workers in the industrial sector.

Almost absent from public service (5.8 per cent against 23.2 per cent for French born) and from jobs with the highest level of security, foreigners are over-represented in the categories 'temporary employment' (7.8 per cent against 5.7 per cent) and 'private sector salaried, permanent' (76.4 per cent against 56 per cent for French born). They are, therefore, more vulnerable to the effects of economic fluctuations.

Upward mobility does exist however and foreigners in management practising liberal or intermediate professions were proportionately more numerous in 1990 than they were in 1982. However, they only represent, respectively, 3.7 per cent and 3.2 per cent of those active in these jobs. As for the increase in self-employment and independent work (about 4 per cent of active employees at the last census) these cover a variety of situations but a number of observers emphasise that 'setting up your own business' frequently represents a strategy for avoiding unemployment without any guarantee of success.

A number of sectors in which a large number of foreigners work are in decline or have less need than before for unskilled work. But it is in the sectors where labour conditions are the hardest, less 'modern' (and thus the most exposed to restructuring) that foreigners find it easier to find a job (for example, in construction work and mining). This labour force also interests the sectors where short-term profit imperatives are strong and dependent on the hazards of the overall economic situation (for example, consumer goods, trade). The sectors where foreigners work are in fact those where the unemployment rate is the highest, where there is a rapid turnover of staff, and where workers occupy the least senior positions.

Statistical data cannot measure the role played by the informal and underground economy and, thus, irregular employment, which although affecting foreigners and non-foreigners alike, nevertheless employs a great number of the foreign population.

A Higher Proportion of the Unemployed

Between 1980 and 1992 the unemployment rate rose from 6 per cent to 10 per cent. For foreigners it grew from 9 per cent to nearly 19 per cent. It is twice as high for that of French people (9.5 per cent) with differences between nationalities being more pronounced. (Marchand 1991)

This unemployment is particularly likely to affect those who come from countries outside the European Union, with the exception of the Portuguese. Thus the rate of unemployment for North Africans is triple that for French people (28 per cent for Moroccans, 29 per cent for Algerians, 34 per cent for Tunisians). Youth unemployment is also higher for foreigners than for French people. Globally, 'the displacement of unskilled work in favour of the SME of services and commerce is the origin not only of the increase in insecurity of young foreigners but also of the difficulties in redeploying the older workers from the industrial sector' (Marchand 1991). Thus, the duration of unemployment has on average increased by seven months between 1980 and 1992 for foreigners compared to an increase of four months for French people.

BEING A FOREIGNER, IN FRANCE, IS A HANDICAP

Behind problems particular to immigrants[8] there probably is the handicap of having discovered France and the French language recently. It is estimated that about one immigrant out of three doesn't speak French correctly. But this doesn't explain everything: the Portuguese, who've immigrated more recently and who do not speak French any better, have less difficulties than Algerians. Other factors come into play, such as the vitality of each community. Among Portuguese workers, the female activity rate is very strong and many of the construction workers create their own businesses: these are all assets that help overcome the industrial decline and the threat of unemployment. The particular case of Portuguese workers may also reveal a different policy of the employers who consider them as a culturally closer European workforce: in the industry sector, for instance, the promotion from unskilled to skilled worker is four times more frequent among the Portuguese than among North Africans. The latter seem to have more problems integrating into the firm. (Maurin 1991)

As can be seen, the reasons used to explain the inferior situation of foreigners, and particularly of certain categories in the job market, are many, but none directly falls under ethnic or 'racial' discrimination. The reasons for this 'handicap' experienced by foreign populations in employment are first sought in the 'characteristics' of the groups themselves: low qualifications, difficulty in adapting, poor command of the French language. The differences between foreign population groups are also taken into consideration as consequences of their 'particularities': some 'seem to have more difficulty to integrate into the firm', while others 'show real dynamism'.

Finally, when neither of these two explanations seems sufficient, one can always call upon the famous '*cultural proximity*' that is supposed to reduce the 'distance' between a non-French-speaking Portuguese farmer and a chief executive and to increase that which separates this same chief executive from a French-speaking Algerian worker.

This last explanation deserves a closer look. In France, 'cultural proximity' is considered a relatively objective, rational or at least reasonable basis for an employer's choice. If 'in industry, for example, the promotion from unskilled to skilled worker is four times more frequent among Portuguese workers than among North Africans', this is probably, as E. Maurin writes, because employers adopt a 'different policy towards European manpower'. There is a name for this 'different policy', based upon a supposed 'cultural distance': discrimination. Using this so-called 'cultural distance' is an ideological trick: it 'objectivises' a stereotype and legitimates the practice. Used in a scientific article, whether the author is aware of it or not, and whether he has been censored or has censored himself, it appears as a justification. The explanation by discrimination is thus generally avoided. It could, nevertheless, offer less ambiguous, less tortuous and a less ideologically oriented means to understand the facts. For if the data are few and incomplete, as we have already stressed, they are not completely non-existent and they could be further investigated. Amongst the groups of workers who, in 1981, had no qualifications, 6 per cent had become qualified workers, 6.5 per cent employees and 3.5 per cent technicians or managers in 1989. For North Africans, these proportions are significantly less: 3.5 per cent had acquired a vocational qualification, 3.5 per cent become employees and 2 per cent technicians or managers. Because of insufficient data concerning the situation of 'immigrants' in the labour market, in jobs and inside the firm, we started a qualitative investigation using, on the one hand, the press, and on the other hand, interviews with various informants (employers' organisations, trade unionists, recruiting agency staff, representatives of anti-racist and solidarity associations, government departments, tribunals and lawyers). The following elements concerning discrimination are taken from this investigation.[9]

EMPLOYMENT DISCRIMINATION, COLLECTIVE AND SOCIAL RIGHTS

During the last decade or so, almost every aspect of foreigners' life in France has been subjected to restrictive legal measures in response to the will to control frontiers and to check unauthorised immigration. Whereas the general evolution of French (and European) legislation tends more and more to assimilate foreigners into the host community through the granting of various rights, the subordination of these rights to the legality of the foreigner's residence in the country creates numerous restrictions. This is the reason why we have seen the reappearance of short-term visas, the creation of 'on-the-spot' illegal immigrants – foreigners who before were legitimately settled in France (children and husbands/wives of foreigners, parents of French children), the suppression or reduction of certain acquired rights, the limitation of family re-groupings, the control of 'mixed' marriages and the possibility for public authority to oppose them, the reduction of social and health protection, the drastic limitation on the right to sanctuary, the extension of administrative custody and of estrangement.[10] Most of these measures are officially applied to illegal residents or in cases of threats to law and order, but they also concern their dependants and, because they make the 'regular' situation more and more precarious, they, in fact, threaten all foreigners. (GISTI 1993)

There also exists a series of laws against racism and discrimination that have been progressively applied since 1972.[11] However, discrimination remains, the origins of which are legal, just as there remains a whole series of illegal discriminatory practices that are either not sanctioned – or only moderately so – because they are not recognised as such.

Employment

Foreigners' access to employment is subject to an administrative police regime which compels them to obtain residence permits that allow them to work. The 10-year permit equals an authorisation to work. Those who possess a permit are accorded the same treatment as French people and they have the same degree of access to private sector jobs. Obtaining this permit is easier for EU nationals.

Since 1975, the rule laid down by decree is to oppose 'the present and future possibility of employment in professional areas requested by foreigners' to each and every authorised demand for a salaried job, whether it is a first request to settle on French territory or a request to change status (as for students or shopkeepers, for instance).

Legally, the access to a certain number of jobs is limited or forbidden for foreigners. Until 1991, civil service jobs were prohibited to all foreigners.[12] They are now open to EU nationals, except for the police force, the army, the magistrature or central government, which all involve exercising state authority. State enterprises (Electricité et Gaz de France, Société Nationale des Chemins de fer Français, Régie Autonome des Transports Parisiens) apply this same exclusion principle. Three and a half million public servant jobs and 2.5 million quasi-public jobs are thus denied to non-EU nationals. Most of them do not involve any particular public power prerogative. In fact, many non-EU nationals take part in public utility services and are at the same time excluded from the corresponding status, either through contracts (assistant professors and foreign doctors, for instance) or through the use of employing associations (particularly in welfare departments).

Many freelance professions (such as head of communication agencies, of entertainment businesses, tobacconists or landlords of public houses and professions are also closed off to non-EU nationals. Health professionals are even submitted to the double imperative of both nationality and French diplomas.[13]

To these discriminations brought about by law, one can add illegal discrimination. This is not investigated. As we shall see it is, in fact, so difficult to prove that the victims and their defenders are discouraged from taking out lawsuits.

During these last few years, a certain number of court judgments have, nevertheless, enabled already old measures that make provisions for sanctions against discriminatory job offers, included in the Penal Code and the 1972 law against racism, to be finally applied. Breaching the law in this matter is rarely punished when the offender is a public service. The directors of the ANPE (French National Employment Office) (a public utility service) who allow discriminatory job offers to be published or posted in their agencies are condemned only in exceptional cases, even if they are legally responsible.

Discriminatory types of job refusals are often mentioned as common practice,[14] by victims as well as by trade unions or anti-racist associations. Any type of action in this matter is very difficult. The employer has a right to hire whomever he chooses as long as he does not do so according to criteria prohibited by law. But since he is not compelled to defend his choice, it is easy for him to escape any accusation. Two types of freedom thus come to oppose each other: the employer's right to hire whomever he wants without having to justify his choice and the individuals', whose rights to equal treatment are also enshrined in law (Ray 1990). Of course, the bad overall economic situation makes it easy for employers to operate in this way.

In the case of a refusal to recruit someone based upon the number of foreigners already employed, tribunal judgments are contradictory. One employer lost his case because it was his job to organise work in such a way that antagonisms could be avoided, while another employer was discharged on the basis that his decision was not inspired by racist or xenophobic motives. Here again, where public administration is concerned, impunity seems to be the rule. As the MRAP (Mouvement contre le Racisme et pour l'Amitié entre les Peuples) stresses, 'it seems that when summoning bearers of public authority one is often confronted by the dilution of responsibilities inside the administration'.

Unequal wages, when applying rules concerning minimum wages or extra hours, access to promotion and to professional training, discriminatory granting of bonus payments (merit awards, output bonuses, and so on)[15] between foreigners and indigenous French workers can sometimes be seen in statistics, where such statistics exist. They prove the existence of what some American authors term 'institutional racism', a phenomenon that is totally ignored in France.

Collective and Social Rights

Foreign workers now have the same rights as French workers as far as trade union rights and representation inside the company is concerned (1972, 1975 and 1982 laws). However, there remain discriminations, particularly legal ones, in terms of access to some equal-representative or consular institutions and to professional councils.

Although they are eligible to vote for the Conciliation Boards (made up of employers and workers, these boards having jurisdiction over industrial disputes) foreigners cannot themselves be elected to them. They are excluded from commercial courts, chambers of commerce and industry, and from chambers of agriculture, as well as mediation and conciliation offices. They are not allowed to hold office on either Regional or National technical committees for the prevention of industrial injuries. When it is known that, statistically, foreigners occupy particularly hazardous jobs, it is hard to understand such an exclusion, which dates back to 1946.

It is well known that participating in trade union activities or using one's right to strike is riskier for foreigners, for those who are French by acquisition and for 'coloured' French people, than for the French ancestry – the so-called French 'de souche'. Once again, the proof of this discrimination is often hard to demonstrate. This is why actions more often cite other breaches of law and do not mention – or only secondarily so – the discriminatory character of the incriminating evidence.

The benefits derived from various rights as a wage-earner are often hard to obtain for 'immigrants' (foreigners, French of foreign origin, 'coloured' French). This is particularly true in the case of housing obtained through the 'Employers' 1 per cent' (the contribution made by firms with more than 50 employees to social housing, giving firms control over a certain amount of 'reserved' housing).

As far as social rights are concerned, the equal wage principle has slowly asserted its presence and is explicitly stated in most international conventions relating to the protection of migrant workers and their families. The main discrimination still in judicial existence is a consequence of regulations that concern a foreigner's stay in the country. Children of foreigners who were not born in France, or who did not enter France on a regular family reunification basis, do not have the right to receive family allowances (even if they are of French nationality). Today, the payment of social security benefits (health insurance, maternity allowances, disablement and whole-life insurances, housing allowances, and so on) is generally subordinated to the legality of the stay, not only of the direct beneficiary, but also of any indirect beneficiaries. A great many of these dispositions seem in contradiction with international treaties signed by France.[16]

Another source of legal discrimination can be found in the enforcement of the territoriality principle. Family allowances are fully paid only for children living in France. For children left behind in the country of origin, they are paid according to a less generous scale based upon bilateral conventions and, furthermore, cease to be paid in the event of unemployment or early retirement. It is impossible to settle one's retirement pension from abroad and just as impossible to export disablement and industrial injury pensions. The Conseil Constitutionnel has refused to grant any constitutional weight to this territoriality principle. In cases such as those mentioned above, the enforcement of this principle, nevertheless, leads to the erosion of workers' rights acquired through years of working and paying contributions.

Because there are no reciprocal agreements with their country of origin, various solidarity allowances were for a long time refused to foreigners (for example, the complementary allowance from the Fonds National de Solidarité which 'tops up' incomes lower than the legal minimum for pensioners, disabled adults' allowances, mothers' allowances and so on).[17] These exclusions were declared unconstitutional by the Conseil Constitutionnel, and abolished by a new law passed in June 1998.

Within the bounds of legal and illegal discrimination are differences generated by public administrations regarding public utility services or public programmes as set out in law. The discretionary power which the administration possesses *de facto* in this general framework is more often than not supported by the courts that rule on the misuse of power and fraud than on the equality principle (Lochak 1987). The Conseil d'État and the Administrative Courts have, nevertheless, condemned municipal by-laws which tend to reserve for French people only, the benefit of social allowances created by local authorities (for example, education parental allowance, unemployed workers' allowances, and so on).

WORKPLACE RACISM AND DISCRIMINATION: A HIDDEN REALITY

The Syllogism of Company Rationality

Why do you want employers to introduce inside the company, management elements that are foreign to its vocation as producer, that is to say elements which are not linked to economic or financial profitability?

This excerpt from an interview is a perfect example of the way in which job discrimination is treated in France: through denial. As we have already said, the first reflex is to deny racism, or at least to treat it as unimportant. One of the essential arguments rests upon the so-called 'rationality' of the worlds of labour and companies which are ruled by abstract regulations and principles: ability, duty specialisation and seniority. This is, in fact, how the French public office presents itself, *as by right* reserved for native French people and subject to a multitude of bureaucratic rules, behind which, the practice of the state as an employer disappears as it evades its own rules by way of subcontracting. The non-racist character of the world of labour is thus 'proved' by an argument that takes the form of a syllogism: a company lives in a world of rationality, racism isn't rational, therefore they are incompatible.

What is more, private or public enterprises and administrations, just like all major organisations, function on a structural 'opaqueness' that is erected as a management principle. This opaqueness is all the stronger since it rests upon the legal interdiction – a translation of the Republican ethic inside the field of employment – to categorise French people by ways other than sex, qualifications, professional status, and so on. This opaqueness is only slightly tempered by the legal obligation to present statistics concerning foreigners. On top of all this one can add the difficulties for trade unions, even for work inspectors, who, like researchers, have a legal entitlement to access to workers' biographical data. The company, in fact, considers itself a private place.

If the existence of discrimination, when applying for a job, is more or less acknowledged, what happens within the company remains largely unknown. It seems particularly difficult to prove discriminatory practices concerning job conditions, wages, career development and promotion and laying off workers. Most of the people we interviewed, whatever their status or position, had little information on what happens inside the firm. The discrimination cases which have attracted most attention from trade unions and work inspectors have been, and still are, those against trade union leaders.

Since, despite a few 'atypical cases', there is no real discrimination inside the firm, it becomes easy to prove that it is the so-called 'victims' who invent them. This is what one is led to believe by employment agency staff in charge of unskilled workers. They said: 'It is the foreign workers themselves who are the most worried: "Did you tell him I was African?" They're afraid they're going to be rejected. And when they are rejected, they reassure themselves by thinking it is due to the colour of their skin. In fact, when they are not chosen, it's because they're not suitable.'

In fact, external to anti-racist and solidarity associations, the methods used to analyse labour market processes exclude racism and discrimination. It is as if there were *isolated* cases only, cases that are condemnable – and sometimes even actually condemned – but which are seen to result from acts that are reduced to individual behaviour, described as 'stupid' or 'clumsy' and considered merely as anecdotes.

One can thus readily understand that before even considering procedures that would enable the identification of racist acts, and to measure their effects in terms of their importance within a firm, one is confronted by a pure and simple non-acknowledgement, which completes the trail of denial over racist practices. This denial arises from the firm's culture as well as from the national culture. This universalising culture is not challenged by workers' unions, by employers' federations nor by anti-racist associations. The universalism of the class vision of some thus comes to oppose the liberal universalism of the others, in a common ideological field where 'pluralist' and, *a fortiori* 'communitarian' references are absent.

Avoiding 'Undesirable Elements'

Practically all those we spoke to mentioned the efforts made by some employers not to recruit certain candidates, and particularly those of North African and African origins. The pretexts vary according to professional sectors and the jobs to be filled. Some employers refuse systematically, whatever kind of job is being offered, for no other reason than the fear of being unable to 'control' these persons should they form a group. Others refuse on the pretext of 'non-acceptance' of foreigners or 'coloured' people by other employees inside the firm, and others still use the pretence that the idea of recruiting immigrants would 'discredit the firm's corporate image'. Finally, one of the main arguments is based upon the so-called impossibility of allowing the public or clients contact with 'coloured people' or with people whose foreign origins are 'visible'. Training course refusals are also frequent and based upon the same reason.

There are more subtle preventative strategies for avoiding 'undesirable' candidates. Some public utility services or employers, for instance, ask for identity photographs thus completing the sifting process which started with surnames. The use of coded formulas inscribed on job offers intended for intermediate agencies (for example, the famous 'B.B.R.',[18] the '01' notice) is a practice probably already abandoned for others by these agencies, which collude in these *a priori* elimination processes. Also, banks and insurance companies refuse applications on the grounds of place of residence when those places have been widely stigmatised. A Paris suburban town authority, taking the opportunity to benefit from a major urban renewal scheme, has even started to change the names of some areas in order to avoid the 'repulsion effect' of certain, infamous, housing estates.

The preferential recruiting procedure that favours the children of employees in many large public services, means that job offers are already filled when they are publicly advertised. One of our informants told us that in the Paris Region 80 per cent of the Contrats Emploi-Solidarité[19] (government-sponsored contracts for the unemployed, which includes professional training) for a public transportation enterprise had been offered in that way. In certain public institutions, half of the employees have at least one family member also working there. The concentration of a large number of people of common geographical origin (Auvergnats, Corsicans, West Indians or Bretons) reveals the existence of what is delicately called 'informal recruiting networks' (Bouvier 1989; Giraud and Marie 1990). These practices constitute an obstacle to recruiting people who, although French, have no access to restricted or informal information. In fact, their parents, as foreigners, could not be recruited because of the nationality clause. This preferential recruiting practice also exists in the private sector, where it is a tradition and where it sometimes works as a consensual, unwritten law and, often, is backed by trade unions.[20] Thus the current situation differs according to whether or not firms employed many immigrants, say, 15 or 20 years ago. Unfortunately, the firms that did are in decline (the car industry and building and public works companies, for instance) and they do not recruit many new employees.

One can also consider as discriminatory the preferential recruitment of foreigners or people whose appearance or 'cultural' characteristics makes it possible to employ them in unfavourable conditions. This is what happened during the 1960s, today being perpetuated through the illegal work offered to 'illegal immigrants'. The employer's 'practical sense' also shows itself in the recruitment of young people available from the pool of North African immigrants, where it is thought that they correspond to the firm's public image, and in their exclusion, where they are considered not to. The issue then is that of their job conditions.

The Deprofessionalisation of Recruitment Procedures

Generally, recruitment procedures have evolved over time and give a growing emphasis on interviews, where enquiries are made about 'personality', personal opinions and certain aspects of the applicants' lives which have less and less to do with professional qualifications. All this takes place at the expense of written tests (Lyon-Caen 1991). Multiple ways are used to guarantee to the employer the freedom to recruit according to apparently objective and legitimate criteria: psychological or graphological tests, claiming an applicant is over-qualified, questions about hobbies, leisure-time, and so on. These changes also affect public offices which used to boast they recruited on the grounds of written and anonymous 'examinations'.[21]

THE HAZARDS OF DEFENDING DISCRIMINATION VICTIMS: HOW CAN ONE FIGHT SOMETHING THAT DOES NOT EXIST?

All the evidence confirms the following facts: it is difficult to be informed about racism and discrimination within the firm, and to have it established and qualified as such, in order to bring a court action. The fight against racism faces many difficulties which can be detailed as follows: victims do not speak out; trade unions or anti-racist intermediaries are not always present nor able to defend the victims; the choice of methods is a complex task; a legal fight is largely inefficient and can sometimes even be dangerous for the victims.

Victims Do Not Speak Out or are Not 'Heard'

Racist remarks at work, an atmosphere where 'questionable' jokes are frequent, common use of stereotypes by employers, managerial staff or work colleagues (who can also belong to minority groups) are common features. But the perception of the racist character of these interactions is not at all uniform. There is little consensus on the definition of what is considered 'racist' and even less consensus about how to appraise the seriousness of racist remarks and the degree of their 'banality'. In France, one is far from the 'political correctness' era, and there is not even a 'code of good behaviour'. On the contrary, ordinary verbal racism – which is regarded as posing no real threat – is very commonly tolerated and indulged (in fact, as with 'ordinary' sexist remarks). This is why those who make racist remarks – and, often, those who are victims of these remarks – do not always recognise that an offence has been made.

This also explains why victims of racism think they are not 'heard', psychologically speaking, that is to say: no one can imagine and understand their suffering, and that the prejudice they endure is underestimated. They are, in fact, twice aggrieved: they are victims of racial discrimination on the one hand and, on the other, of a general suspicion about the reality of the facts they report. They are believed to be readily prone to exaggeration, even 'paranoia'. The experience of discrimination is thus both disputed and acknowledged as attributable to personality and even psychological problems.

The 'euphemisation' of racism by these effects and consequences is extremely perverse, not only because it weighs heavily on the victims, but also because it contributes to the devaluing of all persons or groups which are 'ethnicised' or 'racialised', or even encourages the act to happen. Some victims even come to the point where they accuse those who bring them into contact with firms of placing them in humiliating situations: *'Why did you send me over to so-and-so? You knew he didn't want Arabs.'* Others practise avoidance strategies, and can anticipate when to escape from potential direct confrontation with racism, suspicion and rejection. More generally, one can say that ethnic or 'racial' discrimination has not acquired, in the general view, a sufficiently illegitimate status for victims to feel authorised to act, to publicise their situation and to hope that support structures can be set in place. Legal action is thus even more hindered.

**Discrimination that Cannot be Proved Does not Exist'
(Lochak 1988)**

There is a fundamental gap between law texts and the possible conditions that could lead to their enforcement. French law, in this respect, is governed by the 'presumption of innocence' principle. The plaintiff is thus obliged to prove ethnic or 'racial' discrimination has taken place. Furthermore, because structural or institutional racism is not acknowledged as such, and because of the existence of indirect discrimination, he or she must prove discriminatory intent.

French trade unions, the only mass organisations present in all companies of a certain size, are not really equipped to take out civil actions in discrimination cases. Trade unionists themselves are steeped in a general atmosphere of 'euphemisation' of racism. Those willing to act admit they are afraid of not being backed by all the employees. According to them, it is mostly the growing precariousness of jobs and the fear of unemployment which bring victims to accept humiliating conditions, as a justification for escaping their responsibilities. Because they have not changed their status, they are unable to bring a civil action in court. Thus only the victims are entitled to act with, at best, the help of anti-racist organisations external to the firm. Finally, they consider that the legal action framework does not offer sufficient guarantees for an efficient defence.

It is a fact that the problem of providing proof more or less paralyses them. The pressures placed on witnesses dissuade them from testifying; the 'group cultures', which themselves are not exempt from xenophobia, make it very difficult, both for the victim and for potential defenders, to gather sufficient evidence to bring a case to court. Finally, proving that someone is deprived of normal career development because of 'ethnic' origin demands a protocol (which only the work inspector can establish) that facilitates the collection of evidence that other workers, comparable in all respects except racial origin, have experienced more favourable career development. Who is going to approach the work inspector and ask him to undertake this task?

Doing so means that one expects a legal type of follow-up to an eventual official report. In fact, it turns out that suing an employer or his representatives for discrimination is a very serious procedure. If successful, the discriminatory act may be redressed (where a person who was dismissed must be reinstated). However, it is more often the case that the employer will be asked to pay damages.[22] Where prosecutions result in failure, the employer can sue the victim for libel. This is why those we spoke to say they prefer to organise the victims' defence along more 'classical', more certain and, *de facto*, more efficient lines.[23] One work inspector even told us that in the case of a mass dismissal of 'African' unionists, he based his plea on articles of the Labour Code relating to the protection of trade unionists without even mentioning racial discrimination, which he himself thought was blatant.

An efficient workers' defence thus tends to discourage resorting to legal remedies against discrimination and thereby colludes in the perpetuation of the ignorance of such situations and in the non-acknowledgement of racist motives. The Presidency of the Paris Conciliation Board has stated that, never, amongst the 17,000 cases brought to court every year, has the accusation of racism been presented. They added – despite the existence of article L 122-45 of the Work Code – that should it happen, 'we would not want to hear it and we would send these people back to common law courts'. It seems that an evolution in thinking by conciliation boards is possible on this issue, as has been recently shown by the sentence passed on an employer, stating that the plaintiff was the victim 'of a certain discrimination due to his Cameroon origin' (GISTI 1994).

As for the Central Offices of the Paris Work Inspection, they declare that having never studied this issue they are unable to make any contribution. How is it that well-known institutions that specialise in labour law and disputes between employees and employers know nothing or almost nothing? It is simply because, as we have already stressed, racial or racist discrimination is by no means their major preoccupation. Even worse, it seems that suing on these grounds runs the risk of taking plaintiffs down a cul-de-sac, and of depriving them of the benefit – if one can call it a 'benefit' – of a more efficient and safer line of defence.

In France, racism and racial discrimination are not primary arguments, nor even secondary ones. Most of the time they are not even mentioned: 'discrimination on racial grounds is often not even mentioned by the plaintiff who is certain he won't be able to bring proof of the discriminatory foundation' (GISTI 1994).

Occultation and 'euphemisation' of ethnic or 'racial' discrimination, in France, build a 'wall of silence' which is further consolidated 'for the good cause' by some of those who, in France, are amongst the best defenders of immigrants and equal rights. The equality principle itself now comes to 'shelter' racist practices, the condemnation of which remains purely on the basis of 'principle'.

Those we talked to nevertheless seemed more aware of the discrimination problem than was the case a few years ago. This is probably due to the fact that this discrimination does not only affect foreigners but, more and more, people with French nationality. Its racist character can thus no longer be denied. For a large number of people acting in the labour market, the refusal to recruit people who have lived in France for a long time or were born in France, appears as an obstacle to integration and as one of the main threats to the 'virtues' of the French 'assimilation model'.

There is thus, today, an urgency, felt in varying degrees by militants and other social actors, to bring these practices into the light. Research in this matter can bring to the surface precious pieces of information as to the extent, the ways and the processes of discrimination. But there needs to be a political will to encourage such work. And, as we have tried to show, it is as if the simple fact of 'recognising' discrimination presents, in itself, a major risk of social and political destabilisation.

Translated by Jean Duriau

NOTES

1. 1985 'Loi Informatique, Fichiers et Libertés' creating the 'Commission Informatique et Libertés' holding extensive powers to investigate, control and accuse.
2. Amongst the first group counted, not only the descendants of French parents but also all those who were born on French territory benefit – under certain conditions – from the rule of the double *jus soli*. The second group fall under different procedures including that of naturalisation.
3. According to the 1990 census, there were 4.1 million people amongst whom 1.3 million are French and 2.8 million foreigners. This definition

    includes – although they are neither foreigners nor French by acquisition – native French born in the Départements et Territoires d'Outre-Mer (in particular, the West Indies).

4.   It is interesting to note that 'immigré' has no translation in English. The word 'immigrant' also exists in French, but is very seldom used. It seems that in English, or at least in the American use of the word, 'immigrant' is someone whose intention is to settle inside the nation. True or not, this is not the presumed intention of the term 'immigré' when used in France.

5.   'Immigration' statistics are those, already mentioned, provided by the Ministère de l'Intérieur, that are, on the one hand, the flow (number of foreigners entering France) and, on the other hand, the amount (number of valid residence permits).

6.   'Over a long period of time (since 1971), the proportion of foreigners amongst wage-earners tends to decrease ... whereas the immigrant population represents a more and more important part of the Ile-de-France Region population ... This can be explained by the fact that the children of immigrants disappear from statistics once they reach 18 years of age since they then become French' (Martinielli 1990).

7.   A subtitle the author introduces states: 'neither the social mobility of immigrants nor that of their children correspond to pre-conceived ideas. An important part of the first generation and especially of the second generation, has managed to reach a "higher" social position than that of their parents.'

8.   Foreigners, here, in fact.

9.   For more information see De Rudder, Tripier and Vourc'h, 1994.

10. See 1986 and 1993 so-called 'Lois Pasqua'.

11. Besides the major reference texts (Déclaration des Droits de l'Homme 1789, Déclaration Universelle des Droits de l'Homme 1948, Préambule to the 1946 Constitution, and article 2 of the 1958 Constitution), there is a 1972 law against racism, completed in 1990 and a law against discrimination introducing new articles in the Penal Code and the Labour Code.

12. Except for scientific and technical establishments as well as higher education establishments since 1983 and 1984.

13. For more details concerning these interdictions to exercise freelance or liberal professions, see Lochak (1991). The recruiting of foreign doctors in public health hospitals under highly discriminatory conditions has been the subject of many disputes (De Rudder, Tripier and Vourc'h 1994).

14. Irregular residence in France is a legitimate reason to refuse employment.

15. 'The "equal pay for equal work" principle forbids the employer to pay, differently, women and men, foreigners and natives ... but does not forbid him to differentiate wages according to each individual's merits and output or to grant bonuses that jurisprudence recognizes as lawful' (Lochak 1987).

16. Rome Treaty; OIT Convention No. 118 which speaks of 'usual residence' and defines the principle of 'lack of residence administrative condition' in matters related to social security; Cooperation Agreement between the EU and Algeria, Tunisia, Morocco and Turkey assimilating, in matters of social benefits, all those who have these nationalities with those who hold EU Member State nationalities and thus to natives of these countries; Lomé Convention; European Social Charter; Children's Rights Convention.

17.   In this last case, the nationality condition concerns not only the mother, but also the children, since this allowance is only given out to French mothers of French children.

18.   'Do you know the BBR? Behind these letters hides the code word "Bleu, Blanc, Rouge" (Blue, White and Red) which, far from indicating the Republican flag, indicates that the employer seeking a temporary collaboration wishes to recruit a White, preferably French "de souche" person' (K. Yamgnana 1992).

19.   C.E.S.: Part-time work contracts reserved for those unemployed for more than a year, partly sponsored by the state.

20.   In a large car factory of the Sochaux region, an announcement that the firm was offering jobs to 600 young people led an FO trade union representative to demand a priority for (1) children of staff, and (2) people originating from the region, on the basis that 'they have a Sochaux heart and it's good for the region' (*France-Info*, Saturday 11 May 1994).

21.   Which, probably, historically favoured the recruitment of women of whom there are many in the civil service.

22.   There is a jurisprudencial opposition to reintegration (GISTI, 1993). As J.J. Dupeyroux observes: 'In practice, a racist dismissal can happen without the victim obtaining reinstatement. At best, this person will be able to obtain damages based upon the abusive nature of the dismissal.'

6 Migrants and Ethnic Minorities in the Netherlands: Discrimination in Access to Employment

Mitzi Gras and Frank Bovenkerk

INTRODUCTION

Under Dutch law, it is illegal to discriminate on grounds of race. Article 1 of Dutch Constitution states, 'All persons in the Netherlands shall be treated equally, in equal circumstances. Discrimination on the grounds of religion, belief, political opinion, race or sex, or any other ground whatsoever, shall not be permitted.' However, formal equality in the law does not always mean equality in practice. A clear example of racial discrimination is shown below:

> A newspaper advertises a vacancy for an experienced waiter to work in a restaurant. Mustafa El Mansouri, a young man of Moroccan descent, decides to apply for this job. He is an experienced waiter, of the required age and possesses the necessary certificates. He also speaks fluent Dutch. He telephones the employer but is told that the vacancy has already been filled and that he is too late. Five minutes later, Jan de Wit telephones the employer and applies for the same job. He is the same age as Mustafa and is also an experienced waiter. The employer informs him that the vacancy is still open and invites him for an interview.

In 1978 Bovenkerk and Breunig-Van Leeuwen demonstrated that despite the illegality of discrimination in employment it was widespread in the Netherlands. Bovenkerk and Breunig-Van Leeuwen used the experimental technique of 'situation testing', which had previously been applied in the United Kingdom to measure the incidence of racial discrimination in the British labour market. The principle of the method is as follows: two equally qualified applicants apply almost simultaneously for the same advertised job vacancy. Both applicants have the same age, work experience and education and differ only in one respect; one applicant is white and native while the other is black or has an identifiable foreign background. The extent to which one applicant is treated more favourably than his or her paired partner provides a direct index of discrimination. In 1978, Bovenkerk found that applicants from ethnic minorities encountered discrimination in 20 per cent of their applications for semi-skilled jobs. The research results caused a stir in the Netherlands. The Dutch had considered themselves to be very tolerant. Racism and discrimination were viewed as abhorrent, and many people denied the fact that this was actually occurring in the Netherlands.

There have been many amendments to racial policy since the research was undertaken. The legislation on discrimination has become more detailed and more stringent. The 'Equal Treatment Act' has come into force and prohibits both direct and indirect discrimination. A special policy for ethnic minorities has been set up to improve the position of disadvantaged groups in society. The National Bureau for Combating Discrimination has been created and 40 other anti-discrimination agencies have also been established to prevent and combat racial discrimination. There are more than 350 institutions currently engaged in organising racism awareness training and running education programmes and information campaigns aimed at changing people's attitudes towards ethnic minorities. Codes of practice have been drafted, which describe the laws against discrimination for the benefit of both employers and employees.

In the light of these new measures, it is pertinent to consider whether the measures have been effective. Does discrimination occur to a lesser extent now than in the 1970s? Do migrants have equal access to employment opportunities at present? To answer these questions, Bovenkerk and Breunig-Van Leeuwen's study (1978) was repeated under the auspices of the International Labour Organisation (see Bovenkerk et al. 1995). Discrimination against Surinamese and Moroccan immigrants was tested at the semi-skilled and the highly skilled job levels. The Dutch study was part of a wider ILO project on racial discrimination and measures to combat it. Comparable studies using identical methodologies have been carried out in several other industrialised countries.

This contribution will briefly describe the history of migration into the Netherlands and discuss the disadvantaged position of the most significant groups of immigrants in the labour market. The chapter will also include various pieces of evidence demonstrating the occurrence of racial discrimination in the Dutch labour market and will describe the methodology and the results of the situation testing experiments.

IMMIGRANTS IN THE NETHERLANDS

Which ethnic groups or immigrants are most likely to experience discrimination? International immigration has generally fallen into five categories in most West European countries. First, there is the frequently disregarded constant flow of managers and international capital owners from America, Japan and other countries where multinational firms are based. Although their numbers are sizeable, these groups have not been considered either as a social problem or a potential financial burden on the state. Neither colour nor ethnicity seem to matter as their economic and social functioning depends on international global economy developments rather than on national or regional labour markets. It is not expected that American or Japanese personnel will be potential victims of racial discrimination in the labour market.

A second wave of mass emigration into Europe resulted from the process of decolonisation. Many Algerians, Moroccans and Vietnamese migrated to France, whilst many West Indians, Indians and Pakistanis entered the United Kingdom. East Indians and West Indians emigrated to the Netherlands. During the 1950s, the Netherlands experienced the greatest level of immigration in its history. The immigrants generally came from Indonesia. They were Eurasian political refugees (300,000) and a tiny remnant of the Dutch East Indian Army of the Moluccan island in the eastern part of the Indonesian Archipelago. Fortunately, these immigrants arrived at a time of economic reconstruction after the Second World War which resulted in a substantial expansion of the labour market. Eurasians were easily absorbed into the economy of that time. Although Eurasians may be recognised phenotypically, their 'racial' characteristics have never been considered to be negative. They are now considered to be assimilated and neither their first nor second generations produced a clear record of discrimination.

Emigration from the other colonies in the Dutch West Indies provides a very different picture. During the 1970s and the 1980s more than 250,000 people emigrated from Surinam, Curacao, Aruba and other small islands of the Dutch Antilles. Economic push factors in the countries of origin caused this movement of people rather than the needs of the Dutch labour market. In this respect, the Dutch experience differs fundamentally from that of the United Kingdom where immigration was triggered as a direct response to acute labour shortages in certain sectors of industry. In fact, the Surinamese, Antilleans and Arubans could not have arrived in the Netherlands at a worse time as the oil crisis and the ensuing shrinking of the labour market coincided with the peak in the numbers of immigrants. Immigrants with little education or few occupational skills, who formed the majority of the new arrivals, have found few openings in the labour market. Lower-class Creole and Hindustani-speaking Surinamese, as well as the worst educated Antilleans and Arubans, have produced a second generation that may encounter social rejection because these ethnic groups as a whole have been typified as unfit for 'legitimate' work.

A third group of immigrants includes the descendants of Mediterranean male migrant workers who arrived in the 1960s. Generally, Turks, Moroccans, Spaniards and Greeks came to fill the vacancies in the metal, textile and chemical industries as well as in certain sectors in the service industry such as cleaning. As economic prosperity continued, their contracts of employment were extended. Migrant workers who did not return to their country of origin and who were reunited with their family in the Netherlands, produced a second generation. Migration still continues in the form of secondary family reunion: second-generation men and women find spouses in the country from their parents' country of origin. However, for these workers, the 1980s brought a formidable restructuring of the Dutch economy which pushed unskilled first-generation migrant workers out of the labour market and required of second-generation job-seekers, educational and occupational skills at a level that they had not at that time attained. As it currently stands, the smaller groups of migrants from Southern European countries such as Spain or Greece seem to have fared well in the new post-industrial economy, whereas Moroccans and Turks have been excluded.

A fifth category of migrants include political refugees and asylum-seekers from countries including the former Yugoslavia, Sri Lanka and Iran. Because of their recent entry into the Netherlands, their social position has not yet been established. It is not possible to make even an educated guess as to their degree of exposure to racial discrimination in the labour market.

In the light of the above, it was decided that the most likely candidates for discrimination in the labour market would be Surinamese, Antilleans and Arubans, Turks and Moroccans. Do these groups constitute little more than a heterogeneous category who have in common nothing but a poor labour market position? Or will they begin to merge into a more generalised social group suffering from disadvantage? As all immigrations discussed occurred only after the Second World War, and most of these have not yet produced a second or third generation, it is hard to predict the end-result. The thesis of one group of Dutch authors (Roelandt 1994) puts forward the argument that continued disadvantage will result in an ethnic sub-proletariat or an ethnic underclass. However, research undertaken by social psychologists such as Hagendoorn and Hraba (1987) showed racial gradations and differences between the ethnic groups. Their 'social distance scale' research demonstrates that Surinamese and Antilleans experience greater social acceptance than Turks. Moroccans were generally held in the lowest esteem by the Dutch. If the first interpretation is correct, we would expect equally high discrimination scores for Surinamese and Moroccans. The second view would predict more discrimination against the Moroccans.

ETHNIC MINORITIES IN THE DUTCH LABOUR MARKET

In today's labour market, the position of ethnic minorities is unfavourable in every respect. The unemployment rate among Turks, Moroccans, Surinamese and Antilleans is very high. Among the Dutch, the unemployment rate is 7 per cent for men and 13 per cent for women. Among Turks it is 34 per cent for men and 48 per cent for women and among Moroccans it is 39 per cent for men and 66 per cent for women. The Surinamese unemployment rate is 27 per cent for men and 35 per cent for women and for Antilleans it is 32 per cent for men and 48 per cent for women. The percentage of non-working women is higher than the percentage of non-working men in all of the ethnic groups (Roelandt et al. 1992).

The percentage of long-term unemployed is higher among ethnic minorities than it is among the Dutch population. While 35 per cent of the Dutch job-seekers are unemployed for a period of longer than two years, this contrasts with 57 per cent of the Turkish job-seekers, 55 per cent of the Moroccan, 49 per cent of Surinamese and 39 per cent of Antillean job-seekers (Roelandt et al. 1992).

Furthermore, ethnic minorities are highly over-represented in industry and in jobs at the lowest occupational levels. For example, the number of Turkish and Moroccan men working in industry is about double that of Dutch men. They are also highly under-represented in jobs at the top end of the occupational hierarchy. Only a small number (2 per cent of Turkish men and 5 per cent of Moroccan men) occupy highly skilled jobs. The position of Surinamese and Antilleans is slightly better than the position of Turks and Moroccans, but in all respects, it is still less favourable than that enjoyed by the Dutch.

A Special Policy for Ethnic Minorities

A special minorities policy in the Netherlands aimed at improving the social position of immigrants was introduced in 1983. A primary objective of the programme is to reverse the high unemployment figures among immigrants.

In the 1980s, combating racism and discrimination took a high priority because it was realised that ethnic minorities were being denied equal opportunities. In recent years, however, discrimination has been almost brushed aside as a cause of high unemployment. At present, the immigrant's disadvantaged position in the labour market is explained by a low level of education and a generally poor command of the Dutch language. As a result, the government's policy has been aimed mainly at upgrading levels of qualifications. Thus, more language courses have been made available to teach ethnic minorities to speak Dutch more fluently and supplementary education and training courses have also been provided, together with increased possibilities to acquire work experience.

Moreover, special employment policies have been set up to remove the disadvantageous position of immigrants in the labour market. Several companies in the public sector, and to a lesser extent in the private sector, have launched positive action programmes for the integration of ethnic minorities and have set goals and timetables aimed at increasing the percentage of minorities working in their company. In 1990, employers' organisations and the trade unions signed an agreement to use their best efforts to hire 60,000 members of ethnic minorities within five years (1991–5) (The STAR agreement). Recently, the Act for the Promotion of Proportional Labour Participation of Immigrants was established. This Act requires companies with more than 35 employees to employ ethnic minorities in proportion to that of the local available workforce. In order to achieve this goal, companies must draw up a plan as to how they will do this. Furthermore, the companies are committed to producing and publishing an annual report on the contribution made by ethnic minorities in their workforce.

Nevertheless, despite all of these public and private efforts, the minorities' disadvantage in the labour market is increasing rather than diminishing. Up to now, the employment policies have been less than successful; positive action programmes do not seem to result in companies hiring more workers with ethnic backgrounds and 60,000 jobs for minorities, promised in the STAR agreement, will not be realised on time. The apparent failure of these schemes raises the thorny question: Why does nothing seem to work? Why do ethnic minorities not get a job, despite their qualifications and despite all these initiatives?

Discrimination: an Explanation?

In the Netherlands, an enormous amount of social scientific research into ethnic minorities and their position in society has been carried out. It has been repeatedly demonstrated that racial discrimination in the labour market is a structural phenomenon – offering a possible explanation for the high unemployment figures among ethnic minorities.

Interestingly, it is mainly on the basis of social science research, and not on the basis of legal actions, that we know that discrimination occurs in the Dutch labour market. This reluctance to use the law is explained by the fact that citizens in general do not go to court as readily as they do, for example, in the United States or Great Britain. The reasons for this are fear of retaliation by, for example, the employers, or fear of being considered over-sensitive. Complaints are very often not treated seriously by the police or the Public Prosecutor and, furthermore, it is a well-known fact that most cases do not lead to conviction of the perpetrators. Where prosecutions are successful, the sanctions imposed are insignificant (see Kartaram 1992; and Berghuys and Zegers de Beijl 1993). In the case of a conflict, pressure groups will not try to fight for their rights through the courts, but instead, try to effect change through negotiation, for example, with the government.

A variety of methodologies have been deployed to study racial discrimination in the labour market. Researchers have interviewed employers and personnel managers about their views concerning ethnic minorities and have demonstrated that when they are given the choice between hiring equally qualified ethnic and native applicants, a majority of the employers and personnel managers would prefer to choose the native applicant (Van Beek 1993; Hooghiemstra 1991). Van Beek (1993) also used the method of 'conjoint analysis' to study the selection behaviour of employers. Employers are presented with profile descriptions of applicants. Characteristics of applicants which might influence selection procedures, like education, experience, age, sex and ethnic background are incorporated into the profiles. The profiles of persons with an ethnic background appeared to generate a considerably lower preference than those of white Dutch persons.

Other researchers have interviewed victims of racial discrimination and have demonstrated that migrants are experiencing discrimination not only when applying for jobs, but also with respect to promotion, dismissals and conditions of employment and working conditions (Essed 1984; Biegel et al. 1987; Bouw and Nelissen 1988). Discrimination is also experienced on the shop floor, especially where the distribution of duties is concerned, and in interactions with native employees (Brassé and Sikking 1988).

Veenman (1990) and Kloek (1992) analysed the unemployment rates of both native Dutch and of ethnic minorities and found a discrepancy between those figures, even after matching a number of characteristics, such as age, education, sex, occupation and regional unemployment figures. They found that only a small part of this unemployment discrepancy can be accounted for by levels of education and other characteristics. Therefore, they had to conclude that discrimination plays a substantial part in the disadvantage of ethnic minorities in the labour market.

Den Uyl et al. (1986) used the situation test as a means to explore discrimination against ethnic minorities in private employment agencies.

On the basis of these results a 'Code of Practice' for these agencies was drawn up in 1987. In 1991, Büyükbozkoyum et al. carried out a small-sample correspondence test and observed no discrimination against highly educated Turkish engineers in hiring procedures. They went on to suggest, therefore, that the rate of discrimination varies with the level of occupation.

THE OCCURRENCE OF DISCRIMINATION IN THE NETHERLANDS

To demonstrate the occurrence of discrimination in hiring procedures in the Netherlands, we repeated the situation tests along the lines of Bovenkerk's earlier design, because it has important advantages over other methods. Usually, discrimination does not occur overtly, which makes it difficult to demonstrate its existence. In the majority of cases, ethnic applicants will not be told that they were turned down on the grounds of race, but because there were other, more suitable candidates. As people do not readily admit that they discriminate against ethnic minorities, interviews with personnel managers and employers about their prejudices and views concerning ethnic minorities lack reliability. Situation testing studies the behaviour of personnel managers and employers directly and thus provides an insight into what happens in practice rather than what is claimed to happen. The tests are objective and resemble everyday life experiences of people trying to find a job. This methodology can also detect the more subtle discrimination that migrants often encounter. Situation testing is therefore the most suitable research method to study the occurrence of discrimination (Fix and Struyk 1992).

In total, three experiments were carried out. In the first experiment, the rate of discrimination against semi-skilled Moroccan applicants was examined. The second experiment examined the experiences of semi-skilled Surinamese men. The difference was incorporated in the research design to determine whether the rate of discrimination varied by ethnic group. To find out whether the rate of discrimination encountered by migrants varied by educational/job level, a third experiment was carried out, in which discrimination against highly skilled (that is, college-educated) Surinamese applicants was examined. The methodology and results of the three experiments will be described separately.

1. Discrimination against Semi-skilled Moroccan Men

Two Moroccan and two Dutch students were selected as test applicants. They were all of a conventional appearance (average height and weight, conventional dress and haircut and conventional dialect), and possessed good communication skills and the ability to improvise, and they looked credible as semi-skilled job-seekers. They resembled each other as much as possible in overall demeanour, appearance and other relevant characteristics. The Moroccan 'candidates', selected to act as test subjects, were born in the Netherlands, integrated into Dutch society and spoke Dutch fluently. They were trained to behave as similarly as possible in different situations and they were taught to match their answers to the different types of questions usually encountered in job interviews.

Prior to each test, fictitious biographies were drawn up for all four, in accordance with the advertised job requirements. They gave the same age and cited the same work experience and education. The Moroccan test subject could be identified by way of a typical Moroccan name: Mustafa El Mansouri. The Dutch subject used a typical Dutch name: Jan de Wit. In total, the four subjects applied for 175 semi-skilled jobs in the service and retail trade sectors, including waiters, kitchen porters and shop assistants. Only the private sector was tested, as job vacancies in the public sector could not be found. The vacancies were always advertised in newspapers and the first contact was always made by telephone.

The application procedure in essence comprised of three stages, where unequal treatment could, in theory, occur. First, for example, one applicant might be rejected immediately ('Sorry, the job has just been taken'), while the paired applicant might be given a brief interview by telephone, concerning work experience and education. Second, one applicant might be rejected after a brief interview by the employer ('Sorry, you are too young') while the paired applicant was invited for a personal interview. Third, one could be offered a job while the other was turned down.

In 43 of the 175 tests, the Moroccan was rejected immediately ('Sorry, but the job has already been taken') while the equally well-qualified Dutch subject, who telephoned ten minutes later, was treated as a serious candidate. Only in two cases did the opposite outcome occur; the Dutch tester was rejected while the Moroccan tester was accepted. To eliminate cases of unequal treatment due to random factors, the cases of unfavourable treatment of the Dutch tester were subtracted from the cases of unfavourable treatment of the Moroccan tester. This resulted in a net discrimination rate against the Moroccan applicant of 41 cases (23 per cent) in the first stage of the application procedure. In practice, this means that even if the Moroccan applicant has by far the best qualifications, is born in Holland, speaks Dutch fluently and might be a much better candidate than all of other applicants, he will be eliminated from the competition beforehand in one out of every four applications for no other reason than his name is Mustafa El Mansouri. The following example illustrates this point:

> A Moroccan and Dutch subject applied for a job as a shop assistant. The Moroccan tester telephoned the employer first and asked in perfect Dutch whether the vacancy was still available. The employer's answer was as follows: 'Hi, Mustafa, brother! It is a shame, but you are too late! Thanks for calling!' Ten minutes later, the Dutch tester telephoned and asked the same question. The employer's answer was: 'Can you tell me something about yourself? ..., sounds good, you can come for an interview?'

Where the Moroccan applicant was not rejected immediately after revealing his name, he was briefly interviewed by telephone by the employer about his age and qualifications, in a way similar to that used with the Dutch candidate. However, it frequently happened that only the Dutch subject was invited for a personal interview and that the Moroccan was rejected with an excuse:

> A meat and sausage company advertised in a newspaper for experienced help. Both testers were asked their age and whether they had any experience with boning meat. Both said they had never boned meat, but were willing to learn. The employer said to the Dutch tester, 'It is not really necessary that you are able to bone meat, you will get on-the-job training. It is more important to fit in the team and your age (20) is an advantage. You can come for an interview.' To the Moroccan tester the answer was, 'Sorry, but it is very important that you have experience in boning meat and making sausages. We really need someone who is able to do this.'
>
> Both applicants applied for a job as a salesman for a solarium business. The Moroccan tester called, but was asked to telephone again because things were too busy at that moment. The employer was able to talk to him only after four calls. She was clearly very irritated by his perseverance, but asked for details of his age and work experience. Unfortunately, he was considered to be too young and to have insufficient experience. He also did not have the required knowledge about skin allergies and skin diseases. The equally qualified Dutch tester was given a chance to apply immediately and was invited for an interview after a short conversation about his age, experience and education. Nothing was said about experience of dealing with skin allergies or skin diseases.

When the Moroccan applicant was fortunate enough to move on to the third stage, the following scenario often occurred:

> A vacancy for a shop assistant in a men's clothing store was advertised in a local newspaper. Both testers were invited for an interview. The

Moroccan tester was asked a few brief questions about his former job and his education. A few days later his application was rejected. The Dutch tester went for an interview one hour later. The interview was held in a separate room with two people for 50 minutes. The questions were much more serious and diverse and information was provided about the company, the terms and conditions and salary. The next day the Dutch tester was called and offered the job.

In total, the Moroccan applicant was unfavourably treated in comparison with the equally qualified Dutch tester in 68 of the 175 tests. Opposite outcomes (unequal treatment in favour of the Moroccan tester) occurred in only four cases. In all other cases, both testers were equally treated and both advanced to the same stage of the application procedure. The result is a net rate of discrimination of 64 cases (37 per cent) against the Moroccan applicant. Thus, it can be concluded that discrimination against Moroccan men occurs frequently in hiring procedures at the semi-skilled level. When a young Moroccan man applies for a semi-skilled job, there is at least a one in three chance that he will be rejected because of his ethnic background.

2. Does Discrimination Vary by Ethnic Group?

The experiment was repeated in the same way with black Surinamese applicants. The only difference was that now the application procedure was terminated after two stages. The testers did not go to the personal interview when invited. Surinamese applicants encountered discrimination at a slightly higher rate than Moroccan applicants (40 per cent compared with 32 per cent) but this difference was not significant at the 5 per cent level and therefore should be interpreted as zero. It can be concluded, therefore, that the rate of discrimination against men from an ethnic minority at the level of semi-skilled jobs does not differ by ethnic group. Despite their perceived greater social acceptability, Surinamese men encounter discrimination to the same degree as Moroccan men. This shows that discrimination is not just an isolated problem of one group only, but is a general characteristic of how the labour market functions with respect to immigrants.

3. Does Discrimination Vary by Educational/Job Level?

Is racial discrimination a problem only at the semi-skilled job level, or is it also a problem at the highly skilled job level? To answer this question, a third experiment was undertaken in which college-educated Surinamese and Dutch applicants applied for jobs at the highly skilled level, such as financial manager, personnel manager and teacher. As Büyükbozkoyum et al. (1991) had already found no discrimination against highly educated Turkish engineers, it was expected that the rate of discrimination would be less than at the semi-skilled level.

Because it is more usual to apply for highly skilled jobs by letter rather than by telephone, we used a slightly different technique, known as 'correspondence testing'. Instead of sending test applicants for a position, two standard application letters were sent simultaneously to the same advertised vacancy. One letter was signed by a well-qualified Surinamese applicant and the other signed by an equally qualified Dutch applicant. In order to avoid detection the letters could not be identical, but they were as similar as possible. The (fictitious) 'candidates' were matched in all applicant characteristics, such as age, work experience, education and reasons for applying for another job. The only difference was their ethnic background. The Surinamese applicant was identifiable by a typical Surinamese name, Errol Rozenblad, and his place of birth, Paramaribo, in Surinam. The Dutch applicant used a typical Dutch name, Paul van Bergen.

Where both applicants were immediately rejected, this was counted as a non-observation, as no information about an employer's preferences was available. If both applicants were offered an interview, or if both names were to be kept on file, or if both applicants were rejected but sent a new vacancy to apply for, this was treated as a case of 'equal treatment'. If only one applicant received a positive answer, while the other was directly rejected, this was treated as a case of 'unequal treatment'. The application procedure was terminated after an invitation had been obtained by one or both applicants.[1]

In total, 182 applications were made for jobs, requiring a college education. The private sector as well as the public sector was tested. Companies advertising their preference for minority applicants in the event of equal suitability, were also tested. Equal treatment, where both applicants received an invitation for an interview, or both were kept on file or both were sent a new vacancy, occurred in 93 cases. In 62 cases, the Surinamese applicant was rejected, while the Dutch applicant was sent a positive reply. An example is given below:

> Both applicants applied for a job as an administrator in a private company. Their letters were identical, but the employer's response was different. To the Surinamese applicant the answer was, 'Thank you for your application for the position of administrator in our company. However, we must inform you that this vacancy has already been

filled.' The same day, the Dutch applicant received the following answer: 'Further to your letter, we would like to invite you for an interview on the 25th of February.'

In 27 cases, the Dutch applicant was rejected, while the Surinamese applicant received an invitation for an interview or had his name kept on file. Consequently, the net rate of discrimination against the college-educated Surinamese applicant was 35 cases (19 per cent). This shows that discrimination occurs not only at the semi-skilled level, but also at the highly skilled level. Surinamese male immigrants encounter discrimination in one out of every five applications for jobs requiring a college education. This means that education alone will not help to end the disadvantageous position of immigrants in the labour market. Even with a college education, immigrants will have difficulties in finding a job because of the discriminatory behaviour of employers.

The results do not correlate with those obtained by Büyükbozkoyum et al. (1991), who observed no discrimination against highly educated Turkish engineers. However, this might be explained by the low number of observations in this study and by the fact that engineers are in greater demand than the occupations tested in our study.

At the highly skilled level, the private sector was substantially more disposed to discriminate than the public sector (31 per cent compared with 14 per cent). Companies with a positive action programme for ethnic minorities were not likely to discriminate against ethnic minority applicants or Dutch applicants. In fact, a net rate of discrimination against the *Dutch* applicant had been expected, because those companies had stated in their vacancies that in the case of equal qualification, preference would be given to the ethnic applicant. In fact, the rate of discrimination observed was 0 per cent for firms with a positive action programme in force, while this was 21 per cent for firms without a positive action programme. In other words, positive action programmes do not result in preferential treatment for the minority applicant but do seem to be an effective instrument for reducing racial discrimination in hiring procedures.

The rate of discrimination encountered by Surinamese at the highly skilled level (19 per cent) was significantly less than the rate of discrimination encountered by Surinamese at the semi-skilled level (40 per cent). Thus, it can be concluded that the higher the educational level of the applicant, the less discrimination applicants will encounter in hiring procedures.

Why are employers less likely to discriminate against highly skilled immigrants than semi-skilled immigrants? One explanation might be that employers are less prejudiced towards immigrants with a college education;

after all, these applicants have shown that they are able to conform to the high standards of their new society. They have displayed high levels of motivation and perseverance. Employers may also have had better employment experiences with this group than with immigrants who had received little education.

Another explanation for the discrepancy might be that the application procedure at the highly skilled level (where written applications are required) gives less rise to discriminatory behaviour by employers than the application procedure at the semi-skilled level (where the initial contact is made by telephone). When an employer or personnel manager receives an application letter from a minority applicant, he not only notices the foreign name, but at the same time he observes that the applicant is qualified. In the case of an application by telephone, the employer notices only the foreign name of the applicant and can reject him/her before the applicant has had an opportunity to provide information about qualifications.

Finally, the discrepancy might also be due to the fact that at the highly skilled level there were vacancies for jobs in the public sector as well as in the private sector, while at the semi-skilled level, there were vacancies for jobs only in the private sector. As discrimination occurs less often in the public sector than in the private sector (14 per cent versus 31 per cent), this might account for the lower rate of discrimination found at the highly skilled level. Within the private sector, the difference in the rate of discrimination between the semi-skilled level and the highly skilled level diminishes (40 per cent in comparison with 31 per cent).

CONCLUSION

The results of the research demonstrate that racial discrimination in employment recruitment occurs to a considerable degree throughout the Dutch labour market. Despite the integration process of immigrants into Dutch society and a plethora of anti-discrimination measures, the rate of discrimination against ethnic minorities has doubled over the past 17 years. The high rate of discrimination encountered by immigrants forms a serious impediment to their chances of finding and securing employment and the conclusion can be drawn that the unfavourable position of ethnic minorities in the Dutch labour market is not only due to their low levels of educational and language problems, but is, for a substantial part, caused by discriminatory behaviour on the part of employers in hiring procedures.

Discrimination in access to employment is encountered not only by Moroccans but also by Surinamese men. Discrimination was in evidence both when applying for jobs at the semi-skilled level and at the highly skilled level and both in the private and public sectors. Employers tend to discriminate less when the educational level of the ethnic applicant is higher. It would seem, therefore, that the extra education facilities provided for minorities, as advocated in the Netherlands' minority policy, seem to be effective. However, discrimination at the higher job/educational level is still considerable and therefore education alone will not end the disadvantaged position of minorities in the labour market. Discrimination in hiring procedures should be actively combated to help reduce the high unemployment figures among ethnic minorities.

In this study it was found that companies advertising a preference for minority applicants in the case of equal qualification, did not, in fact, treat the ethnic applicant more favourably than the Dutch applicant. However, they did not treat the ethnic applicant unfavourably. Positive action programmes, therefore, appear to be an effective instrument for eliminating discrimination in hiring procedures and to bring about equal treatment and opportunities for migrant workers in access to employment.

NOTE

1. At the highly skilled level, it was not possible to send 'real' test persons to a personal interview, as was the case in the experiments at the semi-skilled level. It would have been very difficult to select two equally qualified persons, able to play the role of these highly skilled candidates. Thus, the correspondence-testing identifies discrimination only at the initial stage of selection.

7 The Labour Market for Immigrant Women in Sweden: Marginalised Women in Low-valued Jobs

Wuokko Knocke

Immigrants are not just immigrants – they are also women and men. Why do I find it necessary to begin with this apparently self-evident statement? Quite simply because this trivial fact is, remarkably enough, often overlooked. Both in the public debate and in everyday discourse this fundamental and obvious fact is hidden by the gender-neutral and socially equalising term 'immigrant'. In many respects both men and women are, of course, affected by the structural subordination and powerlessness that is part of being an immigrant. But in ignoring the obvious truth that immigrants come in two sexes, one also disregards the fact that, like Swedish men and women, they are being located in the gendered social system. Women encounter the difficulties that are part of their status as immigrants, while at the same time being confronted with the social subordination of women and the gender segregation in the labour market. Or, as expressed by Annie Phizacklea: 'Migrant women are thus placed at the intersection of two processes, gender and racial subordination ...' (Phizacklea 1983: 6–7) or, as in the Swedish context, subordination on ethnic grounds, for being 'foreigners' and 'the others'. With some remarkable exceptions produced by female scholars, such as, for example, Phizacklea's anthology *One Way Ticket* (1983), women in migration were for decades, by and large, ignored in international and, definitely in Swedish studies. Research either dealt exclusively with men as immigrants, while women were, and to a large extent still are, invisible or treated as dependent family members. Alternatively, research findings on male immigrants were generalised to apply to women as well (Morokvasic 1983, Bretell and Simon 1986; Knocke 1986 and 1991; Boyd 1991). Neither have formal regulations contained in the legislation on gender equality considered the specific interests of immigrant women (Expert Report to the European Commission 1986). Despite statistical evidence of their high levels of labour force participation in many of the Western

European economies, women have been ignored as economic actors in the labour market (OECD 1985; Knocke 1991). There are also wide gaps in our knowledge about their educational backgrounds, their social and economic situation and daily working and living conditions in receiving countries (de Troy 1987). As a result, a simplified and distorted picture of immigrant women has become integrated into everyday thinking and existing conceptions about immigrant women. The purpose of this chapter is to provide an overview and insight into the employment patterns and the situation of immigrant women in the Swedish labour market. The chapter begins with a theoretical discussion, analysing how dominant images and conceptions of the abstract and reductionist notion of 'the immigrant woman' have been created within majority society and the way in which these conceptions affect the position of immigrant women in the society at large and in working life. This theoretical discussion then forms a basis for presenting and discussing concrete conditions in the labour market in terms of labour force participation, occupational patterns, career opportunities and unemployment patterns. The article also examines and comments on the similarities and differences at the aggregate level between the occupational status of Swedish and immigrant women, and concludes with some reflections on immigrant women's chances of maintaining their position in a changing labour market.

ON REPRESENTATION AND NAMING

Because women in migration have been ignored for so long in both public discourse and research, they have become locked into a vicious circle from which it has been difficult to break free. I argue that 'invisibility', a central concept in feminist research, is one of the fundamental causes of their marginality, and the crucial factor that has perpetuated their subordination and powerlessness both in society at large and in the world of work. As Jenson and Mahon (1992) argue, the possibility of representing oneself and one's interests is a matter of having access to power. As immigrant women have had no power and influence, they have had no public platform or strong collective interest groups that could have taken them out of their invisibility to a place in the public arena. As Ålund (1991) shows, in their private world they have built up strength and positive self-esteem. But they have not been able to mobilise the power resources required to represent their interests, or to put forward more balanced or alternative images that could have thrown into question the definitions presented about them and their life situations. Instead, they and their interests have been represented by the political, ideological and economic power holders of the dominant majority. Naming and labelling is also a way of exercising power, which socially defines and places powerless groups in society (Knocke 1991). Thus, I argue that the commonly used term 'the immigrant woman' – including the stereotypes and negative images related to it – is an expression of the exercise of power by the dominant majority over women immigrants. The abstract term 'the immigrant woman' totally anonymises the women, who come from varied backgrounds in terms of origin, education and experience. Their collective identity is presented as problematic, where they themselves are usually being associated with problematic characteristics. The complex problems include their non-defined cultural background, an assumed lack of education, an absence of work experience, a poor command of the Swedish language, strongly traditional gender roles, including oppressive husbands, social isolation and being tied to the home, in short termed as 'problem ideologies' by Ålund (1989; cf. also Phizacklea 1983: 3). By unilaterally explaining immigrant women as carriers of problems, ensuing stereotypes have helped to disregard and block awareness of the discrimination and structural barriers these women encounter in the community and in working life. Complex circumstances have been given a simplistic explanation, with the blame largely being laid at the door of the victim (Knocke 1991). A less ideologically loaded and factual way of becoming invisible, at least where statistics are concerned, is to become a Swedish citizen. Becoming naturalised is a relatively uncomplicated process: five years of settlement (for Nordic citizens, two years), being 18 years old and an absence of a serious criminal record are the only requirements.[1] Fifty-three per cent of immigrants and refugees had taken Swedish nationality by January 1989. Preferences differ according to place of birth and the motive for migrating. Worker immigrants from Finland have tended to naturalise more frequently than, for example, worker immigrants from former Yugoslavia – 57 per cent and 31 per cent respectively. Refugees from the former Eastern European countries such as Hungary (84.2 per cent), Czechoslovakia (83.3 per cent) and Poland (59.7 per cent) have naturalised more frequently than refugees from Chile (32.8 per cent) due to the intention of the latter to return to their country of origin. Different naturalisation patterns imply that certain nationalities 'disappear' from the labour force statistics more often than others. Unfortunately, though, naturalisation is no guarantee for not being treated as an immigrant when searching for work. In this chapter, I use the term 'foreign-born', where data apply to both foreign nationals and naturalised persons, and in all other cases, the terms 'foreigners' or 'foreign nationals' is used. There exists no unequivocal definition of the term 'immigrant'. In both popular and official discourse it often refers to all persons born outside Sweden, both foreigners and naturalised. Even children born in Sweden, normally referred to as the 'second generation', where one or both parents have or have had foreign citizenship, can be included in the immigrant population.[2]

MULTICULTURALISM OR CULTURAL HIERARCHIES?

Since the Swedish Parliament, in its immigrant policy of 1975, has officially adopted cultural pluralism, there is special reason to question the problematisation of a different cultural background. Research in other European countries, where multiculturalism is the official norm, has provided us with evidence that shows how the culture of immigrant populations is problematised in relation to the country's own culture (Essed 1991). A closer look at multicultural Sweden also reveals the existence of a value hierarchy, which implicitly posits the culture and norms of the dominating majority as being superior and worth striving for (Ålund and Schierup 1991). Members of the dominant group perceive their own values and world view as that which is 'normal'. Even when looking at apparently rational social institutions that are supposed to help various categories of clients – such as day nurseries for children, healthcare and hospital services, employment offices, social welfare facilities, and so on – they are in fact creations of the dominant culture and entirely based on the majority's standards and values (Hannerz 1981). People who fail to adapt to these standards or unhesitatingly adopt accepted patterns risk being labelled as deviant or are defined as a social problem.

Adherence, at least rhetorically, to the immigrant policy's cultural freedom of choice with simultaneous demands of adjustment to Swedish values, may sometimes result in paradoxical formulations of objectives that highlight the ambivalence and contradictory reality of multiculturalism. In a spirit of well-intentioned paternalism, a government commission report (SOU 1979: 89) states for example that 'the immigrant woman' needs help to choose her path into Swedish society. Among other things, she is supposed to understand and accept Swedish ambitions to achieve gender equality both in the family and the world of work. The women are expected to adapt to the Swedish patterns of gender equality while, as a concession to the freedom of choice, they are also supposed to maintain their own cultural background. On the other hand, it is exactly this different cultural background that is considered to make it difficult for immigrant women to adapt to the rules prescribed by the host country. According to

Hannerz (1981: 214), even the most benign and generous attitudes towards immigrant cultures are entirely permeated by 'Swedishness'. Thus, deliberate action need not necessarily be a component in ethnic discrimination (cf. Essed 1991). Social relations between majority and minority are systematically shaped by value hierarchical thinking, passed on through a complex institutional process, for example, written texts, public discourse, the media – from the macro level of the experts and holders of power down to the micro level and everyday discourse and practice.

THE POWER OF NEGATIVE CONCEPTIONS

Ethnocentric perspectives and ethnicism, that is, cultural depreciation of 'the others', have given rise to the negative conceptions and images surrounding immigrant women. These negative images have had a considerable impact. They have become 'truths' that have affected both the way these women see themselves and also the way society sees them. The risk in being described as a 'problem' or – as happens with some nationalities – as a weak group (SOU 1981: 87) by significant others, is that immigrant women will internalise a negative perception of themselves. I have come across examples where a group of women who are normally considered 'strong' – Finnish women in this case – have accepted negative perceptions of themselves as poorly educated women with inferior language skills. This must be seen in the light of the fact that Finnish women, in reality, have had better formal education and normally speak better Swedish than many other groups, and even better than Finnish men (SOU 1981: 87). Generally accepted stereotypes thus seem to be more powerful than concrete facts.

From the second half of the 1940s, until the ban on non-Nordic worker immigration in 1972 when there was a shortage of indigenous labour, male immigrants were in demand and were recruited to meet the need for labour in an expanding industrial production. Although only male workers were mentioned in discussions on the labour shortage, women also started coming in the early 1950s, or were recruited to a certain extent in the 1950s as domestic workers and in the 1960s, for example, as nurses and textile workers. Many women, not least women from Finland, came to Sweden on their own initiative. Otherwise the majority of women came either with their husbands or arrived later in the framework of family reunion. The women who came when there was a shortage of labour rarely had any difficulty in gaining entry to the labour market. Evidence collected in a study confirms that most women, whether coming by themselves or with husbands, were motivated to come because they knew there was work for them too (Knocke 1986). They were needed to fill jobs that were not attractive to Swedes, and were therefore functional in terms of labour market needs. In this context, I argue that their social invisibility, in combination with the stereotyped images that were created, has played a decisive part in the process of marginalization and a continued peripheral placement in the hierarchy of the working world. As stated in a government report, immigrant women were given work 'mostly in the occupational areas where little or no knowledge of the Swedish language is required, such as cleaning and restaurant work' (SOU 1979: 89, p. 165). They also found work in other typical female occupations in the public care sector. Far more often than Swedish women, they were found in female-typed industrial work – the most monotonous and low-valued jobs – 9 per cent for Swedish women as compared to 30 per cent for foreign women until around 1981 and 25 per cent in 1985 (AKU 1976–85). I shall return to their occupational pattern after first presenting their participation in the labour force.

CHANGES IN IMMIGRANT WOMEN'S LABOUR FORCE PARTICIPATION

The Situation in 1981

The proportion of foreign women in the female workforce has, over the years, been just above 5 per cent or around 90,000–100,000 persons. Together with naturalised women they have made up more than 9 per cent of the female labour force, which amounts to around 200,000 persons. Throughout the 1970s and, as Table 7.1 shows, still in 1981, foreign women had a high degree of labour force participation.

In 1981 all groups of women with foreign citizenship had a higher labour force participation rate than Swedish women when comparing the entire 16–74 age span. However, this is something of a statistical illusion. With the exception of a couple of age groups among Finnish women, and the youngest group among other Nordic citizens, in most age groups the labour force participation rate was lower among foreign women than among Swedes. The explanation for the higher percentages for the entire 16–74 age group was the different age structure shown for foreign women. As many as 80.3 per cent of all foreign women were in the 16–44 age bracket, while the same figure for Swedish women in this age bracket was 52.9 per cent. Barely 20 per cent of foreign women were in the

Table 7.1 Relative activity rates for women by age and citizenship, 1981 (%)

Age	Swedish	Finnish	Other Nordic	Other Foreign*	All Foreign
16–24	67.8	73.4	73.6	58.2	67.7
25–34	83.8	85.8	79.2	72.2	79.5
35–44	86.9	85.4	80.9	79.3	82.3
45–54	85.0	72.8	63.8	74.3	71.7
55–64	57.6	56.5	50.7	50.5	52.8
65–74	4.0	7.4	0.0	6.5	6.0
16–74	65.3	77.8	71.1	68.1	73.0

Source: AKU (The Labour Force Survey). Average annual figures 1981, raw tables (foreign women have been subtracted from the total population).
*The figure was 81.3 per cent for Yugoslavian women and 73.7 per cent for Greek women for the entire age group, 16–74. No spread by age is given.

45–74 age bracket, against about 47 per cent for Swedish women. Another expression of the greater concentration of foreign women in their best working years was the average age, which in 1981 was 33.6 for all employed foreign women against 38.9 for employed women in the population as a whole. Foreign women were quite simply in the most productive and most reproductive age brackets, and this reflected to a certain extent in their pattern of labour force participation (Knocke 1983).

Although foreign women were in a phase of their life cycle when their children were small and needed looking after, measured in working hours or the intensity of gainful employment, their attachment to the labour market was stronger than that of Swedish women. In 1981 the percentage of part-time working Swedish women was 52.6 per cent against 43.8 per cent for foreign women. As a result, average working hours for foreign women was higher at 32.8 hours a week, as against 30.9 hours for all women. High percentages in full-time work were particularly evident among women with nationalities that had traditionally supplied Sweden with labour. The women from Yugoslavia were at the top of the table (69.0 per cent), followed by Greek and Finnish women (64.0 per cent), while the figure for other non-Nordic women was 61.0 per cent.

Comparable figures for women who had more recently arrived in Sweden as refugees were not reported in the 1981 labour force survey. Usually, groups with a large proportion of refugees have, at least initially, shown low values. The 1980 National Census reports for some of these groups the proportion of women in employment for all foreign-born, that is, both foreign and naturalised women, which then was 47 per cent for

Chilean women, 54 per cent for Polish women and 40 per cent for women from Turkey. Low activity rates can partly be explained by a high proportion of women being involved in studies: 27 per cent for Chilean, 10 per cent for Polish and 15 per cent for Turkish women. The percentage of women included in study activities, for example, language courses, was 6 per cent for all foreign-born women (Statistics Sweden 1984). Jonung (1982: 30) suggested a number of other possible explanations for the lower level of labour force participation in these groups: differences in the motives for immigration, shorter periods of residence in the country, and either very low or very high levels of education that were not easily adaptable to the corresponding type of employment in the new country.

Having children was, in certain age groups and nationalities, a concrete reason for lower activity rates. It was characteristic of foreign women in 1981 that far more of them than Swedish women had children of school age: 31.8 per cent of foreign women against 16.4 per cent of Swedish women. Notably, the youngest group of foreign women, up to the age of 24, had twice the number of children than had Swedish women. A far higher proportion of women from Turkey and Greece became mothers before they had reached the age of 25 than was the case among Swedish women. Having a greater number of children at a relatively young age thus delayed the entry into the labour market for women of some nationalities, while for other nationalities this had less effect on workforce participation. Gainful employment was less frequent for mothers of young children (under the age of 11) from Finland, Poland, Turkey and Latin America, while the workforce participation of Yugoslavian and Greek women was not affected at all by their having children (Ds A 1981: 2: pp. 79 and 81; Knocke 1983). Access to public childcare facilities, parental insurance and paid parental leave up until the child is 18 months old, including the right to return to their jobs, has made it possible for all women, both foreign citizens and Swedish, to remain in the paid labour force after becoming mothers.

There are at least two conclusions that can be drawn from the high labour force participation rates of foreign women in 1981. First, the figures show that the majority of them wanted to go out to work and that there were jobs for them. Secondly, the very fact of their high rate of workforce participation refutes all statements about 'the immigrant woman' being isolated and tied to her home. To quote the Finnish sociologist Elina Haavio-Mannila, this is a myth built upon false premises: 'Immigrant women certainly do not sit "imprisoned" in their homes, provided for and oppressed by their men, as is often stereotypically described' (1981: 155).

The Situation in 1991

Having reviewed the rate of labour force participation in 1981, we now look at the position ten years later, in 1991, with some reference to the 'boom year' of 1988. First, some important changes must be mentioned. The strong link that existed between immigration and the economic cycle from the end of the 1940s to the mid-1970s is no longer there (Ekberg 1990). Today, immigration is no longer determined by the labour needs of industry and the public sector. With the exception of citizens from the other Nordic countries, the halt on immigration, introduced in 1972, has limited the right to migrate to Sweden to cases of family reunification and the immigration of political and humanitarian refugees. With every major war or world crisis, Sweden has received groups of refugees from new, and often increasingly remote, countries. Sweden's populations of foreign origin therefore are different today, both in terms of the motive for immigration and the composition of nationalities, than was formerly the case when most immigrants came to Sweden to work.

What, then, was the labour force participation rate of foreign women in 1991? What changes have there been since 1981? The 1991 Labour Force Survey shows that 81.7 per cent of the total female population between the ages of 16 and 64 was in the labour force while the percentage for foreign women had gone down to 67.1 per cent. The labour force participation rate for the total female population with children under the age of seven was as high as 85.7 per cent. These figures are no longer extracted separately for foreign women. As a rule, women with foreign citizenship still have children earlier than do Swedish women. But, with the exception of Turkish women, whether they be naturalised Swedes or foreign citizens, there is now no longer any major difference in the fertility pattern of Swedish and immigrant women (Statistics Sweden 1991). Since 1983, fertility rates have risen among Swedish women and fallen among immigrant women.[3] With the exception of Turkish women, the difference in the number of children should therefore no longer be a decisive factor in explaining the differences in labour force participation rates. What can be said is that the figure for Swedish women's entry into the labour market has continued to rise while, compared to Swedish women, foreign women have lost their strong position in the labour market.

Yet Finnish women still manage to hold their position well. Their participation rate (81.4 per cent) was, in 1991, virtually the same as for the female population as a whole and actually higher than that of Finnish men (79.9 per cent).[4] The figure for Yugoslavian women, who, at 81.3 per cent, had the highest labour force participation rate in 1981, dropped to 68.8 per cent by 1991. This should be set against the fact that in the 1988 boom they still had an activity rate of 77.5 per cent. Within three years their rate had dropped by almost 9 percentage points. I shall return to some of the probable reasons for this pronounced drop among Yugoslavian women. The reduction was less dramatic for foreign women as a whole, from 69.9 per cent to 67.1 per cent. When looking at some nationalities or refugee groups with low rates in 1981, we find that women from Turkey, Chile and Poland actually increased their economic activity over the ten-year period; 52.0 per cent of Turkish women, 64.8 per cent of Chilean women and 65.6 per cent of Polish women were in the labour force in 1991. In 1991, foreign women still had a higher total number of working hours than all women: 69 per cent of them worked 35 hours or more a week against the average of 59 per cent for all women. The gap between average weekly working hours was however less pronounced now than in 1981, being 34.7 hours for foreign women against 33.6 hours for all women.

THE UNEMPLOYMENT PATTERN FOR IMMIGRANT WOMEN

According to the economist Jan Ekberg (1990), immigrants who arrived before 1970 have a very different position in the labour market from those who arrived after 1970. The labour market situation for early immigrants, who also often became naturalised, is about the same as for the total population. The frequency of gainful employment drops and unemployment increases among immigrants from later years. In particular, both women and men who migrated since 1984 have very low activity rates and a high incidence of unemployment. Strikingly low labour force participation rates are reported in the 1991 labour force survey for women from Iran (39.1 per cent), while their unemployment figure was 14.3 per cent for that year. Compared to 1987, where their activity rate (for 20–64 years of age) was only 18 per cent and unemployment 16.6 per cent (Ekberg 1990), we see that their activity rate increased and unemployment slightly decreased. Their activity rates were, however, nowhere near the percentages for the women who came to Sweden in the early wave of labour immigration.

As a complement to the section on immigrant women's participation in the labour force, Table 7.2 presents details of how they have been affected by unemployment in different years. Irrespective of whether the economy was expanding or shrinking, unemployment for female foreign citizens has been higher, often twice as high, as the figure for all women. Even in 1988, a year of acute labour shortage, their unemployment level was 2 percentage points higher than that of the total female population. A comparison of the different age brackets shows that it is always the youngest women who have been the hardest hit. The low unemployment figures in 1981 and

Table 7.2   Unemployment by age and citizenship (%)

Age	Foreign Women			Total Female Population		
	1981	*1988*	*1991*	*1981*	*1988*	*1991*
16–24	9.8	5.0	10.3	6.6	3.5	5.4
25–54	4.0	3.6	5.0	1.7	1.2	1.8
55–64/74	0.3	0.6	3.8	1.6	1.6	2.0
16–64/74	5.1	3.7	5.8	2.6	1.6	2.3

Source: Labour market survey average annual figures (conversion of selected raw data tables).

Table 7.3   Relative unemployment figures by citizenship (%)

Citizenship	1981	1988	1991
Finnish	4.8	2.9	3.0
Danish	6.2	2.9	3.9
Norwegian	5.1	3.6	6.7
Yugoslavian	4.0	0.8	8.1
Turkish	–	1.7	6.3
Polish	–	6.5	6.5
Chilean	–	–	7.7
Iranian	–	–	14.3

Source: Labour market survey, annual average figures.

1988 for the oldest foreign women are partly explained by the fact that they were few in numbers in these age brackets, both in the population and in the workforce. This age group was larger in 1991; it had a higher activity rate and unemployment was now higher than for the corresponding group of the female population.

As an illustration of variations in the unemployment pattern, the unemployment figures for women of different nationalities are presented in Table 7.3, in so far as the labour market survey statistics allow these figures to be extracted.

The highest unemployment is to be found among refugee women, and in particular among the most recently arrived women from Iran, whose unemployment rate has rocketed to 55.5 per cent in 1993. There are fairly strong variations in the pattern of unemployment for the other groups, both between different years and between different nationalities. The relatively high unemployment figure for Finnish women in 1981 was affected by the fact that unemployment in the youngest age bracket (16–24 years), was 10.7 per cent in that year. As mentioned above, the youngest foreign women always had the greatest difficulties in the labour market. Among those who came in the initial wave of labour migration, the increase in unemployment between 1988 and 1991 is strikingly high for women from Turkey and Yugoslavia. For the latter group the increase from 0.8 per cent in 1988 to 8.1 per cent in 1991 and then to 18.7 per cent in 1993 is astonishing, since they were over many years one of the most highly integrated groups in the labour market with more than 50 per cent working in manufacturing jobs. Before proceeding to the issue of immigrant women's occupational profiles and the changes that have taken place over a number of years, a few words should be said about the social protection and material security of the unemployed. Thanks to the intervention of the state and the powerful position of trade unions in matters of immigration, most immigrants, both women and men, have from the very beginning of labour migration to Sweden, joined the trade unions. As union members they have been entitled to equal wages for equal jobs and they were insured against unemployment with the same unemployment benefits as their Swedish co-workers (SOU 1967: 18; Knocke 1982). Until 1993 unemployment insurance benefits amounted to 90 per cent of a person's salary, but since then have been lowered to 75 per cent of the salary level. The non-unionised or those who do not qualify for unemployment benefits in terms of length of service, are entitled to a daily cash allowance or to social assistance, when the duration of unemployment exceeds the time limit stipulated for insurance benefits. Insurance against unemployment was introduced as early as 1947 in the first bilateral agreements for worker immigration. Social protection of foreigners in other respects was introduced by the Swedish welfare state in the 1960s through a number of reforms, which aimed at giving foreigners the same social privileges and standards of living as those of native Swedes. Social protection of unemployed immigrant workers is far better than in many other countries. It is comparable to that of Swedes and, in spite of recent deteriorations in benefit levels, saves them from material misery.

SIMILARITIES AND DIFFERENCES IN IMMIGRANT AND SWEDISH WOMEN'S OCCUPATIONAL PATTERNS

The occupations of immigrant women are very similar to those of Swedish women in a number of respects. At least, that is the impression we get from a first glance at the statistics. In contrast to both Swedish and immigrant men, more immigrant women are concentrated in a small number of occupations. The 1985 Population Census showed that only about 25–7 per cent of men are to be found in the ten most common male occupations against the women's concentration of 44–7 per cent in the most common female occupations. Except for the occupation of cleaner, which, as one of the top ten occupations for immigrant men is an indication of their relatively subordinate position, no occupations were common to both women and men in the 1985 population census. Table 7.4 offers a comparison of the ten most common occupations ranked in descending order, for Swedish and foreign-born women. I shall then comment on certain changes in the occupational patterns for immigrant women between the 1985 population census and earlier population and housing censuses.

Cleaning has always been the primary occupation for both foreign and foreign-born women. This was the case in 1975 and 1980, and remained so in 1985. Cleaning is a traditional female occupation and is also one of the ten most common occupations for Swedish-born women, ranking fourth. At the top of the league for Swedish women is clerical work, an occupation that is in third place for foreign-born women. This occupation

Table 7.4 The ten most common occupations among foreign-born and Swedish women (%)

Foreign-born Women	%	Swedish-born Women	%
1. Cleaner, etc	10.5	1. Other secretarial and typing jobs	8.3
2. Nursing assistant, ancillary nurse	6.7	2. Nursing assistant, ancillary nurse	7.3
3. Other secretarial and typewriting jobs	5.7	3. Sales person (Retail trade)	6.0
4. Childminder, etc.	4.0	4.Cleaner, etc,	5.3
5. Kitchen/restaurant assistant	3.9	5. Childminder, etc.	4.3
6. Hospital auxiliary, home nurse	3.5	6. Hospital auxiliary, home nurse	4.2
7. Sales person (retail)	3.5	7. Secretary, stenographer	3.3
8. Secretary, stenographer	2.4	8. Kitchen/restaurant assistant	3.1
9. Nurse	2.2	9. Nurse	3.0
10. Teaching, incl. home language teaching	1.8	10. School teacher	2.4

Source: Statistics Sweden, Population Census 1985.

is in fifth place for women with foreign citizenship, indicating that naturalised women, more often than foreign women, are to be found in this typical female occupation. Special processing of the 1980 national census shows that office work was in third place among Finnish women, but as low as seventh and tenth place for Yugoslavian and Turkish women (Leiniö 1986). In neither the 1975 nor the 1980 population census did any pedagogical work feature amongst the ten most common occupations for immigrant women. The 1976 home language training reform for children gradually opened up an 'ethnic niche' for foreign-born teachers. Another substantial change compared to 1980 (when 'machine assembler' was the seventh most common occupation among immigrant women), was that in 1985 no manufacturing occupation appeared among the ten most common occupations. In 1980, two of the most common occupations for Finnish women, four of the most common occupations for Turkish women and five of the most common occupations for Yugoslavian women were in the manufacturing sector. After cleaning, the second most common occupation for women from Yugoslavia, with high concentrations in industrial jobs in general, was machine assembler (Leiniö 1986).

What is the explanation for this change in the occupational pattern of immigrant women? For women who came as labour migrants it has been much more common than for Swedish-born women to have female-typed jobs located in the male industrial sector. The structural transformation over the last 15–20 years has successively reduced the size of the industrial sector, which has led to a sharp reduction in manufacturing occupations (DS 1990: 35). The reduction in industrial sector employment should also have affected immigrant women's work in this sector. New technology may also have replaced some of the work tasks that were previously performed by immigrant women. But the information no longer agrees here. For example, the Swedish Metalworkers' Union 1989 Congress Report states that, measured in the number of employees, growth had been higher in sectors with a large proportion of unskilled jobs than in sectors with a large proportion of highly skilled jobs. And it is women who ended up in the jobs that require little skill and that create severe strain, according to the Swedish Metalworkers' Union (1989: 72). There are no data on the extent to which this has affected immigrant women. But what we do know is that so far the current economic downturn has primarily affected employment in the industrial sector. Considering that Yugoslavian women were strongly over-represented in manufacturing occupations, we have here one important factor that explains the reduction in their labour force figures and the sharp increase in the level of unemployment in this group. Below, I shall analyse one more effect of their occupational concentration.

At all events, their high degree of penetration into the engineering industry has made them particularly vulnerable to the decline in employment in this sector.

Immigrant women thus found themselves, much more often than Swedish-born women, in jobs in the male industrial sector. They were given jobs considered 'light' and that were reserved for women. Thanks to the critical analyses of feminist research, we know that the traditional division of work into 'heavy' male jobs and 'light' women's jobs does not reflect the strain that these 'light' jobs actually involves (Fürst 1985; Knocke 1986). Monotonous, repetitive jobs were the norm for immigrant women, often paid on piece rates that pushed up the pace of work and that tied women to the machines or the assembly-line. Repeated lifting and repetitive movements were physically strenuous and caused repetitive strain injuries, while the machines and tools used were not ergonomically suitable for women. As a number of studies have shown, more often than for comparable Swedish groups, their work environment was both physically and mentally sub-standard (Statistics Sweden 1977; Statistics Sweden 1984; Knocke 1986; Knocke 1992).

IMMIGRANT WOMEN: DISPOSABLE COMMODITIES?

The effects of monotonous and strenuous jobs may be seen today in the high degree of redundancy in the form of long-term illnesses and disability pensions. In a study of sick leave broken down by citizenship in 1988, the National Insurance Office (1990: 4) found that the sickness figures (days of sickness benefit paid per person covered by the health insurance scheme) among foreign citizens were, on average, about 70 per cent higher than the level for Swedish citizens. Women had a higher sickness rate than men in all the groups covered by the study. A high variation in sick leave was also found between different nationalities. Southern European women had the highest number of days of sick leave per year, 82 days, compared to 28 days for Swedish women. Most notably, long-term absenteeism was higher for women than for men. The entire difference in the sickness figures between the sexes was explained, for the women from Southern Europe, Eastern Europe and the Nordic bloc, by differences in long-term sick leave (lasting at least 90 days per year) for which sickness benefit was payable. Long-term sick leave is part of the marginalization process that leads to early retirement and disability pensions. When considering the reduction in labour force figures for the immigrant workforce, the National Insurance Office does not hesitate to state that 'to a not inconsiderable degree, the low frequency of gainful employment ... depends on a high incidence of disability pensions among immigrants'. A survey of urban areas that covered immigrants resident in the Stockholm county showed that approximately 75 per cent of Greek women in the 50–64 age bracket were receiving disability pensions or sickness allowance. The figure for Yugoslavian women was about 60 per cent and about 35 per cent for Turkish women, against 15 per cent for Swedish women in the same age bracket (SOU 1989: 111).

In a research project at Volvo-Torslanda Works a special analysis was undertaken on long-term absenteeism among assembly-line and other engineering workers (Paulson 1994). The findings confirmed that immigrants – both men and women – were harder hit than Swedish workers by long-term illnesses. Here too, major differences appeared between different nationalities and between the sexes. Swedish men had the lowest incidence of long-term absenteeism at 4.7 per cent, the next lowest being Finnish men with 12.2 per cent. The total percentage of women with long-term illnesses was about three times greater than the proportion of long-term illness for all men: 13.5 per cent of Swedish women suffered from long-term illness, 20.8 per cent of Finnish women, 45.9 per cent of Yugoslavian women and 64.3 per cent of Turkish women (who, however, were very few in number). Primarily, for the Yugoslavian women, the proportion of long-term illness sufferers went up sharply after the age of 25. The proportion also increased among Swedish and Finnish women, but not as dramatically as among Yugoslavian women. To give an example, as much as 54.8 per cent of Yugoslavian women in the 35–44 age group suffered from long-term illness, against 26.4 per cent of Finnish women and 22 per cent of Swedish women.

Separate figures broken down by length of employment and gender were not available. However, a total of two-thirds of the Swedish workforce had been employed for less than five years, while that was true of less than a quarter of the Yugoslavs and about one-fifth of the Finnish workers. Paulson (1992) found a strong correlation between age and length of employment in terms of sick leave.

Personal interviews at Volvo with a number of Yugoslav and Finnish women revealed employment periods from 8 to 20 years for the former and from 2 to 20 years for the latter, with the majority having been employed for a long time. My study 'Gender, Ethnicity and Technical Change' (Knocke 1994) shows that for women, gender and immigrant status have led to a similar imprisonment and subordination in the hierarchy of work. Irrespective of their ethnic origins, they were taken on and became trapped in monotonous jobs on the assembly-line. They were

clearly aware of the health hazards involved in their work and wanted to
'get away from the assembly-line for the sake of their bodies'. The pay was
valued in the context of the severe wear their bodies were exposed to: 'The
pay does not correspond to the work input and the hard physical wear of
one's body.' Others felt that the women had already paid too high a price:

> The only profit we have made are our damaged backs, which now iron-
> ically are the more or less real reason why people cannot get ahead or
> train for better jobs. The women see no point in struggling on – they
> have paid too high a price already. You can't buy health with money.
> Why should you squeeze the last drop from yourself? (Yugoslav
> woman, age 50, at Volvo 23 years)

Perhaps the sub-heading of this section may be regarded as extreme.
But the statistics that show the proportion of immigrant women suffering
long-term illnesses and on disability pensions, taken together with the
empirical workplace studies of their work situations, provide clear evidence of their vulnerability both in the labour market in general and within
the work organisation of individual companies.

PERSONNEL TRAINING AND PROMOTION

It is no coincidence that the women – mainly Yugoslavian, Greek and
Turkish, but also Finnish – who came to Sweden in the early years of
immigration as labour, are over-represented among those suffering from
long-term illness or being forced into early retirement. They came here
when young, rarely over the age of 30, and have worked in Sweden for a
long time. What does not emerge from the cross-section statistical data on
allocation by occupation is that the majority of these women were
assigned to – and stayed in – the same low-status and physically hazardous
jobs; jobs that rarely allow any development of skills or new qualifications. Very few of them were given the chance of attending in-house
training courses and advancement to better jobs. In an interview study
(Knocke 1986) with 111 women from Finland, Yugoslavia, Greece and
Chile, none of the 66 women working in factories had been offered company training courses, even though most of them had been employed at the
same workplace for ten years or more. Thanks to their trade union, 2 out
of 45 women working in hospitals had attended training courses during
paid working hours. Some women suffering from work-related injuries as
cleaners had been given lighter work.

As early as the 1975 survey of immigrants' living conditions (Statistics Sweden 1977) a clear hierarchy can be seen in terms of the development of skills and occupational training, both between the sexes and by nationality. Approximately 60 per cent of male Swedish citizens, including second-generation and naturalised immigrants, reported that they had the opportunity to do learning on the job, and just over 30 per cent had attended training courses at the workplace. Of female Swedish citizens, 45 per cent said they could learn something in their work, while about 23 per cent had attended some form of training course at the workplace.

Barely 45 per cent of male foreign citizens could acquire new knowledge at work, and 22 per cent had attended courses. Only about 28 per cent of female foreign citizens could learn something in their work, and only about 18 per cent had been given some form of training at the workplace. There are no current national statistics on personnel training or in-house training for immigrant women. However, Statistics Sweden (1991) has published figures on employees attending staff training in the spring of 1987 for the entire labour force by groups of citizens. While 26.1 per cent of the Swedish labour force had attended either short or longer courses, the proportion for naturalised immigrants was 17.5 per cent and 16.5 per cent for foreign citizens. At 21.3 per cent, the 'other Nordic citizens' and American citizens had the highest proportion of participation in training courses. Most neglected and with the lowest attendance were citizens from the African or Asian countries. Less than 10 per cent of these people had been given any kind of personnel training. The time factor may be a partial explanation, since people from these countries had probably been in Sweden for a relatively short time and had not had time to learn Swedish well enough. However, this can hardly be seen as a full explanation. The Volvo survey's questionnaire gives an up-to-date and detailed picture of Yugoslavian and Finnish women's participation in company in-house training and the degree of skill their work requires (Schierup and Paulson 1994). A general tendency was that a larger number of younger employees had completed courses than had older employees, and far more men than women. At 70 per cent the proportion of employees who had attended internal training courses was highest amongst Swedish men in the 19–30 age bracket, followed by young Finnish men at about 60 per cent. Only about 28 per cent of young Yugoslavian men had attended any form of internal training (except for Swedish language training courses). About 58 per cent of young Swedish women had attended internal training courses, about 40 per cent of young Finnish women and barely 20 per cent of young Yugoslavian women. Despite their long periods of service, the older Yugoslavian women had the lowest percentage at 15 per cent, or two of the 14 women in the survey. The gender pattern was broken by the older Finnish women, about 30 per cent of whom had attended internal training courses against 20 per cent of older Finnish men. When school education, length of employment and age are controlled for, the probability of having a 'skilled job' was 25 per cent higher for people who had completed a course of in-house training than for people who had not. The correlations were, however, not entirely consistent. The frequency of internal training was twice as high for young Finnish women than for young Yugoslavian women. Despite this, about 95 per cent of young Finnish women, against about 88 per cent of young Yugoslavian women, were in unskilled or semi-skilled repetitive jobs. Only one in ten young Finnish women had a 'skilled' job, against three in ten of both Yugoslavian and Swedish women. One explanation would appear to be that a lower percentage of Finnish women had upper secondary education than both Yugoslavian and Swedish women. Irrespective of age and education, it was more common for women than men to have unskilled, repetitive jobs. A comparison of men's and women's situations broken down by citizenship reveals that the greatest similarity between the position of men and women was in the Yugoslavian group, while the contrast between Finnish men and Finnish women was striking, above all in the younger generation (Schierup and Paulson 1994).

These results agree with the analysis of interviews in my study (Knocke 1994), where different sets of stereotypes between men and women, on the one hand, and between men from different nationalities, on the other, led to differences in the reception given to them by work supervisors and in their opportunities for training and promotion. Negative experiences associated with some individual Yugoslavian men led to a collective labelling and stigmatisation of all Yugoslavian men. Positive stereotypes of Finnish men as good and reliable workers gave them advantages in both internal training and career opportunities. Irrespective of their ethnic background, the women were disadvantaged in terms of internal training and career opportunities. A Finnish woman employed at Volvo for 20 years gives the following description of the systematic labelling of work tasks by gender.

As I see it women may have lighter work tasks, but they are the most monotonous jobs and they cause the greatest amount of physical harm. I think it is wrong that women always get the most monotonous jobs, that they are said to be women's jobs and that women are the weaker sex. Men doing the same jobs would get the same injuries. It is much easier for men to change jobs in the factory.

In the following quotation, two Yugoslavian women express their dissatisfaction about missed training opportunities.[5]

The big problem for us foreigners is that our work supervisors give Swedes priority over us when it comes to further education. That is where the big discrimination lies. We are prevented from moving forward. It is sad that Volvo shows no interest in giving me the opportunity to get more training. Sometimes I think immigrants have one chance and one chance only - to qualify for a disability pension at the age of 37.

An analysis of the advantages and disadvantages of hierarchical work organisations compared to non-hierarchical organisational forms would be relevant in this context, but is not contained within the framework of this chapter. However, this much should be said: that the traditional, mostly male, supervisors emerged as the personification of power on the shop floor. They were identified as the 'gatekeepers', who prevented advancement and erected barriers to immigrant women's educational ambitions and their chances of promotion. Other investigations have also confirmed the central role of work supervisors, both in terms of the psycho-social working environment and the chances of immigrant employees advancing to better jobs (Zander and Höglund 1992).

CONCLUDING REMARKS

When examining some of the factors that have contributed to creating the stereotypes surrounding immigrant women, a closer look reveals that the negative images splinter up into a far more nuanced picture. The image of the home-bound, 'isolated immigrant woman' is confuted, as I have shown, by their high rate of participation in the labour force. On the same grounds, the assumption that their 'culture' – the components of which are rarely defined – and a traditional female role were serious obstacles to their entry into the labour market, fails to stand up. What is true is that the younger women in some nationality groups have had their entry into paid work postponed due having children at a young age, and that the women in some nationality groups also had more children than Swedish women. With the exception of women from Turkey, the fertility pattern has gradually come more into line with the fertility pattern of Swedish women. Having a large family should therefore only in exceptional cases be an obstacle to gainful employment.

Among the stereotypes, there have primarily been two factors that have played a decisive role in affecting immigrant women's chances in the labour market. The first is their educational background, or the idea of the 'poorly educated immigrant woman'. The second factor is knowledge of the Swedish language which, often without any empirical basis, has been generalised into the assumption of the 'linguistically deficient immigrant woman' (cf. Phizacklea 1983: 3).

Against these negative assumptions stands, for example, a 1977 survey of non-Nordic immigrants from the age of 18 upwards that showed that people with upper secondary education, or higher, were over-represented, both among women and men, compared to the population in Sweden as a whole (SOU 1981: 86). Admittedly, just over a quarter of the women had less than nine years of education. But this means, on the other hand, that three-quarters of them had at least the equivalent of a normal nine-year compulsory education and many of them had more years of education than that. Similar results are reported from other investigations, including the Volvo study (Schierup and Paulson 1994) and my study of 111 women (Knocke 1986). Thus, in summary, it may be said that there have been, and still are, immigrant women who are poorly educated or even with no education at all. But the occurrence of poorly educated women is far from as 'extensive' as the generalising perception would have us believe. Neither, therefore, should it be taken to justify their entrapment at the bottom of the labour market and their exclusion from companies' in-house training programmes.

The language issue is a complex one, and it appears to be difficult to arrive at uniform measurements of verbal and written language skills. Needless to say, newly arrived immigrants do not understand Swedish and some, mainly the older ones, never really manage to learn the language well. It is also known that differences in language learning ability is a function of educational background and the linguistic similarity to Swedish of the individual's mother-tongue, making the acquisition of the Swedish language easier for certain groups and individuals than for others. Equally important, and often more decisive, is, however, the fact that many people find themselves doing jobs that constitute particularly unfavourable environments for learning and developing language skills. Piecework in a noisy factory and cleaning work carried out in isolation with no social contact effectively prevents language acquisition (Leiniö 1980; Knocke 1986). Demotivation in a job that affords no prospect of career develop-ment is very likely to cause a lack of ambition to learn more Swedish. Another issue that has never been seriously considered or examined sys-tematically is the kind of demands on language skills a given job actually involves. Immigrants and refugees themselves attach great importance to better Swedish language training. In my investigation of 111 women in industrial and hospital work, better structured Swedish language courses were given top priority on their list of wishes (Knocke 1986). The Swedish National Audit Bureau's survey of highly educated immigrants also noted that changes in Swedish language training was put at the top of the list. More specifically, the requests were for a grouping of students by level of education, and targeted training for different occupational groups (The Swedish National Audit Bureau 1992: 11). Refugees who arrived in Sweden in the 1980s have been very badly affected by unemployment, irrespective of the economic cycle and despite the fact that a relatively large number of them are well educated, often with university degrees. This indicates, according to Ekberg (DS 1990: 35), that there was little demand for their labour and their skills and as a concomitant to this weak demand, supply (that is, people offering their skills on the labour market) may have been negatively affected. The Swedish National Audit Bureau's (RRV) five-year follow-up study with a sample of highly educated refugees (year of immigration, 1985 and 1986) shows that the preparatory period, including Swedish language courses, generally took two to three years before the people in the investigation were 'ready' to begin applying for qualified jobs or starting vocational or supplementary training (1992: 11: 78). With the exception of medical doctors who, after supplementary training, found jobs equivalent to their qualifications relatively easily, the proportion of others who after five years had found work equivalent to their earlier skills and qualifications was 10 per cent, comprising 7 per cent women and 14 per cent men. This figure includes the people who had obtained jobs as home language (that is, mother-tongue) teachers.

The worth of foreign education compared to corresponding Swedish education is a matter that has been discussed over many years. So far, the responsibility for establishing equivalence standards for these qualifications has been divided across many government agencies. The National Audit Bureau recommends that a central body be set up for assessing completed or uncompleted foreign education or vocational qualifications (The Swedish National Audit Bureau 1992: 9). This could help newly arrived refugees to have their qualifications recognised more quickly, or take the requisite courses to supplement their foreign education. When facing the changing labour market and assessing future chances for immigrant women, there are two possible scenarios. The trend we see today is that the kind of manual jobs that were available for immigrant women will become fewer in number. Lower activity rates and rising unemployment for the women who came to Sweden as labour indicate that they are in the process of losing their position in the labour market. Women who have arrived more recently as refugees have difficulties in gaining entry at all into the labour market, despite the high proportion of highly educated women among them. If these trends continue, they form a basis for negative future prospects. A more positive scenario would be that concrete measures are taken to create opportunities for immigrant women and that the negative images are being replaced by more balanced descriptions based on factual knowledge about the resources and potential of immigrant women. As it is today, they are, for example, despite high membership figures, heavily under-represented in influential trade union positions.[6]

A government commission appointed in 1993 to evaluate immigration and integration policies, works without having any representation of the immigrant population, neither woman nor man, among its members or its group of experts. Swedish women's organisations of any kind, be they political, feminist or research-related, almost totally ignore the presence of women immigrants and their different realities (Knocke 1991). A move towards equal chances in society and at work would require that immigrant women are empowered, that is, are given seats and voices in decision-making bodies, where they can represent themselves, their realities and interests.

NOTES

1. Until 1977 seven years' residence were required before naturalization was possible (Statistics Sweden, 1993).
2. In 1992 the population of immigrant origin was composed of 67 per cent or 835,000 persons born in a foreign country (first generation) and of 33 per cent or 406,000 persons born in Sweden (second generation) with at least one parent born abroad. This amounts to 1,241,000 individuals of immigrant origin or around 12 per cent of the total population.
3. In 1991 Turkish women were expected to have 3.4 children over their lifetime, Greek women 1.8 children and Swedish women 2.1 children. This is a big change from 1976, when the expected lifetime fertility was 6.2 children for a Turkish woman, 3.1 children for a Greek woman and 1.7 children for a Swedish woman.
4. The economic recession has so far been hitting the industrial sector, and thus male jobs, harder than the female job sectors. Not only Finnish men, but all men, both foreign nationals and Swedes, had higher unemployment figures in 1991 than women: 7.4 per cent for foreign men, 5.8 per cent for

foreign women; 3.0 per cent for Swedish men, 2.3 per cent for Swedish women.

The National Labour Market Board foresees increasing unemployment for women over the coming years due to cut-backs, savings and privatization of public sector jobs, which are mainly female.

5. The research leader for the Volvo study was Carl-Ulrik Schierup, University of Umeå. The interviews with women from Yugoslavia were conducted by Aleksandra Ålund, University of Umeå.

6. The Female Equality Officer of the Trade Union Confederation (LO) gave the following answer about addressing the specific interests of women immigrants: 'We look at each other [in the equality committee] and say that we should do something. But we never seem to find time.'

8 Young People of Foreign Origin Born in Switzerland: Between Invisibility and Diversity

Francesca Poglia Mileti

SWITZERLAND AND ITS FOREIGNERS

Introduction

More than a decade later than some other European countries, Switzerland is facing an economic crisis with resultant unemployment. In this economic context, it is worth raising the issue of both the status and condition of young foreigners who are born and living in the geographical centre of Europe where a wind of nationalist withdrawal is blowing.

Italians, Spaniards and Portuguese (in smaller numbers) came to Switzerland more than 20 years ago, retaining their nationality. Although they were employed at the lower levels of the job hierarchy, these immigrants have experienced a good integration into the labour market. Their children have apparently succeeded in becoming culturally integrated. Indeed, as members of their community since their early socialisation and primary education, when and where a collective knowledge could develop, they have taken part actively in social and cultural life. But hit by unemployment, an increasing number of them are now excluded from the labour market. Although their motivation and ideals are quite similar to those of Swiss people belonging to the same age groups, for example, internalisation of the imperative for individual success and mass consumption, they are no longer benefiting from available social resources.

Behaviour, attitudes and social representations might be influenced by a variable such as unemployment, given a context of varied and changing social relationships between foreigners and natives, based on an ambiguous and reciprocal imagery. Thus, the social position of young people from long-standing immigrant communities, who recently succeeded in gaining some social recognition, at least officially, could be challenged. Not only could their new experience of unemployment modify their self-perception but also the understanding of their status and role in the immigrant community as well as the appreciation of their life prospects. This chapter begins with a short assessment of the political and economic environment of ethnic relations. It presents a brief overview of the Swiss political situation based on results of recent referendum (*votations populaires*) in the course of which some issues related to foreigners and to the entrance of Switzerland into the European Economic Area (EEA) were discussed and voted upon. After a short presentation of data relating to the foreign population and unemployment in Switzerland, the chapter focuses on the young foreign jobless – Italian, Spanish and Portuguese – aged from 20 to 30 years old, who are living in the canton of Neuchâtel.[1] This chapter aims at showing the impact of job loss, looking at several aspects related to both labour and immigration spheres, such as possible 'return' to the country of origin, links with the immigrant community, the representation of immigrants, and so on.

The Swiss Political Context: No Opening

For more than ten years negative votes against foreigners have followed one another, on topics as different as the abolition of seasonal worker status, the right for established foreigners to vote in local elections, naturalisation procedures, and so on. We shall focus our attention on the four recent popular votings that dealt with these issues.

On 6 December 1992, a referendum resulted in a 'no' vote for Switzerland's entrance into the European Economic Area. Let us here emphasise that the main concern of the vote was the adherence to the Economic Area and not to the European Union. (Extreme) right-wing parties were at the forefront of the 'no' campaign. Christoph Blocher, representative of the radical side of the UDC, a so-called populist politician, was among the 'no' propagandists. He took this opportunity to give renewed approval to the ideas of the (former) British Conservative MP, Enoch Powell, Powell having been considered as the 'racists' leader' since 1960 (Solomos 1993). Although more balanced in his opinions, Blocher has raised the spectre of a foreign invasion, stressing the danger of racial inter-breeding and of the loss of national identity should Switzerland join Europe.

Paradoxically, the outcome of that popular vote dramatically disturbed the 'national identity' by worsening the already existing gap between French-speaking and German-speaking cantons. These traditionally have diverse views on various subjects, the French-speaking cantons being more favourable to an open policy. The results of the vote, energetically criticised by a section of Swiss youth, have once again increased the so-called 'rösti barrier' (taken from the name of a Swiss-German dish) that separates cantons favourable to Switzerland's entrance into the EEA from cantons with majorities in favour of the opposing view – the 'Nein-sager'[2] – who are against joining Europe, irrespective of how it is undertaken.

The closing of the geographical and then symbolic borders has been reinforced by the results of a referendum held on 12 June 1994. On that day, the Swiss population decided not to revise the national constitution and, consequently, not to make it easier for young foreigners born in Switzerland to undergo naturalisation procedures. Let us not forget that in Switzerland, citizenship, and consequently the right to vote, is reserved for Swiss nationals, except in two cantons: Jura and Neuchâtel. (In the latter, established foreigners have been able to vote at the local level since 1849.) This attitude towards 'foreigners' can be explained by the will to maintain a specific population in a differentiated status, because that population is achieving successful assimilation and is thus becoming less and less visible. The fear of being unable to recognise 'foreigners', an ability which strengthens the possibilities of unequal treatment between immigrants and natives, implies a refusal to grant them membership to 'the fictive society' (Rath 1993), a society whose members decide, at any moment, who can belong and under what conditions.

Nevertheless, another referendum held on 25 September 1994 showed a slight sign of opening up. Reluctantly, Swiss people agreed to modify article 26 of the Constitution in order to introduce sanctions against racial discrimination into the penal law. In doing so, William Tell's land chose to join the 137 states that ratified the International Convention passed by the UN in 1965. Despite a positive vote gained by a majority of 54.7 per cent, some 939, 738 Swiss citizens opposed the 'anti-racist law'. On one hand, the 'no' propagandists argued that adhering to the UN would muzzle Switzerland and, on the other hand, that such legislation would jeopardise freedom of expression.

But again, on 4 December 1994, Swiss citizens expressed their fear of the foreign population by voting in a new federal law that provides restrictive measures regarding foreigners' rights – as previously approved by referendum. This new law, which had the initial aim of dealing with foreigners involved in drug trafficking, resulted, in its final version, in highly discriminatory provisions against foreigners, especially asylum-seekers and undocumented people. The law states, for instance, that in specific circumstances a foreigner can be held in custody as long as no decision about his/her right to stay has been taken.

As illustrated by the results of the referendums mentioned above, immigration still lies at the heart of major social, economic and political challenges, even in a country where immigration issues have seemingly been less conflictual than elsewhere.

Foreigners in Switzerland: Some Facts and Figures

Several waves of foreign workers have flowed into Switzerland since the beginning of the twentieth century. In the period following the Second World War, in the context of rapid economic expansion, employers confronted by a national labour shortage turned to foreign sources of labour. Between 1960 and 1970, the foreign population doubled in Switzerland, the major part of it coming from Italy. The immigration flow reached its peak in 1964 with a foreign workforce accounting for up to 27 per cent of the economically active population. The number of non-nationals decreased steeply over the following ten years as a result of the restrictive measures taken by the Federal Council, an economic crisis and a heightened level of xenophobia. Because of the very strict control of the foreign population by Swiss authorities, Switzerland succeeded in exporting a great part of its unemployment problems. The crisis hit primarily its foreign workers. Between 1974 and 1976, 330,000 jobs were lost but only 25,000 of those were registered as unemployed. The remainder can be explained by forced or semi-voluntary departures (according to the point of view adopted), of 245,000 foreigners (Flückiger 1992). Between 1980 and 1990, a new immigration wave from Portugal reversed the previous trend. In the recent years, a great number of people coming from former Yugoslavia have entered Switzerland.

What is the situation now? At the end of December 1993, 1,277,106 foreigners were registered, representing 18 per cent of the total resident population (Office Fédéral des Etrangers, *Les étrangers en Suisse*, 1 et 3 1993). This figure includes permanent resident population excluding annual and seasonal workers, asylum-seekers and international officers. If the figure seems to be high in comparison with other European countries, it should be remembered that Switzerland does not automatically provide Swiss nationality to foreigners' children and grand-children, even if they are born in Switzerland. The red cross passport can only be obtained after lengthy administrative procedures, following an individual request for naturalisation. These procedures are described by anthropologist Pierre Centlivres as a real assault course (Centlivres and Centlivres-Demont 1991). For instance, it should be mentioned that in 1993 foreigners who acquired Swiss nationality represented less than 1 per cent of the total foreign established population.

Italians are the most represented group in Switzerland (29 per cent). Nationals from former Yugoslavia account for 20 per cent of the foreign population. The Portuguese represent 10 per cent of established foreigners and Spanish immigrants about 8 per cent. In 1993, 117,636 foreigners, both economically active and non-active, came to Switzerland. Compared to the previous year and taking account of changes in work and residence permits (A, B or C) and births,[3] it shows an increase of about 4 per cent. Among new incomers, 35 per cent are former Yugoslav, 12 per cent are Portuguese, 7 per cent are Italians and 3 per cent are Spaniards. A total of 71,164 foreigners left Switzerland during the same period.

As far as Neuchâtel canton is concerned, the average of the foreign permanently residing population is higher than in the rest of the country. It accounts for 22 per cent of the population, 35,805 people, with more than half of them economically active. Among foreigners established in Neuchâtel, the number of Italian and Spanish immigrants are proportionally similar to national averages. Conversely, the proportion of Portuguese (27 per cent) is more than twice the national average. Yugoslavs are underrepresented in Neuchâtel as they account for only 4 per cent. All these figures exclude asylum-seekers who are relatively numerous in the region.

THE ECONOMIC SITUATION IN SWITZERLAND

A Renewed Rise in Unemployment[4]

In Switzerland, talks about the economic crisis only started in 1992. According to a process that is apparently already in operation, the new economic and social deal could challenge the attainments of the immigrant population established in Switzerland. In 1990, the active population counted up to 75,576 job-seekers, that is to say an unemployment rate of 2.08 per cent. Since then, the situation has considerably worsened.

In August 1994, the unemployment rate had risen to 4.6 per cent with 164,187 jobless, more than twice the figure registered four years earlier. If these figures are far behind European averages, unemployment, nevertheless, generates strong feelings of economic crisis and insecurity among the indigenous resident population. It is worth underlining that unemployment insurance is limited to a specific period of time corresponding to a maximum of 400 daily allowances (that is, nearly two years duration). If job-seekers do not succeed in getting a job, or if the cantonal employment offices are unable to offer them one, they find themselves without any financial resources. The fear of not getting a permanent position is thus emphasised by a social insurance system unable to provide long-term security.

As noted by several authors (e.g. Ledrut 1966; Cornioley 1994), unemployment does not affect individuals equally. It proceeds selectively according to regions, age groups, activity sectors, gender, nationality, and so on. In August 1994, because of having the highest unemployment rates, the western and southern cantons of the country, the French and Italian-speaking ones, were among the most disadvantaged. With an employment rate of 6.5 per cent, Neuchâtel, where the watchmaking and machine industries are experiencing a marked decline, is ranked as the fourth most disadvantaged Swiss canton. Besides, and paradoxically, the cantons characterised by a very high unemployment rate and a higher proportion of foreigners were also those that were more in favour of an open policy for Switzerland.

As far as age is concerned, it should be noted that the 20–24 year group has experienced the highest unemployment rate (5.9 per cent), followed by the age group 25–29 (5.5 per cent). Compared to 1990, both age groups registered an increase of 65 per cent of joblessness (34,797 to 53,149). Also, a high majority of foreigners born in Switzerland, the so-called 'second-generation immigrants', are to be found in those age groups. The distribution according to gender shows that the unemployment rate for women was higher than the national average at 5.1 per cent, compared to 4.1 per cent for men. The proportion of unemployed women and men was, respectively, 55.8 per cent and 44.2 per cent.

Foreigners, as a category, encounter strong discrimination in the labour market. Although, quantitatively speaking, they were less numerous among the jobless than Swiss nationals, their unemployment rate was more than double: 8.5 per cent for foreigners as against 3.5 per cent for Swiss nationals. Foreigners were over-represented among the unemployed (39.4 per cent) whereas they represented only 22 per cent of the active population. Most of them were, indeed, working in relatively unskilled jobs in sectors severely hit by the economic crisis. Moreover, their vocational experience was less transferable on the labour market.

Sectors[5] that had the highest concentrations of unemployment were clerical and administrative jobs, the metallurgy and machine industry, the hotel trade, the domestic economy and the building industry (Office Fédéral des Etrangers, *Les étrangers en Suisse*, 1 1993). In fact, in Switzerland, foreign workers were mainly occupied in the building industry (12.5 per cent), in services (12 per cent), in the machines industry (11.5 per cent), in the hotel trade (10.25 per cent) and in personal care services (7.5 per cent).

Their distribution, by nationality, within the various economic sectors has been determined by various factors, such as the different opportunities on offer from the labour market during different waves of national immigration, and vocational traditions, as well as social reproduction processes inside the immigrant population. At the Swiss level, and regarding the communities that we are interested in, we see that Italians were distributed mainly in the following sectors: 15 per cent in building and civil engineering industries, 14 per cent in trade, 14 per cent in the machines industry and 9 per cent in metallurgy. Portuguese immigrants especially were engaged in services: the hotel trade (23.5 per cent), the building industry (21 per cent), trade (8 per cent), health and personal care (7 per cent). The distribution of Spanish immigrants in the various economic sectors was very similar to that of most foreigners working in Switzerland. They were more active than Italians in the tertiary sector but less active than the Portuguese. Seventeen per cent were working in the building industry and 10 per cent in the machines industry. Unlike Portuguese immigrants, who were concentrated in the hotel trade, Spanish workers were divided into trade (9.5 per cent), the hotel trade (9 per cent) and personal care (9 per cent).

Because of their insertion into sectors and activities that were strongly affected by job loss because of the economic crisis, foreigners were more severely hit by unemployment than Swiss people. Important individual inequalities could be foreseen, especially for young foreigners, as a result of interconnected factors such as social origin (most of them belonged to the working class), residence in a declining industrial region, and membership of an age group that was over-represented in jobless categories, as well as of a nationality encountering discrimination in the labour market.

The unemployment rate of young foreigners aged 20–29 years old was high (8.54 per cent) and nearly twice that of young Swiss people (4.7 per cent). If the figures reveal that foreigners do encounter social inequalities and discrimination, it does not allow us simply to assert that exclusion from the labour market is caused by nationality. First, it should be noted that inside that age group the proportion of young foreigners was higher than that of young Swiss. Secondly, a fair evaluation of the variable 'foreigner' would require a multivariate analysis. Such an analysis, which is not possible to present here, would require the introduction of variables such as social origin, occupation and vocational training in order to make a meaningful comparison between the unemployment rates of Swiss and foreign people with a similar social status. Obstacles encountered by young foreigners on the labour market should, in fact, be considered within the broader context of difficulties faced by young people from the lower classes. Foreign nationality is obviously worsening the already difficult position of those who are more likely to become unemployed because of their low qualifications and social status.

It should also be noted that the gap between the unemployment rates of young Swiss people and young foreigners was lower than that of older people (more than 40 years old) where rates had gone up to 3 per cent for Swiss people and to 7.5 per cent for foreigners. Within the younger generation, the slight difference between natives and foreigners was due to a degradation of Swiss youth's access to the labour market, rather than to an improvement in foreigners' circumstances. Indeed, finding a job and keeping a permanent position is, nowadays, the major problem faced by young people. Despite a decrease in differences between Swiss people and young foreigners born in Switzerland, inequalities still exist.

THE 'SECOND-GENERATION IMMIGRANTS'

We all know that foreigners and immigrants are objects of discourse filled with cultural, ideological, symbolic and emotional connotations. This discourse reveals existing social challenges directly linked to patterns of individual interactions. They also illustrate how relationships to foreigners have been historically built in a national context. All these challenges can be defined in terms of power protest, integration, social recognition and identity. Similarly, the names given to immigrants' children also reveal significant social challenges.

As a matter of fact, the label 'second-generation immigrants' was brought into the Swiss political debate in 1980 through reports published by the Federal Commission for foreigners' problems. In 1988, about 250,000 individuals were registered as 'second-generation immigrants' in Switzerland (Bardet-Blocher et al. 1988).[6] Due to the lack of accurate data available – the Commission does not make any calculation – we will present data in relation to the population belonging to the 20–29 year old age group only. Of course, not all individual members of those categories are 'second-generation immigrants'. There are, in addition, numerous immigrant children who are under 20 years of age.

In 1990, there were 24 per cent of non-Swiss nationals aged from 20 to 29 years old within the population in Switzerland (Recensement fédéral de la population 1990, 3, *Emploi et vie active*, Berne, OFS 1993).[7] Within those groups, the proportion of foreigners was higher than in all other age categories. Furthermore, the proportion of young people aged 20–29 years old was higher within the foreign population (22 per cent) than within the Swiss population (15 per cent). Italians, Spaniards and Portuguese represented nearly one-half of all young foreigners of that age. It should also be noted that within those age groups, in comparison with respective national populations, the Portuguese – mainly as first-generation immigrants – were more numerous than the Italians and Spaniards.

Most of the 'second-generation immigrants' were occupied as skilled workers. Compared to first-generation immigrants whose occupations were limited to unskilled jobs, some social advancement can be registered. However, the social status resulting from better vocational training does not represent a real improvement of the position of immigrants since this qualitative shift is characteristic of the whole economic structure (Bolzman, Fibbi and Garcia 1987: 63). This move is, nevertheless, positively valued by foreigners who do perceive it, in the context of inter-generational comparison, as a sign of real social advancement.

Today, because economic recession and unemployment have severely hit immigrants' children, the issue is put differently. The generational move is no longer considered vertically, in terms of upward social mobility, but horizontally, in terms of inclusion/exclusion from the labour market. Because the immigrants' daughters and sons are better adapted to their host country's lifestyle and because they are better educated, they are no longer willing, as were their parents, to accept any kind of job or treatment. Social reproduction is thus no longer achievable inside the immigrant population, not only because of a lack of employment, but also because young people are no longer mobile and precarious immigrants (Dubet 1989). Unlike immigrants in search of work, characteristically represented by Spanish or Italian seasonal workers, and usually considered as poorly or not integrated, the young foreigners we interviewed presented a low cultural visibility. Their lifestyles, aspirations and ideals were similar to those of their Swiss counterparts, the relationships and contact they have with them being anything but occasional.

For our purpose, we could schematically analyse immigrants' insertion[8] in connection to both socio-economic and socio-cultural fields. The first generations are characterised by opportunities for insertion in the labour market – even if the real situation is getting worse for this category also – but with a lower level of 'cultural integration'. For their children, if the economic recession continues, the trend could be just the opposite. Because of their exclusion from the labour market, the following generations could be 'culturally integrated' without any access to economic resources. Despite the cultural invisibility of young immigrants born in Switzerland, equal opportunities between immigrants and natives do not exist, since diversity, and correspondingly, disparity, have been slipping from cultural to economic spheres (Lapeyronnie 1993: 105).[9]

The sociology of immigration is called into question by this statement, especially in the way it analyses the so-called 'second-generation immigrants'. If that population is, indeed, very similar to Swiss youth, it is differentiated on the basis of cultural and national idiosyncrasies. In the actual political context, it should never be forgotten that nationality is a dominant criterion of categorisation which, in some cases, can lead to discrimination. On the other hand, even if they are very close to the unemployed first-generation immigrants, their children can be distinguished by some identity references and values more oriented towards Switzerland than the country of origin, without asserting any break with the latter. The specificity of the so-called 'second generation' is thus very interesting, even if they are not considered as a homogeneous social category. This is the reason why we consider that the study of this population makes an important contribution to the understanding of modern societies. The main difficulty is, without any doubt, to be able to determine, as rigorously as possible, the sociological criteria used to build on the category.

Although they do not constitute operating concepts, combined notions such as 'visibility/invisibility' and 'diversity/similarity' could help towards achieving a better understanding of the ambiguous status of young foreigners born in Switzerland. In most cases, issues regarding their political status, their cultural memberships or their life trajectories can be enlightened by these notions or, more fairly, by taking all these issues into account. The situations and life experiences of these young people can be described as a dialectic between 'sameness' and 'difference', 'visible' and 'invisible'. It is clear that both orientations or schemes applied to read the immigration problems should be organised in a flexible way and with a variable intensity. It will depend on the population, on socio-political contexts and fields of observation as well as on evaluation criteria, bases of comparison, levels of analysis and adopted viewpoints. Some individuals might, for instance, present a weak social visibility because they achieved 'assimilation' at an individual level or, conversely, because their community of origin succeeded in developing alternative economic networks which are unknown or not recognised by the indigenous population. This is the case, for instance, with women members of some immigrant communities.

In tackling the problem that way we can see that 'immigrant reality' is a many-sided game. The 'intensity concepts' mentioned above not only contribute to an enrichment of our analysis but also represent immigrants' true life experiences. Individuals are able to exploit, with variable efficiency, the ambiguity or ambivalence of 'similarity' and 'diversity', of 'visibility' and 'invisibility' while they are setting up, more or less consciously, collective or individual strategies. These strategies are inserted into a continuum that stretches from a sphere linked to the country of origin (emigration, culture of origin, and so on) to another in relation to the host country (immigration, insertion at local levels, and so on).

For individuals born in Switzerland, socialisation takes place in a dynamic and, at least, two-fold multicultural context. The cultural heritage (values, specific practices, knowledge of the migration family project, and so on) transmitted among members of the nuclear family and, by extension, of the whole immigrant community, is not dissolved but reinterpreted according to a singular history and an everyday life spent in Neuchâtel, Switzerland. Concepts of assimilation and integration are unable to account for the development and patterns of life of older immigrant populations and even less for the life experiences of young people from immigrant communities who are born in Switzerland. That is the reason why their integration should be considered as a many-sided process including diversified and multiple ways of insertion, taking place at various levels, in different spheres and fields, according to variable degrees of involvement. Broadly speaking, it has been noted already that minorities' integration operates according to a differentiation process. The more a population achieves insertion, the more various individual orientations are stressed and become recognisable (Lapeyronnie 1993: 114–15). To summarise, we can agree with Didier Lapeyronnie when he considers that, as time progresses, most populations sharing common origins become diversified, but it does not mean a complete detachment from the country of origin.

To describe the actual condition of young people from immigrant communities in Switzerland (Italians, Spaniards and, to a lesser extent, Portuguese), it is therefore difficult to register a linear process of integration into a well identified entity. On the one hand, at a socio-cultural level, the so-called host society is not characterised by a homogeneous regional structure. On the other hand, young immigrants born in Switzerland are increasingly achieving integration according to diversified individual strategies, through plural identification with various groups, by membership of non-ethnic sporting and cultural organisations and by personal involvement into areas not linked to the culture of origin, and so on. More and more often, the 'second-generation' immigrants, as they are called, develop singular ways of adaptation, individual behaviour and ambitions to fit in the socio-economic requirements of the receiving society (De Certeau 1985). Finally, the way young immigrants do assess their identity is complex. It is a flexible and dynamic network of references, a continuous movement of comings and goings.

ITALIAN, SPANISH AND PORTUGUESE JOBLESS AGED 20–30 IN THE NEUCHÂTEL CANTON

The issues developed in the following section of this chapter are derived from a qualitative study undertaken in Neuchâtel canton with unemployed Italian, Spanish, Portuguese and Swiss young people aged 20–30 years.

We collected our observations during in-depth interviews and proceeded to analyse the 15 most significant interviews. Our sample was composed of four Italians, three Spanish-Italians, one Spanish, four Portuguese and three Swiss respondents. Most of them had received poor vocational training, or no training at all. All unskilled people were women (five among eight). Among the three remaining women, two of them had two years training as beauticians and one undertook an apprenticeship as a sales assistant. All men were skilled workers. The less skilled ones went through apprenticeships (builder, plumber and clerk), two were technicians (Federal Certificate of Capacity, Technical School), one qualified at a Higher Commercial School and the most qualified was an engineer from the Higher Technical School.

Spheres of Insertion

Having seen the complexity and multiplicity of young people's social realities, we decided to interpret the interviews from a perspective based on the various spheres of insertion that they had selected. The concept of sphere has been chosen because it has a broader sense than that of social group or social background. In our study, we gave priority to two specific spheres of insertion, one linked to labour and the other linked to immigration, even though we knew that young people's social participation was not restricted solely to them. The 'sphere' is used not only to cover the topics selected for our analysis, since, for young immigrants, it also represents real fields of insertion with specific social networks, practices, attitudes and behaviour. The notion also encompasses the identification processes involved in them, as well as an imagery translated into explicit discourses along with more or less conscious representations and values. Being a member of several spheres of insertion involves attaching to them more or less importance, according to particular points along their life experience (Dubar 1991). Finally, the concept of sphere also refers to the labelling processes and all the names which result from them. Most probably, the host society describes the population studied using terms like 'foreigner', 'second-generation immigrant', 'worker' and 'unemployed'. Let us state precisely that the categories and expectations attached to these terms are not fixed once for all, and that they can vary according to the type of social groups or individuals who use them.

The Importance of Work to Young Jobless Immigrants

At a time of unemployment, when a person is no longer able to contribute to society by his/her work, the integration role of work becomes lost.

An important identity reference is being eroded as well as the networks of relationships, social recognition, and so on. How important is work to people who are seeking jobs? How do they view unemployment? What do they feel about being unemployed and what strategies do they develop to overcome their situation?

According to authors like Christian Lalive-d'Epinay and Carlos Garcia there is, nowadays, a tendency for greater involvement in the leisure sphere. In their view, work is now viewed more in relation to other aspects of everyday activities and is no longer the sole yardstick of identification, since a new hedonist individualism has developed with self-fulfilment as a central value (Lalive d'Epinay and Garcia 1988). Apart from this cultural shift, changes in how work is represented have also occurred because of the new realities of today's labour market. Structural unemployment has induced young people to see work as having less of a central role in their life experience and their transition to an adult lifestyle (Eckmann-Saillant, Bolzman and De Rham 1994). Thus, not having permanent work has become a normal way of life. Grell considers that a new ethos based on resourcefulness and stability in the social space of 'outside work' has developed in response to the impossibility of identifying with a steady occupation (Grell 1985). This shift in work representation as put forward by the above-mentioned authors can be summarised thus: previously viewed as a guarantee of self-development and as a contribution to society, work is now considered through an instrumental perspective, by individuals who give priority to the 'outside work' sphere for achieving self-development (Lalive D'Epinay and Garcia 1988).

The reality of young unemployed Italians, Spaniards and Portuguese people was far removed from this explanation. For them, work was still a central value. A permanent job was at the top of their hierarchy of values followed by family and self-development activities. '*No family without a job.*' For young jobless people, 'normality' was a permanent position and still considered as the most important link between individuals and the community. It even seemed that, because of its scarcity, work was becoming increasingly valued. Thus, the classical sociological view that suggests we should consider representations according to social class, is still valid. Young people with a low occupational status valued the instrumental dimension of work as well as the role it played to help pass the time, whereas better trained young people were more likely to consider work as a way of gaining social recognition, forming social relationships and to stress the satisfaction of paid work. Individuals (all women in our study) whose lifestyles and activities were considered to be more marginalised, such as involvement in artistic groups or Latin American cultural communities, had a more balanced vision. Without challenging the central value of work, they tried to position it inside a broader life context seeing it to be of major importance to self-development.

If work is a norm it does not automatically mean that unemployment is considered as a sign of marginalization. On the contrary, it seems that unemployment has become an ordinary feature of life. For Gabrielle Balazs, the triviality or normality of unemployment generates a new definition of inactivity among certain social categories, in particular, young people. Official pronouncements induce us to believe that increasing unemployment is an inevitable, thus normal, condition. The unequal situations and forms of unemployment experienced by people out of work, are then hidden (Balazs 1985). If job loss has similar consequences for all people concerned, mainly the rupturing of links with the world of work and its social norms and related social networks, none of the jobless interviewed expressed a feeling of collective membership to the jobless category. Paradoxically, if unemployment is considered today as a fast-expanding 'social phenomenon', it is in fact experienced at a very individual level, in the intimacy of day-to-day living.

Individual strategies developed by the jobless, to help them face up to unemployment and to maintain a consistent self-identity, have been classified into three main categories. The first group represents people who, although they refuted the negative social representation of being jobless, did not challenge it by offering an alternative or more positive image. They tended to develop rather passive attitudes and strategies. The Portuguese, some Spanish and Italian young people belonged to that group. Some of them were not well qualified, others were well qualified but were very disturbed by an identity loss that was the result of being unemployed.

The second category was made up of people who, after having distinguished between the 'goods' and 'bads' among people out of work, came to the conclusion that they were the 'good' ones. All of them were men and in particular Swiss men. They received higher training than the other groups' members and developed dynamic attitudes mainly centred on job seeking.

The last category was made up of unskilled women. They stressed the positive aspects of unemployment such as enjoying free time to think about oneself or undertaking new activities, and so on. During the interviews they wanted to value the outside work sphere in stressing the wealth and plurality of experiences offered by cultural activities.

Links with the Immigration Sphere

What is the impact of job loss on the links and relationships established inside the immigrant sphere? Do young people reconsider their position as immigrants' children when experiencing unemployment? Does vocational inactivity lead them to get involved in the 'immigration sphere'? Do young foreigners born in Switzerland develop claims and protest strategies similar to what the young '*beurs*' are doing in France?

Generally speaking, the young people interviewed did not express any explicit causal link between unemployment and immigration. Job loss did not call into question their stay in Switzerland. This view illustrates a broader vision of immigration: work (or no work) that caused the first generations to emigrate does not represent, in their children's eyes, a pertinent reason for being resident in the immigration country. Even more important aspects than that solely of working were taken into consideration, such as the length of stay of their community of origin, being born in Switzerland, feelings of integration or of attachment to the host country as well as even the simple will to stay. Work is in fact only one side of life in Switzerland. In saying so, young people revealed their desire not to have to justify their presence any more.

Of course, every individual was affected by unemployment in his/her daily life but this did not challenge his/her self-perception as an immigrants' child. Young people did not consider themselves as targets for social inequality; neither did they view their unemployment as a consequence of racial discrimination. The content analysis of interviews revealed the existence of a hierarchical social representation of various immigrants' categories according to nationality, date of arrival and progress towards integration. Italians, Spaniards and Portuguese did believe that, in Switzerland, racism and discrimination were targeted against new immigrants coming from Turkey and former Yugoslavia, or against asylum-seekers, and so on. However, Italians and Spaniards sometimes considered that the Portuguese were encountering racial intolerance. This representation is factually confirmed since only the Portuguese declared they had recently been subject to racial attack at work.

In general, unemployment was perceived as a personal situation and not as a result of being an immigrant. Second-generation immigrants were hardly conscious of the fact that they were members of a group severely hit by unemployment. The main reason for this is not only because the unemployment statistics were unknown, but also because of their lack of collective and thus political involvement. Their individual behaviour did not allow them to generate a collective consciousness and to view problems within a global and long-term perspective. On the other hand, they did think that their extraneous status was not the best way to define their membership of a particular group. This is the reason why they asserted both the existence of cultural specificities and the refusal to be categorised as immigrants. They wanted to be a part of youth in general.

Finally, the absence of an established link between unemployment and immigration could also be viewed as the outcome of a special insertion process, that enabled the young people socialised in Switzerland to acquire values such as industrial peace, consensus, compromise and neutrality. This way of thinking, somewhat stereotyped for the purpose of our description, reflects a Swiss propensity to mist over social inequalities and social issues.

If being jobless does not directly throw into question their presence in Switzerland, then what about practices and real relationships developed inside the immigrant community?

Few changes caused by unemployment could be noted from the interviews. It seemed that there was no increased distance from, or solidarity towards, the immigrant communities and networks. Apart from tangible support by the closest members of the young people's families, we could not find evidence of a real involvement in the community of origin. Surprisingly, immigrant associations were not required to help the jobless. They were not asked, for instance, to support them in administrative procedures or to provide them with information on job opportunities in businesses run by employers of the same nationality. This illustrates the fact that first-generation immigrants and their children have experienced diversified trajectories. Young people from immigrant communities, involved in various fields, did not consider unemployment as a fate befallen on specific categories of people, but rather as a personal misfortune. Consequently, they expected more from the unemployment offices than from the immigrant community. From that point of view, it can be said that unemployment is, paradoxically, establishing a fundamental link with Swiss society since it is perceived by second-generation immigrants as a national and relatively new phenomenon, hitting Swiss people and foreigners alike.

In contrast to most foreigners living in other European countries, and because of geographical proximity, foreigners living in Switzerland could conceivably return to their countries of origin. However, return was not viewed as a solution to unemployment for most young people, but only as a possible measure of last resort. In any case, for many of those who have never lived in their family's country of origin, this would not mean a return but a real new-life experience. Return was conceivable for some of the Portuguese who came to Switzerland less than ten years ago. Single people and people who married a Swiss national did not wish to go back to a country or a region where services and leisure activities were said to be less developed than in Switzerland. Portuguese couples who had migrated to build a house in their homeland seemed ready, in the mid-term, to return to Portugal in the event they perceived a negative balance (costs against benefits) in terms of their immigration experience. In this last case, the following analysis is obviously less pertinent.

Second-generation immigrants do have strong identity feelings and multiple national memberships even if the impact of their unemployment on the 'immigration sphere' is weak and their visibility is low. All of them said they were proud to be Portuguese, Spanish or Italian. Apart from a few individuals, everyone was reluctant to be seen as Swiss, despite strong links established with the host country. The combination of dual identity feelings hinges on the temporary balancing of one aspect of life in Switzerland against another, according to the life trajectory. In managing different memberships – in relation to nationality, age, occupation, friendships, and so on – individuals are able to develop what might be called 'identity strategies'. Through notions like 'visible' and 'invisible', 'sameness' and 'difference' we can illustrate how concepts like 'immigrants' and 'second-generation immigrants' are used and managed for the development of identity strategies. Both concepts are indeed far from neutral. They induce strong emotional and political meanings connected to very specific social challenges. It is then worth considering how they are viewed by individuals whose relationships to immigration issues represent a fundamental basis for self-definition.

Concepts of 'Immigrants' and 'Second-generation Immigrants'

A cultural reference well short of the dichotomy 'national versus non-national' is slowly being recognised by Swiss public opinion, in relation to those immigrant populations established in Switzerland for quite a long time. Moreover, claims of plural belongings and multiple identity references developed by young people from immigrant communities, in particular Italian, Spanish and, to a lesser extent, Portuguese, are more or less well accepted. Paradoxically, the long-term contact between immigrant and native communities, the supposed existence of a mutual knowledge of practices and representations – even if frequently stereotyped – and a decreasing visibility as foreigners, have led the way to a greater recognition of foreigners' specificities. Finally, because they are born and educated in the country, second-generation immigrants are granted a minimum of acceptance to so-called Swiss culture. Nevertheless, in the host society, the social representation of foreigners founded basically on economic utility still remains. That image, summarised by the phrase 'immigrant equals worker' (Sayad 1991), confines each individual to a single work role and prevents him/her from maintaining any other claim or aspiration.

Given the polysemy of words such as 'immigrants' and 'second-generation immigrants' and given the existence of contrasting socially, politically and emotionally marked representations, the young people interviewed had great difficulty in defining and describing the concepts (Poglia 1993; forthcoming). The terms were indeed defining foreigners as members of objective categories, while also referring to numerous representations of immigration. During the interviews, 'immigrant' was given a myriad of meanings when it appeared to be a social challenge linked to identity definition. Different meanings could be given by the same person according to the thematic context of the discourse, the situation, or the imaginary projection built upon it. All contradictions reflected ambivalent and ambiguous feelings about belonging to a group socially viewed, more often than not, in a negative way.

Although they expressed their solidarity towards their parents or towards foreigners in general, the young people interviewed refused to be called 'immigrants' or 'second-generation immigrants'. The stronger reactions came from Italians and Spaniards who were also those who felt deeply involved in the host society. Conversely, members of families in favour of possible return to Portugal did not consider that their social recognition could be demeaned or threatened by these words. It is worth noting that some individuals developed specific strategies to escape these categories. For instance, in order to heighten perceived differences between individuals inside the immigrant category, they tended to modify their pattern of classification and, through this classifying process, to value better their own position. This is the reason why they did not systematically deconstruct the commonly assumed representations of immigrants. While refuting them for the purpose of self-definition they sometimes agreed on them to describe other populations. The immigrant category was further divided into sub-groups, to which were attached various characteristics, such as unfavourable social status, difficult integration or a marginalised way of life. The respondent then tried to show how his/her own reality was different. Integration was the main criterion used to distinguish the respondent's category from that of 'other immigrants'. Following on from that distinction, non-integrated people were said to limit their social interactions to compatriots and immigrants' groups, misuse their language of origin and be unaware of the French language, and so on. All distinctions applied as much inside, as between, the national categories. The Portuguese were, for instance, frequently mentioned as not being well integrated.

We think that this way of arguing reflects the common images of immigrants in accordance with the Swiss socio-cultural context, where foreigners are tolerated since they are not so very different. It is also in conformity with Swiss integration policies which value individual insertion and discourage any attempt of achievement through immigrant communities. It should be noted that there is no ethnic concentration in Swiss cities similar to that found in France or Great Britain. In Neuchâtel, for instance, the distribution of foreigners according to nationality was the same at both local and cantonal levels.

The phrase 'second-generation immigrants' generated exactly the same kind of reaction. Although conscious that it was used to label young people, all people interviewed agreed that the concept and its use reflected an inappropriate categorisation. To justify their refusal, they mentioned the inadequacy of applying a notion, that implies spatial mobility, to a life trajectory which never implied or involved migration. Birth in Switzerland certified by official documents was an irrefutable proof of major symbolic importance, since it allowed one to justify one's belonging, integration and thus conformity to the local social background. The rejection of membership of a specific category should not be interpreted as a denial of foreign origins. On the contrary, nationality and richness of the other culture were, in certain circumstances, very strongly rated and valued. If they were positively judged, divergences or differences were highlighted, but they were equally quickly dismissed as criteria for any kind of discrimination.

Both examples reveal how people try to manage diversity in culture as well as within a complex system of attributed and felt identities. The most successful strategies for those wishing to escape, as much as possible, any type of social categorisation, are to operate on several levels of thought and to claim multiple links with various, and not necessarily national, social groups.

CONCLUSION

The cultural invisibility allied to the so-called integration of second-generation immigrants from long standing immigrant communities in Switzerland should not lead us to believe that equal opportunities exist in the labour market. Without ascribing any causal relationships between nationality and unemployment, statistics reveal an over-representation of young immigrants among the registered unemployed. However, the results of a qualitative study undertaken with Italians, Spaniards and the Portuguese aged 20–30 and living in Neuchâtel canton, Switzerland, clearly showed that no causal link was perceived between their unemployment and their foreign origin. In the young foreigners' eyes unemployment was, rather, due to a phenomenon that has grown and become a normal feature of life. Job loss was, thus, not challenging their stay in Switzerland since their birth in Switzerland and their integration into the canton were clearly viewed as more important reasons. As for the impact of unemployment on the immigration sphere, our study revealed that economic inactivity did not modify the relationships with the immigrant community, and that return to the country of origin was not considered as a solution to unemployment. The young people's identification was not fixed once and for all, but was a multifaceted, ongoing process. The young foreigners refused to be categorised as immigrants while they were claiming close links to the country of origin. They also expressed their emotional attachment to the host country even if they were opposed to some major Swiss political orientations. Access to an identity reference oriented towards the country of origin reinforced their feelings of being European, gained through national identity, and enabled them to escape the Swiss political closure.

During our study we did not register any collective protests to establish identity, or any claims referring to the immigrant community, culture or religion. We noted a tendency towards 'collective invisibility' even in a difficult unemployment context. Specific cultural features were valued at an individual level. The development of identity strategies to escape unemployment also operated individually rather than through collective membership. The dialectics of combined notions such as 'visibility/invisibility' and 'diversity/similarity' generated some interesting insights into the situation of 'second-generation immigrants' at levels as diverse as social participation, integration into the labour market, the competition for access to scarce resources and decision-making positions, and social recognition as well as cultural and religious options. The current context does not suggest the emergence of claims for rights or collective movements. However, if the situation gets worse, it should be worth considering the consequences for foreigners born in Switzerland of the gap between a weak socio-economic insertion, caused by exclusion from the production process, and a cultural orientation based on a close relationship with the host society.

NOTES

1.   Results of a qualitative study undertaken in Neuchâtel within the context of the research programme, 'COST A2 – Migration and labour force', financed by the Federal Office for Education and Science.

2. The name given to people who voted against EEA membership and were more numerous in Swiss-German cantons.
3. A Permit: seasonal; B Permit: annual; C Permit: permanent residence. Length of stay in Switzerland is determinant upon obtaining a C Permit. Furthermore, the required period of time depends, itself, on the national origin of the applicant.
4. Figures related to unemployment were collected by the Federal Office for Industrial Arts and Crafts and Labour (OFIAMT) and published in September 1994 in a report entitled *Situation sur le marché du travail en août 1994*.
5. Figures are rounded off to the nearest unit.
6. They 'are considered as second-generation migrants children born of foreign parents in Switzerland as well as children born in Switzerland within the context of family reunion as far as they accomplished the major part of their schooling in our country.'
7. Figures are rounded off to the nearest unit.
8. We do not enter the discussion concerning the use of words such as 'assimilation', 'integration' or 'insertion'. Nevertheless, it should be noticed that we do not consider migrants' integration or that of their children as a linear or step-by-step process oriented towards a predefinite goal.
9. Didier Lapeyronnie considers, indeed, that the position of numerous 'second-generation' members is characterised by a high level of integration but a weak level of participation.

II
New Flows

9 Seasonal Work in Italy: Flexibility and Regularisation
Giovanna Campani and Francesco Carchedi

INTRODUCTION

Immigration into Italy for the purpose of work is a quite new phenomenon in the general landscape of migrations which have interested, and still interest, European countries. In Italy, the transition from emigration country to immigration country took place in 1975, when, for the first time since the unification of the country (1870), the migratory balance showed 200,000 arrivals more than departures. Approximately 20 years on, this foreign presence has multiplied by a factor of five[1] such was the impact of the new arrivals – first on an illegal basis, but attaining legal status during a second period. The importance of the foreign presence became evident after the promulgation of the regularisation laws (No. 943 in 1986 and No. 39 in 1990), and the family reunification, family reasons and study permits. Laws 943 and 39 have given a legal status to foreigners in general and to immigrant workers in particular. They have also 'legitimised' this presence in Italy, introducing the 'universal' principle of equality of rights as well as rights on an economic and civil footing, independent of national origin. Italy may therefore be considered, from all points of view, a country of immigration with inward flows from the developing countries and from Eastern Europe, representing around 180 nationalities, distributed across the national territory.

Starting from these schematic considerations, whose aim was to present the general framework of immigration in Italy, this chapter will focus upon:

1. certain dynamics of the labour market with some interpretation, including comment on the role and function of immigration into Italy and in the labour market itself;
2. that segment of the labour market concerned with the demand and the offer of seasonal work, characterised by flexibility and, often, by uncertain conditions and the impact it makes on some local and regional areas.

155

IMMIGRANTS' PRESENCE IN THE LABOUR MARKET

Since immigration into Italy began in the 1970s, the role and function of the immigration presence has, in the internal labour market dynamics (at macro-level) and in regional and local labour market dynamics (at micro-level), been an important topic of debate, first inside the trade unions and second in the academic field. At the beginning of the 1980s, the census (1979) offered a first general interpretation based, essentially, on the fact that immigration, for its own internal characteristics, is a structural phenomenon, which restores equilibrium to a national labour market otherwise characterised by a lack of balance and contradictions. In practical terms, an inadequate demand response to internal job offers, particularly in terms of professional skill-holders, has led to security and guarantees of work, social security, and so on, as well as job satisfaction, becoming both the principal originating cause of foreign immigration and its justification.

The apparent contradiction, existing between the active presence of immigrants and high unemployment, is explained through the specific characteristics of unemployment itself: the unemployed are mainly young people who do not want to adapt themselves for labour activities requiring no qualifications and offering little in the way of personal fulfilment. Indeed, they wait for better employment opportunities. This condition of 'waiting' unemployment and/or under-employment which can provoke high levels of social suffering – varies in duration for important sectors of the labour supply. In the meantime, the unemployed young people benefit from:

- family revenue (income);
- indirect income (services, economic assistance, and so on);
- different forms of subsistence, related to unconventional, even marginal, life-styles.

In practical terms, the period of 'waiting' plays a function of reducing the supply, particularly in the case of younger people, who tend to be a stable and immobile group. This happens even with an important demand for labour, when the type of work offered fails to conform with the expectations of potential workers from various unemployed categories. Mingione (1983: 21; 1985) considers that the arrival of immigrants is also the consequence of some structural changes, that have taken place in industrialised societies, which connect and mesh with those effects arising from technological progress and by the processes of tertiarisation of the economy. These effects produce dual forms which tend to split on different poles, often in antinomic opposition: high/low productive development, in connection with the use (or not) of technology, inclusion/exclusion from the guaranteed areas of employment, continuity/discontinuity of the services, regularity/irregularity of the contractual positions in relation to the different employment forms, security/insecurity in terms of working and living conditions.

These mechanisms produce within the manufacturing sectors a bloc of job offers requiring no qualifications, having little professional content, demanding a highly flexible approach and with long working hours and constantly renegotiated, irregular wages (Chiapparugi 1983: 415). These characteristics in some local contexts, especially in southern Italy, concern job offers made to nationals as well as immigrants (Calvanese 1983). The latter group would take the jobs not taken by the local labour force but they would often be exposed to objective competition.

The difference among Italians and immigrants experiencing competition is mainly that Italians have access to a localised social network that is much more structured than the sources of information available to immigrants (for the traditional settlement, knowledge of contractual dynamics, and so on), which, somewhere, 'amortise' or at least slow down/oppose the processes leading to less secure work conditions. The condition of non-protection (lack of institutional guarantees, norms, and so on) makes immigrants more open to the risk of insecurity, which is more and more marked in comparison to that of the indigenous population, employed (or waiting for employment) in the formal sectors and/or in parts of the secondary, mainly informal or 'invisible', labour market (Carchedi and Ranuzzi 1987).

The issue of the employment of immigrants in an informal economy, according to Enrico Pugliese (Pugliese 1985: 70; 1990: 71), is not simply the fact that they take jobs refused by national workers, but that they accept work conditions that the Italians try to avoid, because these work conditions are below accepted levels of guarantees, security, income and social protection considered socially appropriate in the present phase of Italy's economic and civil development. Consequently, the maintenance of levels of 'backwardness' in particular demand sectors, as structural effects inherent to technological progress and tertiarisation, according to Mingione's theory, keeps, with different times and moods, the national workers away from these 'niches', creating 'spaces' for the immigrant component of the labour force. Immigrant workers enjoy these available work opportunities (even with a high spirit of adaptability), in a regime of non-competition, as long as the indirect revenues are not reduced and economic support to the unemployed Italians is not withdrawn.

In these cases (often as an effect of manufacturing recessions of a limited or generalised character), the indigenous workers, who initially refused to enter the labour market, tend to come back to the marginal market, even accepting conditions similar to the ones being experienced by the immigrants, provoking situations of competition. Such situations can often lead to so-called 'ethnic conflicts', as was the case in the summer of 1993 in the Pouilles, where immigrants arriving in search of work during the harvest, were violently expelled. In fact, the state of competition is often seen by the Italians as an ideological matter, without having a real understanding of the concrete conflictual dynamics for the occupations of certain jobs.

In practical terms, some components of the indigenous worker supply play the role of a 'coiled spring', extending or retracting themselves according to the level of demand coming from the 'strong' (and also less strong) sectors of the national economy and also in response to the level of the proposed short- or long-term guarantees. But if, for the native population, the passage from employment to unemployment results in a minimum of guarantees in terms of the family and society resources (indirect wages), for the immigrant, this passage means emphatically going from existence to mere subsistence. The 'citizenship effect' and the benefits which citizenship confers on the native population, plays a key role in the discrimination against immigrants working in the same labour market sectors. Consequently, among natives and immigrants there exists in many ways, a difference in 'vulnerability', both in the conditions of employment and unemployment (or under-employment) (Freyssinet 1984: 44–5, in Thala 1989: 212).

PERIPHERAL POSITION AND TYPOLOGIES OF SEASONAL WORK

According to Pugliese (Pugliese and Macioti 1990: 43), the presence of immigrants in the national and local labour markets cannot be understood and interpreted without considering the segmentation which characterises the labour markets and the structural characteristics which these segmentations assume in relationship to each other. The central labour market as constituted by the big factories of the public and of the private sectors, both supported by solid systems of guarantee and of trade union and social security protection (even though they have been going through more than ten years of crisis), corresponds to peripheral reproductive markets. We can, then, think of these peripheral markets as concentric circles – the one following the other – in relationship to its proximity to the model of social security and of the guarantees of the 'central market', up to the extreme peripheral markets, characterised by the most precarious and discontinuous forms of subordinated or autonomous work. Finally, the peripheral productive markets are characterised by the dynamics associated with small enterprises, where forms of non-institutional employment are common and where generally, the guarantees are less important, and subject to renegotiation at any given time directly between those concerned.

The manufacturing markets represent, in contrast, all forms of employment, developing auto-consumption and domestic survival, that is, the reproduction of the labour force with its different components, who are often unemployed or under-employed. They work in areas with uncertain jobs, often half-illegal, for example, petty street trading, daily labour in agriculture, unskilled labour in construction and in portering services.

Seasonal work, as far as it is carried out by immigrant workers at specific limited times of the year, is situated in the peripheral market, both productive and reproductive. It represents specific and peculiar aspects of the peripheral labour market, occupying – transversally – different compartments of one or the other productive and reproductive, without having any legitimation and, up to now, no legal acknowledgement. Seasonal work, from the point of view of the 'system of guarantees', can be considered to be in the extremely peripheral circles, being characterised generally by:

- low wages;
- high exploitation levels with respect to employed immigrants;
- high flexibility for those specific workers having high geographical mobility;
- low social gratification;
- limited professional qualifications.

The presence of these factors and a lack of legislation covering temporary labour migration brings about very uncertain conditions for immigrants employed in this sector. The level of insecurity varies according to the incidence of the different factors operating in each specific area of seasonal work.

FLEXIBILITY AND PRECARIOUSNESS

According to Thala (1989: 207–8), secondary labour markets tend to produce as part of their internal characteristics forms of growing flexibility and precariousness, as a structural system of defence and compensation. This allows:

1. rapid adaptation to the temporary needs of demand and of the productive-technological structure;
2. being able to face the uncertainty of the economic situation when it is unstable and unpredictable, making long-term planning difficult, for example, in seasonal work;
3. being able to reduce and vary the costs of work and investments, in order to meet needs created by economic and technological change.

Flexibility can, in particular, be defined as the productive system's capacity to react (at both the macro and micro level) by creating or eliminating occupational opportunities according to levels of demand during phases of change and variation (positive or negative) deriving from economic links within socially determined contexts.

In essence, flexibility mirrors the requirements (both quantitative and qualitative) of the demand inasmuch as it is based on the adaptability principles of the labour force and its productivity demands. Therefore, flexibility can assume a quantitative dimension – according to Michon (Michon 1987: 37–8, in Thala 1989: 219–20) – when it responds to the expansion of productive activities and to the necessity of product diversification in relation to the rise and fall of the demand's critical mass. Conversely, it assumes a qualitative dimension when responding to the demand's needs in relation to major or minor requests for specific products, the production of which can develop through a differentiated placement of the available labour force.

In other words, quantitative flexibility responds to the fluctuations of the demand, thereby creating a direct link between the enterprise (or the enterprise system) and the external labour market, in terms of the incoming and outgoing labour force flows. Qualitative flexibility, however, must respond to the necessity for diversification of production and does not determine the link with the external supply. Basically – according to Michon (Michon 1987: 37–8, in Thala 1989: 219–20) – qualitative flexibility is characterised by the transfer of the labour force already employed within the enterprise (or systems of enterprise) from one productive sector to another, determining (or not determining) modifications in the modalities of employment.

Generally, Thala (1989) associates quantitative flexibility with the external mobility of workers and consequently to the expanding labour precariousness in the context of the secondary market. Qualitative flexibility, conversely, is associated with the internal mobility of the employed, and therefore to the stability of employment within the primary labour market. As a result, immigrants can find work within a limited selection of jobs, characterised by quantitative flexibility, that is to say, correlating directly with the oscillations of the demand. This determines, in turn, the coefficient of precariousness, deriving from the structural conditions around which work revolves (contractual modalities, job hours, work schedules, salaries, protective measures, and so on). Thus, along with relative forms of precariousness – characterised, albeit minimally, by the presence of protective measures and recognition of different forms of employment – one will also find absolute forms of precariousness, as, little by little, the conditions at the foundations of job modality are reduced to subsistence levels. In this way, we can relate permanent forms of precariousness to forms of social exclusion.

The pendular movement (commuting) between employment, underemployment and unemployment – relative to the duration of work or nonwork – places the largest number of immigrant workers, in varying degrees, within the flexibility–precariousness link, where one becomes the consequence of the other (and vice versa), especially during periods of seasonal labour. Such a process should not be interpreted deterministically, in that the position the immigrants hold within this pendular movement can remain stable for long periods or undergo modification in positive directions; it is not always a given fact that the beginning of the pauperisation process swings from relative to absolute precariousness.

THE PRINCIPAL TYPOLOGIES

Seasonal work – according to Mottura (1992: 88) – can assume two specific forms based on the immigrant's relationship to work (in relation to time and the modalities of job practices) and their respective employers. On the one hand, those who find work in the same firm all year round can therefore be considered 'stable' (in which case we can, with due caution, talk of qualitative flexibility). These immigrants do seasonal jobs, although continuous, changing job tasks in a cycle based on the manufacturing needs of the firm.

On the other hand, there are those who not only change job functions or work activities, but who also go from one firm to the next, in that they move around according to the production cycle that characterises seasonal labour, in relation to the specific demands of particular employers. These immigrants carry out seasonal jobs all year round, regularly changing job tasks according to the productive necessities of the firm.

(a) Concerning mobility:

- commuting is characterised by town–country movement, that is, those migrant workers moving back and forth daily, or for short periods from residential urban areas to agricultural ones, and vice versa.
- commuting, characterised by town–country displacement, either daily or for brief periods, where the place of residence and the place of work are seen in a rural agricultural context and where mobility follows the cycle of local labour demand (or inter-regional).
- commuting characterised by town–country displacements on a daily or brief period basis, in which case the rural agricultural areas become the place of residence and the urban areas become the place of work. One finds in such a typology immigrants alternating between agricultural and urban jobs, in periods where the former is in weaker demand (especially during the intermediate seasons) and therefore unable to satisfactorily supply labour.

The first kind of typology seems to attract the immigrants the most, in that the nature and the modalities of seasonal work practices require an enormous amount of displacement between town and country during periods with greater labour force demands. The other typologies, although significant in their own right by the nature of the problems they raise, seem to carry less weight.

(b) Concerning geographical areas that characterise displacements:

- in communal-provincial areas, defined as being within the local territory of legal residency and domicile.
- in inter-provincial/regional areas, defined as being within a greater area where displacement takes longer, making daily commuting impossible. In this case, it becomes a true displacement – with a temporary abandonment of the domicile – in relation to the labour demand.
- in inter-regional areas defined as being within a larger area that follows the agricultural cycle on a national scale, in relation to local agricultural market demands. In such cases, displacement occurs according to the local labour force demands during different periods of the year and within different agricultural sectors. Displacement therefore takes much longer, including radical changes of residence that can last from two to three months.
- in areas outside the nation, defined as areas that include either different European countries, one European country, or the country of origin. Migratory workers with such seasonal characteristics are to be found in Italy (as well as Spain, Portugal and former East Germany) and are

interested mainly in the agricultural areas near the borders. In this case, we are dealing with 'frontier' labour (of brief and medium duration) in the sense that it includes an area immediately next to the country of origin and only a part of the others.

Taken together, these typologies – through which all seasonal work is classified – produce different needs and expectations on the part of the immigrants, who require differentiated modalities of involvement and engagement (even existentially speaking) in order to receive adequate professional satisfaction.

These expectations range from a need to find acceptable temporary lodgings to that of a ruling that regulates and equalises their conditions as compared to those of the indigenous workers. These conditions are minimal and would allow the employed immigrants in the sector not to be subjugated to the almost total discretionary power of the employers. In fact, such discretionary power often produces, on the one hand, forms of social and economic discrimination between the immigrants and the native population (competing simultaneously for the same jobs), and on the other hand, uncertainty and disorientation in terms of stabilising work schedules and stipendiary modalities and conditions.

QUANTITATIVE DATA AND NORMATIVE PROPOSALS

According to the data gathered from the residence permits registered in the Ministry of the Interior as at 31 December 1993 (Caritas di Roma 1995: 93), the number of legal foreign residents in Italy amounts to 987,405 units, which represents 1.7 per cent of the entire Italian population. Of this group, about 85 per cent, representing 834,451 units, is comprised of citizens coming from Third World countries, whereas the remaining 15 per cent (152,954 units), are European citizens. Amongst the non-EU citizens, about 60 per cent, as deduced from information taken from the residence permits, reside in Italy in order to work (a total of 467,420 units): 94 per cent represent the condition of subordinate worker (equal to 467,224 units), with the remaining 6 per cent in a position to work autonomously. Those employed amount to 63 per cent of the total (312,979 units), whereas the unemployed represent 27 per cent (equal to 134,358 units, all to be found, unsurprisingly, in the context of subordinate jobs). The remaining 11 per cent are either attached to other positions, or are waiting for completion of documents giving proof of contractual certification.

It should be noted that the number of unemployed has grown considerably since the provincial Unemployment Offices have been receiving applications for residence permits. In any case, we are dealing with a majority within a component of immigrants in conditions of under-employment, or taking jobs on the black market (that is jobs without contracts). This last item is not always to be compared to situations of economic and social precariousness, especially in the centre–north regions.

It appears more and more appropriate, as further data in the field emerge, to speak of adequately remunerated informal employment (that is, not regulated by formal contracts). Conversely, this phenomenon does not exist in the southern regions, inasmuch as informal labour is very often synonymous with social and economic precariousness.

SEASONAL EMPLOYMENT DATA AND PROVENANCE OF NATIONALITY

Seasonal employment data, and in particular data relating to non-EU immigrants, was obtained from the Ministry of Labour and based on research done since 1991. Therefore, the most complete information we have dates from 1992, a year noted for having the highest recorded number of immigrants present in the sector (Caritas di Roma 1995: 225). The incidence of non-EU immigrants is 2.6 per cent in relation to the overall total, which amounts to 1,130,746 units. This incidence, according to the Caritas Diocesana, represents almost double the percentage reported in other data on labour issues. In other words, and still drawing from Caritas (Caritas di Roma 1995: 225), one finds a high demand for seasonal workers due to their greater flexibility and capacity to adapt. In practical terms, the admission of the immigrant component into this sector allows almost total coverage of national seasonal employee needs by employers, to the extent that during 1992 only a few hundred jobs remained unfilled.

It is clear that the agricultural sector absorbs the greatest number of non-EU immigrants, with about 14,000 units (equal to 1.95 per cent of this sector's total). However, an analysis in terms of percentages that relate to the total number of indigenous workers shows that the construction sector absorbs more skilled immigrant skilled labour (with 6.34 per cent out of a total of almost 24,000 units). Second to this, is the incidence in the hotel/tourism sector of 4.15 per cent (an overall total of about 234,500 units). If one adds catering to this sector (catering being closely linked to tourism), the percentage of immigrants employed in this sector is considerably higher (6.87 per cent). The percentage of seasonal workers aggregated to 'other sectors' amounts to a total of about 116,000 units, of which only 3,000 are non-EU immigrants. This number, generally, includes domestic help, personnel involved in the care and supervision of children and caring for the elderly, as well as sailors and those holding positions of trust (such as doormen, factory guards, chauffeurs, bodyguards, and so on).

It is important to reiterate and emphasise what has been said in the preceding paragraphs: that of the 28,700 units legally registered in 1992, almost one immigrant in six (representing 4,438 units), resided in his/her country of origin prior to having employment in Italy. In other words, about 15 per cent of the total of non-EU immigrants hired for seasonal labour were hired direct from their respective countries of origin (in line with an established ruling, that is, article 8 of law 943/86, relating to the so-called 'nominal summons' for labour where workers are sufficiently qualified to satisfy specific on-location job requirements). A significant distribution of the hired labour is classified by geographical areas of origin:

1. over half the number of hired seasonal labourers present in Italy are represented (14,811 units out of 24,552) by North Africans (in particular Moroccans and Tunisians);
2. about two-thirds of the total number of workers hired through the nominal summons route are represented by citizens coming from Eastern Europe (especially Poles and Albanians), and citizens from former Yugoslavia (Bosnians in particular) (3,563 units out of 4,438).

Such subdivisions can be explained by the fact that the first type of immigrant labour, when entering Italy, needs to be checked by the authorities. This involved lengthy procedures, which employers found very inconvenient. For the second type, for varying reasons, there are no rigid obstacles to entering the country. These reasons are often humanitarian in essence and should not be underestimated when one considers the citizens of former Yugoslavia. Another example comes from Polish citizens, who have the right to enter Italy and other European countries without a visa.

ESTIMATES ON THE NEED FOR SEASONAL LABOUR

In 1993, for the first time in Italy, the Ministry of Labour required all regional offices and employment agencies to quantify the need for immigrant seasonal labour based on information taken from the preceding years and evaluations made by competent local authorities. The data that emerged from this study show the 1994 labour requirement estimates reported by each regional commission, to the central authorities. Unfortunately, the actual 1994 data are not available.

As one can deduce from these data, not all regional commissions responded to the information request. Within this group are the regions with the highest incidence of immigrant labour (Lazio, Emilia Romagna, Veneto, Campania and Sicily) and with productive areas where seasonal labour, both in tourism and agricultural sectors, is historically significant. However, the need for immigrant labour amounts to about 22,440 units, according to the estimates. If one adds to such a number, on average, 1,500 requests for each region that did not quantify its own need, one is faced with an additional 7,500 units, giving a total of about 30,000 units requested at a national level. It is a total that corresponds closely to that registered at the offices of the Ministry of Labour in 1992.

It is appropriate to point out that some regions, for example Campania, Sicily and Lazio, are noted for their high absorption of immigrant labour in the agricultural sector, especially during the summer harvest periods, for fruit-picking (Lazio, in the Agro Pontino area), tomato picking (Campania, in the Casertana zone), and flower growing under glass (Sicily, from Syracuse to Ragusa). These are areas where the seasonal immigrant presence oscillates, according to research carried out in the field (Calvanese and Pugliese 1991; Pugliese 1995; Carchedi and Ricci 1995; Carchedi 1994), with 7,000–10,000 units, only for harvesting. The type of labour characterised by the irregular component, that is, those immigrants without residence permits, generally predominates. These estimates in small measure (between 3,000 and 5,000 units) concern other Regions (Emilia Romagna, Veneto and Tuscany), pushing up the number of immigrants who find seasonal labour. If the official registrations show around 28,000 units (the number from 1992 concerning all Regions), the unofficial ones, derived from studies in the field, especially in the agricultural sector, amount to, according to our estimates, about 45,000 units (in relation to the Regions that did not indicate their estimated labour needs to the appropriate Commissions). Adding to such an estimate, those 22,500 units registered by the Labour Commissions, one comes up with an estimate of 67,500/70,000 units. Basically, about a tenth of the non-EU immigrants present in Italy in December 1993 were interested in, and found employment in, seasonal labour.

REGIONAL AREAS WITH SEASONAL CYCLES

Seasonal labour (work) configuration, in relation to regional areas, largely depends upon the presence of:

(a) the production of large-scale 'harvestable' crops (fruit and vegetable products, plants and flowers) and animal husbandry for food;

(b) structures for the transformation of harvested products (and other agricultural products), as well as structures to facilitate the transformation of animal farm products;

(c) tourist zones of outstanding natural beauty with efficient infrastructures designed for receiving tourists and supporting recreational activities. There are also economic advantages – in cost/benefit terms – in areas which holiday-makers can choose for themselves.

(d) fast-developing urban areas with a greater importance placed on the labour demands of the construction sector.

These factors, together with others linked directly to immigrants' needs, such as access to adequate accommodation and social services, encourage the immigrants to choose to make a protracted stay (8–12 months) in one area only. In fact, the ability to find employment, either in sectors such as agriculture or the transformation of products, or the catering or hotel industry, with differing time-spans and modalities that follow on, one from the other, requires residing in one geographic area for long periods, even if the job is seasonal in character.

Intermittent employment, characterised by brief periods of non-activity between jobs, is not necessarily as painful as it could be in the light of the immigrant's ability to adapt to different kinds of job situations within the framework of relative precariousness. Conditions are different, however, for those who have limited seasonal employment, and are obliged to find other job solutions elsewhere. Such conditions can be linked to forms of absolute precariousness. From this point of view, and keeping in mind what has been said in relation to geographic mobility, the Regions (or rather, their areas), able to guarantee intermittent seasonal employment, according to the Caritas (Caritas di Roma 1995: 227), are the following: Piemonte, Lombardia, Trentino, Emilia Romagna and Abruzzo. Those that absorb immigrant labour for short periods, (3–5 months) – particularly during the summer months – are: Liguria, Molise and Veneto (May and October), Friuli (June and September), and Puglia (July and September).

Finally, other Regions, such as Tuscany, Lazio, Campania, Calabria, and Sicily, can, based on the above-mentioned research, absorb immigrant labour in large quantities for periods of between 20 to 30/35 days. The reason for this lies in the fact that crops ready for harvesting and requiring immigrant labour, must be consumed (or transformed), in a short period of time, especially with reference to grapes (in Tuscany), water melons (the Pontina countryside), tomatoes (the Casertana area), and flowers or greenhouse products (in certain areas of Calabria and Sicily).

Some of these areas, in particular the Casertana and, to a lesser extent, the Pontina zones (both situated in the Campania and Lazio Regions, close to Naples/Caserta and Rome/Latina), have been the centre of strong polemical and racial tensions emanating from the local populations. In our opinion, the reasons that cause this, are threefold:

1. A large increase in the number of immigrants (an estimated 7,000–10,000 people in all of the areas), and a large concentration of immigrants in specific geographic areas (characterised by small agricultural communities), especially during the harvest. The presence of immigrants, according to those who oppose it, produces problems in terms of accommodation, socialisation and relationships. Last but not least, they speak of landowners cutting labour costs to below the minimum wage, which local workers refuse to accept. However, those who welcome immigrant labour find that it makes up for the gap caused by the historic desertion of the countryside on the part of local populations; the arrival of immigrant labour has reactivated declining crops of a production range which enriched the entire agricultural area. The housing problem should be taken care of by the landowners themselves and the local administrations, and all work contracts should respect the norms established at the national level.

2. Certain stipulations to be made in contracts are not possible, as it is also impossible to organise accommodation, first because immigrants, in large majority, are without residence permits and are therefore illegal according to the bureaucratic norms; second, because the public administration bureaux are powerless to intervene in helping illegal immigrant workers who would have to be sent back over the border in accordance with the deportation laws. Therefore, the only help that the various administrations can offer is purely humanitarian. In order to do this, as the various administrations have been pointing out for years, is to make economic and financial resources available to the smaller agricultural communities, like those already mentioned, who have not been able to avail themselves of such resources by means of the various central administrations. A vicious cycle is created by the fact that these, in turn, are not allowed to offer such resources by law.

3. To avoid such an impasse, and as suggested by voluntary associations and segments of syndicate organisations, one could legalise the situation by the promulgation of a retrospective regularisation process (law), legalising the status of those who have been employed since 1990 (data taken from the last regularisation). Accompanying this proposal are other norms whose goal it is to legalise all seasonal employment,

especially helping to fill the legislative void existing in the agricultural sector. In this way, one hopes to minimise any possible bureaucratic backlash against immigrant seasonal workers who have entered the country illegally in response to a high demand for seasonal labour – especially during summer time.

REGULATION PROPOSALS

In Italy, as things stand, the question of immigration is a marginal factor within the political-institutional debate, in spite of the fact that volunteer organisations and a few trade union sectors, to which some parliamentarians are attached, continually stimulate and apply pressure for removing obstacles and constraints in order to reinforce forms of socio-economic integration and assimilation. Nevertheless, in the last three to four years, Bills have been presented by the different national political parties with the, often contradictory, objective of reducing or extending the normative premises promulgated by the Martelli law (no. 39/90, still operating today).

Schematically, those presenting the Bills can be divided into two parts: on the one hand, those who would like to solve the migration problem in custodial terms (the right-wing: National Alliance, and Northern League and Group League Nord),[2] and on the other, those whose Bills attempt a more positive articulation of the rights and dues owed to foreigners, especially in terms of the immigrant category, aiming progressively at offering more concrete forms of citizenship (the Democratic left-wing and the centre-left Members of Parliament).[3] The first grouping make a principle of their slogan: 'fewer entrances and more expulsions', synthesising their ideas on the subject by emphasising and focusing on the contrast between those in legal and illegal positions, thereby forgetting that often the passage from one state to the other does not depend upon the worker but upon the perverse mechanisms of administrative bureaucracy. The second grouping, however, by understanding the complexity of the phenomenon, and because of its opposition to illegal entry, tries to reconcile labour market demand and the impact made on it by the immigrant presence. Furthermore, they offer immigrants the possibility of acceding not only to formative services, by recognising their former educational qualifications, but also to scholastic qualifications obtainable within a new pact of citizenship operating between the native Italians and long-stay immigrants.

Specifically concerning seasonal labour, the CnEl (National Committee for Labour and Economy, a government consulting agency), in 1993, after numerous meetings with volunteer organisations, trade union forces and experts in the sector, had formulated hypothetical rulings on the question (Caritas di Roma 1995: 228) based upon the following points:

(a) The offer of a three-month residence permit to those immigrants who enter Italy to do a temporary job, with the obligation to return to their home country by a specified date. Those interested in returning during the following year must reserve their jobs with their immediate employers. The jobs must be carried out according to the requirements attached to each job category, including all social security payments based on reciprocal and bilateral agreements between the appropriate institutions of both host and mother countries.

(b) The introduction of measures relating to immigrants already present on national territory, that will enable illegal seasonal workers to benefit from the seasonal residence permit, if an employer is disposed to legalising their status, without being submitted to administrative or legal sanctions. In essence, it is a proposal aiming to break the aforementioned vicious cycle that adversely affects the immigrant's job situation.

(c) The possibility to expand further the regularisation process to other immigrant workers able to demonstrate, not through self-certification, that they have worked for three consecutive months within the last year.

(d) Effective expulsion for those who have not made use of the proposed opportunities, and sanctions against employers who maintain dependants under irregular conditions, as well as opposing those agencies organising the illegal passage of immigrants throughout the country.

This proposal has raised some doubts, especially the part about extending the regularisation to both seasonal workers and illegal immigrants. This aspect of the proposal has blocked all discussion, forcing those who presented the Decree to modify – in a restrictive sense – the ground covered by the amendment. It was proposed that the regularisation process should be extended only to the immigrants' relatives, and to those who had entered as tourists or as students; with such a status it becomes impossible to obtain a job since there is nothing in law that provides for changing the reason from that expressed in the original request for a residence permit. Even in this case, the government reacted positively and so the Decree fell through.

Another attempt to regulate seasonal labour was made by the Ministry of Social Affairs, by taking some of the previous Decree's proposals into account, in a Bill presented in April 1994. It lost by a few votes within the Commission and therefore was not enacted. This Bill is considered to be, however, a good basis for further discussion and amendment if ever it should be presented again to Parliament. Here is a résumé of its contents:

(a) The provision of a six-month residence permit for those carrying out seasonal work, with equal contractual rights to those of the autochthonals, according to the principle of equal treatment (Art.1, Law 943/96).
(b) The determination of the number and the type of seasonal jobs to be decided in the annual programming of labour supply flows.
(c) The taking into consideration of those demands made by non-EU countries nearest to the Italian borders, as well as on the basis of bilateral agreements.
(d) An obligation on the part of the employer to report the number of immigrant seasonal workers s/he needs to employ, to the local provincial 'Office of Labour' (a bureaucratic formality concerning former employees), and offer them adequate housing.
(e) An obligation on the part of the worker, who has received authorisation, to possess all required certification papers and to leave Italy when the residence permit expires: permission to stay longer is granted only after working two consecutive years and where the employment was officially sanctioned.
(f) Precedence to be given to those who have previously worked in Italy, through a system of seasonal employment lists to be held by local consulates and other diplomatic organisations.

Generally speaking, the main aim of this Bill is to regulate the entry of labour flows concerning those aspiring to seasonal employment and to ensure that they respect the obligation to return to their country once they have finished the job in hand. It is also based on an economic differential that could be useful to the immigrant, deriving from the different tenors of life of both host and mother countries. In fact, the seasonal contract offers 151 working days, remunerated at 15,000,000 (liras) and a probable further 4,000,000 (liras) as an unemployment indemnity, even if the working days add up to less. Such a sum would facilitate a comfortable lifestyle for those living in a developing country. What arises, after all of these considerations, is the point that immigration is not only (or predominantly) an economic problem; it is also social, cultural, and often political and religious in nature; these are factors that are not satisfactorily explained, as the literature tells us, within the economic sphere.

BRIEF CONCLUSIONS

So far, an attempt has been made to portray part of the socio-economic complexity that the immigrant presence produces within an advanced industrial society, and the dynamics of its process of integration. Immigration flowing in from third world countries (or from countries of 'blocked' development, as those societies from Eastern Europe may be currently defined), plays an important functional role in the development of a receiving country, in that it is on a level with quantitative flexibility oscillating in relation to the demand. The labour reserve, easily absorbable and just as easily expelled, is comprised primarily of youths and immigrant workers, a characteristic typical of advanced industrial societies; indeed, this has been increasingly evident over the last ten years, where only Welfare State institutions (today in great crisis) have been able to slow down the accelerating process of precariousness.

In the midst of all this, seasonal labour, especially in countries of new migration (of which Italy is one) represents the extreme periphery, being characterised, not only by flexibility, but by forms of precariousness that go from the relative to the absolute. It is a trend that could be arrested, or at least contained within limits, if there existed a normative regulation that could counteract the more deleterious and socially preoccupying aspects. The regulation of seasonal labour, if managed efficiently, could become a decompression mechanism for irregular entry flows. This, in the sense that the proposal to concede temporary permits, once accepted by the immigrants to do jobs within a limited time-span, would help contain the actual number of so-called seasonal flow workers aiming to carry out productive activities in a temporary cycle.

Italy, with its above-mentioned proposals (once they have become state laws) will have no alternative but to follow the road it has chosen, subject, of course, to progressive refinements and revision according to the demands in the sector. The estimates (minimal) that we have put forward, show about 70,000 immigrants interested in seasonal labour work, almost a tenth of the non-EU immigrant presence in 1993, ranging over all national territory.

We must be prepared to give clear and sufficiently adequate answers to the question of the very large number of immigrants and their various work interests, not only because they represent a very important group, but also to combat entrenched forms of social exclusion, racial rejection and xenophobia on the part of the local population.

NOTES

1. December 1993. Estimated residential permits 925,000. Source: Italian Ministry of the Interior.
2. See Law Proposal – Group National Alliance (Martinat and Fini), to change and to integrate the Law 39, and Law Proposal – Group League Nord.
3. See Law Proposal – Democratic Party of the Left, 20 November 1994; Law proposal – Group of the Social Christians, Rome, 20 November 1994 (Tanzarella and Lunia), 26 September 1994.

10 Immigrants in Spain: From Institutional Discrimination to Labour Market Segmentation
Lorenzo Cachón

A DECADE OF IMMIGRATION IN SPAIN

It is only recently that Spain has become a country of immigration but it remains on a small scale, since the number of registered foreigners amounts to only 2 per cent of the total population currently living in Spain. The most significant aspects related to this change are mainly two: first, Spain's transition from a country of emigrants to one of immigrants and, secondly, the great increase over the past few years in the number of immigrants from under-developed countries. The change is relevant if we consider that, for centuries, and particularly during the twentieth century, migration in Spain has meant mainly emigration, first to America, in the first decades of this century, and to EU countries in the period between the 1950s and the 1980s. Throughout the twentieth century around 6 million Spaniards left Spain as emigrants, which represents 15 per cent of the current Spanish population. This means that over 1.6 million Spaniards are still residents in foreign countries. This phenomenon has had such a great social impact that it has led to the creation of the expression 'Spain outside Spain', precisely because this emigration process, together with previous important migrations, has left deep furrows in the country's social structure.

Before the economic crisis of the mid-1970s, Spain was part of the emigrating continuum in the 'European migratory system'.[1] However, with the decrease of Spanish emigration and the increase of immigration Spain's position has changed – in a way similar to that of Italy some years before and to what had taken place during the same period in Portugal and Greece. Consequently, since the mid-1980s, Spain has been part of the centre of attraction of immigration within the 'European migratory system'. In the twentieth century we can distinguish, roughly, five different periods with regard to Spain's incorporation into the European countries with immigration:

1. before 1960, when an increase in the number of foreigners with residence in Spain was very slow;
2. from 1960 to 1974, when the increase was very fast and coincided with an intense period of Spanish emigration to Europe;
3. from 1974 to 1978, when there was a slight decrease, coinciding with the first phase of the economic crisis;
4. from 1974 to 1985, there was a fast increase;
5. up to 1992, there was a progressively faster increase which took place mainly against a background of the regularising process falling between 1985 and 1986 and also between 1991 and 1992.

The first years of this last period coincided with a period of economic growth in Europe and Spain and with the entrance of Spain and Portugal into the EU. The change that has taken place during the last decade is a radical one: in 1983 there were only 210,350 foreigners living in Spain, while ten years later the number had increased to 430,422, that is, a 105 per cent increase.[2] Over half of the foreigners living in Spain at present entered the country after 1985, the year when the Immigration Law was passed. Typical processes of entrance, particularly when coming from under-developed countries, are not through exactly legal channels. A large number of immigrants in Spain were initially been irregular residents: of the present 517,000 legal immigrants, over 25 per cent have been 'regularised' (34,000 in 1985–6 and 110,000 in 1991–2), which means that these immigrants, at least, who are now regularised, had not been so previously.[3] Since the end of the last regularisation process there has been no indication of an increase in the immigration flow, thus following the tendency shown in the years prior to regularisation.

However, the 1980s not only saw the beginning of massive immigration to Spain (massive when compared to the previous volume) but also a change in immigrants' origins. In 1983, 60 per cent of registered residents came from the European Union and 16 per cent from Latin American countries (the two world areas which had been targets of the great Spanish emigrations throughout the century and, still now, places of residence for the vast majority of Spaniards living abroad). Only 2.9 per cent came from Africa and 2 per cent from Morocco. However, 33 per cent of the flow of new legal immigrants during that decade came from Africa, especially Morocco. After this change the number of African immigrants rose to 18 per cent of total legal foreigners in 1993 with Moroccans representing

Table 10.1 Origin of legal foreign residents in Spain (1983 and 1993)

Place of Origin	1983		1993		Change 1983–93		
	N	%	N	%	N	%	Relative increase
Europe	140,095	66.6	217,759	50.6	77,664	35.3	+55.4
– EU	126,388	60.1	189,779	44.0	633,391	28.8	+50.2
– Rest of Europe	13,707	6.5	27,980	6.5	14,273	6.5	+104.1
– Africa	5,982	2.9	79,438	18.4	73,456	33.4	+1,228.0
–Morocco	4,139	2.0	61,793	14.4	57,654	26.2	+1,393.0
– Rest of Africa	1,843	0.9	17,645	4.0	15,802	7.2	+857.4
Latin America	32,875	15.6	81,472	19.0	48,597	22.1	+147.8
North America	13,728	6.5	15,364	3.5	1,636	0.7	+11.9
Asia and Oceania	16,676	7.9	35,421	8.2	18,745	8.5	+112.4
n.c.	994	0.5	968	0.2	−26	–	−2.6
TOTAL	210,350	100.0	430,422	100.0	220,072	100.0	+104.6

Source: Based on statistics taken from the Ministry of Justice and Home Affairs.

14 per cent of this total. There was also an increase, both in relative and absolute terms, in the number of Latin Americans and Asians.[4] To the traditional flow of immigrants in Spain ('European citizens' and 'Latin-American brothers', 'hermanos latinoamericanos') we have now the incorporation of our 'southern neighbours' ('vecinos del sur'), especially Moroccans (see Table 10.1).

Rather than the increase in the number of immigrants, it is the changes in their national and ethnic origin that account for the fact that immigration has become a 'social fact' (in the sense given to the concept by Durkheim), which, moreover, is experienced as a problem by Spanish society.[5] The presence of these new immigrants (the 'real' foreigners) leads to the creation in the mind of an imaginary Spaniard, and of a social image of 'them', different from previous historical 'thems' in Spain, the gypsies.[6]

LABOUR MARKET SEGMENTATION IN SPAIN

In order to understand the position of immigrants in the Spanish labour market we have to remember that this market, like any other capitalist labour market, is segmented, that is, a 'market' that is divided into a series of limited areas or segments, which show no competitiveness among each other, and which are characterised by their idiosyncratic functioning together with effects on the workers that operate inside them. Within each of these segments 'the processes of recruitment, training, promotion, decisions on wages, and so on, in addition to behaviour patterns between workers and employers, are qualitatively different as we move from one market segment to another' (Villa 1990: 48–9). A series of institutional, economic and technological factors define the 'field of possibilities' where an interaction takes place between employers' and workers' strategies, thus determining the structures of the different – relatively closed – markets which constitute the global 'labour market'. Workers' positions within this structure depend, on the one hand, on the 'employment opportunities that are available to them' and, on the other, on the 'working conditions acceptance threshold', that is, on their 'social negotiation power' (Villa 1990: 312). Employment opportunities, from the point of view of the labour force offer, are conditioned by the workers' basic characteristics (sex, age, status, education, qualifications, ethnic origin, and so on) and by behaviour features (reliability, hard work and other personality traits). These features and behaviour patterns tend to be used by employers as discriminating elements (though not necessarily discriminatory) in the selection process of appointing workers to specific posts. The working conditions 'acceptance threshold' is defined basically by the position the workers occupy in the social reproduction system, both in the family and in the class structure: the status the workers have in this system 'delimits workers' positions in the labour market, thus defining their 'acceptance threshold' of the working conditions, below which they would tend to consider their employment opportunities as 'socially' unacceptable. In other words, this defines their '*social negotiation power* ... [which means] there are similar categories of workers at radically different minimum prices, *independent of their potential/real productivity*' (Villa 1990: 312–13).

Both the labour market structure and the workers' position and social negotiation power vary over time and are very sensitive to the cyclical fluctuations of the economic system. These variations not only produce changes in the employment demand in the different segments but also modify their characteristics and range (see Sengenberger 1988: 353–5). This influence of the specific socio-economic situation on structural changes is more dramatic when a labour market is undergoing very active periods of re-adaptation and adjustment.

The Spanish labour market has been suffering a period of deep transformation during the last three decades: its relocation within the framework of the capitalist world economy – with the particularly relevant event of its entry into the European Union – the transformation of its economic

structure, changes in regulations that have taken place since the establishment of the 1978 Constitution and particularly in the last decade, changes
in the institutions of the industrial relations system (especially, trade union
freedom and collective bargaining). All these factors have contributed to a
deep transformation of the labour market agents and segments.

The 1970s economic and political crises stirred the boggy waters of the
Spanish labour market and all the previously latent problems (latent to a
great extent because of the disguise of emigration) exploded simultaneously.
The result was a process of 'employment destruction' which has no parallel
in other OECD countries: the employed population decreased by 20 per cent
between 1975 and 1985. Even if the economically active population
increased moderately during this period, unemployment rocketed sky-high
to the level of 25 per cent. During the following five years (1985–90) the
process was reversed and almost 2 million posts were created, as many as
those that had been destroyed in the previous decade. In spite of this, unemployment only decreased moderately because there was an extraordinary increase in the size of the active population mainly as a consequence of
the massive incorporation of women into economically active life outside the home. These patterns of behaviour of the Spanish labour market are
'anomalous' in the Western context because of their magnitude.

However, it is not only a question of volume and tendencies. At the
same time, there are fundamental structural changes taking place in the
same direction as those we find in other countries, but which in Spain,
have as a result produced a deep reorganisation in the labour market structure: the continuous decrease of the rural population (from 22 per cent in
1976 going down to 9 per cent in 1993) and the movement of the economy
towards the tertiary sector, both in sectorial terms (the services sector went
from 41 per cent to 60 per cent in the same period) and in occupational
terms. Another striking feature is the creation of so-called 'atypical
employment': temporary jobs, part-time posts, and so on. If a guess can be
made that each country has 'its model' of atypical employment – although
the phenomenon has not been analysed in-depth from a comparative view-
point – we can say that the Spanish market is characterised, mainly, by the
development of 'temporary posts': by the end of 1993, a third of wage-
earning workers had a temporary contract (including all 'not indefinite'
working contracts). This kind of contract affects, mainly, latecomers in the
labour market, that is, young people, particularly if they are women.

Unemployment has been the greatest problem in the Spanish social context since the mid-1970s and it still is, at present, with 3,700,000 unemployed (24 per cent of the active population). The Spanish unemployment
rate, which shows no signs of decreasing, is approximately double that of

other EU members. The fact that this unemployment rate has not produced significant situations of social conflict can be explained if we consider the recent development of different areas in the Welfare State. These include free education and health services and the expansion of unemployment benefits, aspects that have improved considerably over the last decade. In addition to these facts, determined by specific policies (for example, around 65 per cent of the unemployed can apply for some kind of unemployment benefit at present) there are other factors, both social (such as 'family solidarity') and economic (such as the hidden economy) which contribute to the softening social effects of unemployment (Cachón 1993a).

The effects of these changes on the labour market structure have been extremely important. The decrease in rural employment, the increase of the economically active population and of women workers, the spread of temporary contracts, the tertiarisation of the economy, the black economy, the rise in the unemployment rate and particularly that of long-term unemployment, a more highly qualified labour force with access to the labour market, the changes in enterprises' policies regarding relations with workers, the end of emigration and the beginning of immigration, are all elements that have contributed to the creation of a labour market that is totally different from the one present in Spain three decades ago.[7]

IMMIGRATION POLICIES AND THE 'INSTITUTIONAL DISCRIMINATION FRAME'

Towards the mid-1980s, at the peak of the labour market transformation, Spain became a country of marked immigration. The position occupied by immigrants will be conditioned by the factors that determine the specific characteristics of this segmented market and, additionally, by two other different kinds of factors: institutional factors and the 'discrimination' against immigrants, or rather, immigrants of specific ethnic or national origins. It is not easy to analyse exactly how the 'discrimination'[8] factor works in the appointment of posts, even though its effects are obvious. Here we will be concerned with an analysis of the institutional factors and their role in the position occupied by immigrants in the Spanish labour market. The formal relevance of this aspect is enormous because the 'range of possibilities' of integration of immigrants in the labour market is defined in legal terms. Outside the legal boundaries, the immigrants' situation is 'irregular' and, consequently, because of this *simple* fact, they are restricted to a specific labour market segment: the black economy of 'illegal foreigners'. However, the fact of belonging to a 'regular' segment does not determine the occurrence of a specific situation: immigration policy has several 'variants' which might lead to different structuring processes of the positions occupied by immigrants in the labour market. In this sense, these 'variants' constitute the 'institutional discrimination framework' against immigrants in the labour market, and as such they create a preliminary framework previous to the possible, more specific kinds of discrimination, immigrants might be subjected to in the appointment of posts or in their working conditions.

The general labour market immigration policy is defined in article 18 of the 1985 Immigration Law[9] (Ley de Extranjería), which establishes that 'the granting of a work permit or its renewal will depend on the following circumstances: (a) the existence of unemployed Spanish workers in the applicant's occupational area; (b) the shortage or lack of a Spanish labour force in the activity or profession and geographical area in which the applicant intends to work; (c) bilateral agreements for reciprocal treatment with the foreigner's country of origin.' This Law has been the touchstone for an immigration policy that is not always consistent with the restrictive character of the Law itself: it is restrictive in the sense that, taking as a point of departure the 'national employment situation' (though this expression is not used in the Law yet), immigrants are being restricted to positions rejected by national workers, that is, positions which are below the Spaniards' 'acceptance threshold'.

The most relevant aspects within the institutional framework created on the basis of the Immigration Law and according to the influence they might exercise on the assumed position of immigrants in the labour market, are the following:

(a) Main Types of Residence Permit

1. General Work Permits (not Self-employed)

Permit 'A': for seasonal or temporary work: 9 months maximum; not renewable.

Permit 'B': for work in a specific profession and geographical area (in the former case it can be restricted to a specific employer); duration: 1 year maximum; renewable for one further year.

Permit 'C': for work in any activity or geographical area; duration: 5 years; renewable.

2. Self-employed Work Permits:

Permit 'D': can be granted for work in a specific area; duration: 1 year maximum.

Permit 'E': without geographical limitations; duration: 5 years; renewable.

This legal pattern of types of work permit establishes a clear distinction between the more unstable permits (A, B and D), which have a maximum duration of one year and which consequently require annual renewal, and the more stable ones (C and E), which have a maximum duration of five years and can be renewed almost automatically. Here, legal guidelines exist which could contribute to the creation of two different types of legal immigrants: a first type characterised by the instability of their situation and a second type with a much more stable situation.

(b) Granting Permits in the Context of the 'National Employment Situation'

The Act for the application of the Immigration Law[10] establishes that 'the competent authority will refuse to grant a work permit when: (a) in view of the national employment situation the competent authority will deem it advisable to do so ...'. In the terms of the Immigration Law outlined above, this means that a permit should not be granted whenever there are Spanish or EU unemployed workers in the activity of work intended to be carried out by the applicant.

Even though it is unlikely that what is actually established by these regulations will be strictly applied in administrative practice[11] the clause explicitly states that immigrant workers will only be allowed to work in sectors, occupations and geographical areas with a shortage of Spanish or EU labour force. This might derive from a general shortage of labour or from the fact that certain posts are below the Spaniards' 'acceptance threshold'.

(c) The Dynamics of the Standard Work Permit and the Annual Quota of Immigrants

Along the same lines, we find the establishment of an annual quota of immigrants – which is independent from the standard work permit dynamics – the aim of which is 'to channel and control the migratory flow', as indicated by the corresponding regulation.[12] For 1993 the established quota was 20,600 permits; the distribution, according to their different characteristics, was the following: 51 per cent, temporary posts and 49 per cent, 'permanent' posts; 49 per cent, farmhands (of whom 70 per cent were temporary); 5 per cent, unskilled construction workers ('permanent'); 29 per cent, domestic help ('permanent') and 17 per cent, 'other services' (given its 'temporary' character, probably catering).

Even though the objective is that of rationalising the immigration flow by directing it to legal channels, the logic of the 'national employment situation' determines the philosophy of the regulation: in its brief introduction it points out three times that its aim is one of negotiating employment offers which 'the national labour market cannot deal with' and this is reflected in the characteristics of the quota fixed for 1993: temporary workers in farming and catering and permanent workers in domestic service.

(d) Regularisation Processes

The priority principle underlying the concept of the 'national employment situation' has taken a different turn in the two regularisation processes relating to immigrants in Spain (1986 and 1991).[13] The new aspects introduced by the 9 July Resolution, which led to the beginning of the process of renewal of work permits regularised in 1991, implies that the different direction in the clause has become consolidated.[14] This Resolution justifies in its introduction the granting of certain types of permits of different duration and extension 'according to the attested degree of integration and settlement' of immigrants and establishes (point I.2.d.) that, in order to apply for a renewal of permits 'B' and 'D', a sufficient condition will be the fact of having 'temporary or discontinuous employment and the exercise of activities which will be a proof of the intention of assuming a regular and stable position during the validity period of the permit to be renewed'.[15]

Extraordinary regularisations and renewals carried out in the framework described above, identify factual situations and, consequently, ignore the limitations imposed by the logic of the 'priority to the national employment situation'. Moreover, a renewal policy, such as the one referred to, allows for a considerable increase in the number of medium duration work permits (over three years). Indeed, in 1992 and 1993 for example, the number of granted work permits type 'C' was 21,667 (not self-employed and of five years' duration) against 5,112 for the two previous years. At the end of 1993 current work permits of 3 or 5 years' duration constituted 36 per cent of the total number of current work permits, while at the end of 1991 they represented only 19 per cent. All this, together with a policy of reuniting families, can contribute to the strengthening of the immigrants' settlement process in Spanish society.

(e) Granting Work Permits: Allocation Criteria

The granting of work permits depends on a system of preferences based on three main criteria:[16] being of Spanish descent or having relatives living in Spain; the period of residence in Spain; originating from Latin America, the Philippines, Andorra, Equatorial Guinea, Gibraltar, Ceuta, Melilla and also the fact of being a Sephardic Jew. On the one hand, we can appreciate here an initial approximation of the notion of 'settlement', measured in terms of the 'period of residence in Spain'. On the other hand, with the establishment of a preference towards foreigners with specific national origins, the result is the creation of 'different' types of foreign immigrants. This possibility is strengthened by the legislation on the concession on Spanish nationality, which clearly underlines the differences between preferential immigrants and the rest: Spanish nationality can be applied for 'after a residence period of ten years ... [but] two years will be enough in the case of nationals from Latin American countries, Andorra, the Philippines, Equatorial Guinea or Portugal and the Sephardies.'[17]

(f) Family Reunion

Family reunion is a key point in an immigration policy aimed at the settlement of foreign workers: in Spain family reunion has been difficult and 'after the (1991) regularisation campaign the granting of family regrouping in the general immigration system has proved to be almost impossible for those relatives still residing in their countries of origin' (Santos 1993: 31). A policy and administrative practice of this kind does not favour the stability and settlement of immigrant workers.

The *simple* fact of being a non-EU foreigner restricts the positions that these workers can occupy in the labour market. Such positions are conditioned by the structural mechanisms of the market, which affect national workers too and, additionally, by specific regulations which constitute the 'institutional discrimination framework' and also by possible specific discrimination against those occupying designated posts – be it in the appointment process or in working conditions. The institutional factors we have described allow us to outline three main types of situations among immigrant workers in Spain: 'settled', 'precarious' and 'illegal'.

THREE TYPES OF IMMIGRANTS IN THE SPANISH LABOUR MARKET

In the institutional framework we have analysed, we cannot talk of an integration of immigrants into the labour market and Spanish society in the singular, as if it was an individualised and similar process in all cases. There are collective and clearly differentiated social processes, where we can distinguish at least three segments or groups of social and labour

positions with different 'ranges of possibilities'. In each of them, there is
the likelihood of finding different types of processes in the appointment of
posts and in the specification of wages and working conditions, as well as
distinct types of workers and employers operating in each area. ISOPLAN
(1991) suggests a differentiation between three groups of immigrants in
the southern countries of the European Union: (1) highly qualified experts
and technicians from EU and other developed countries; (2) workers with
low qualifications from other countries, and (3) illegal workers. This
approach is unduly influenced by Doeringer and Piore's dual labour market conception and by the possible effects of labour market segmentation
on national workers. For us, in an analysis of the *specific* situations of
immigrants in the labour market, a basic distinction is the one produced
when the immigrant manages to 'enter' the labour market segments usually occupied by national workers, though s/he might circumstantially
leave or be expelled. Overcoming this barrier constitutes an extremely
important change which entails completely different structural situations and working and social positions. According to this conception, our
proposal consists in distinguishing three types of immigrant workers:
'settled', 'precarious' and 'illegal'.

(a) 'Settled' Immigrants
Those who have achieved a 'stable' position in the nationals' standard
labour market and a considerable degree of integration into Spanish society. That is, they are immigrants who can be found in some of the labour
market segments usually occupied by national workers. Consequently,
they are subjected to the same regulations and have a similar 'social negotiation power' to that of national workers in any of the mentioned segments. It is a type that is differentiated internally, in the same way as
different Spanish workers tend to be distributed in relatively watertight
compartments in the labour market. However, in the analysis of the integration process of immigrants in the labour market and in Spanish society,
this fact determines a structurally different position. It is an internally
differentiated type because it includes, in the first place, EU workers[18]
who do not have to overcome the legal barriers we have described for
other immigrants and who should actually not be considered as such in
the framework of the European Common Market as established after the
European Union Treaty. In fact, these foreigners' average situation in the
labour market is better than that of the Spaniards'. Secondly, the 'settled'
group includes those immigrants who have been granted a type 'C' or 'E'
work permit, which allows them to work for a period of five years and
with a possibility of renewal.[19] In this group, there has recently been an

important change: some years ago they were, basically, qualified experts and technicians from EU countries (until the 1992 free movement of workers), from other industrialised countries or from certain Latin American countries. They worked in high technology industrial sectors or in expanding service sectors, with similar wages to those of national workers. In recent years, particularly during the last three years, this group of 'settled' immigrants has become diversified because of the improvement of the settlement conditions of an increasingly higher number of workers with lower qualifications, who work in less expansive sectors and come from different national origins. This phenomenon has arisen in the context of the work permits renewal process after the 1991 extraordinary regularisation.[20]

However, even if we classify these immigrant workers as 'settled' this does not mean they have a steady job.[21] Here, we should remember that they share with the Spaniards a segmented labour market where one-third of wage-earning workers have temporary working contracts. Among these 'settled' immigrants we can find a variation and segmentation similar to that found among Spaniards. However, it is precisely the 'similarity' with the heterogeneous group of Spaniards which leads us to consider them apart from the two following groups, which can be defined in terms of negative distancing from the characteristics of Spaniards in the labour market.

Immigrants' social integration varies, depending on the groups we are referring to. The highly qualified ones, who are often from EU countries and with a good degree of integration in the labour market, usually have a stable family situation (as they usually immigrate with their families or are reunited later), high quality accommodation and easy access to training, education, health and social security systems. Their standard of living is similar to that of Spanish citizens with similar professions. However, regular but not very qualified immigrants, who are mainly from the developing countries, tend to arrive on their own, even if they are married, and they seldom achieve family regrouping until after several years have passed. They have low-quality accommodation, often with high rent/bad tenancy conditions, a problematic access to training, education, health and social security systems and their standard of living is below that of nationals with similar occupations.

An important sign of the degree of settlement of 'settled' immigrants, and at the same time a strengthening factor for such settlement, is the constitution of a home.[22] The other groups we analysed live in very unstable conditions and seldom manage to settle down in normal family accommodation. The group of 'settled' immigrants is integrated, in addition to EU workers, by immigrants from developed countries and a high proportion of Latin Americans.

(b) 'Precarious' Immigrants

Those living in a legal situation in Spain but who have not managed to achieve a stable degree of integration in the labour market in the sense described for 'settled' workers and who consequently have not become integrated in the host society. Following Rogers, we describe their situation as 'precarious' because this concept 'implies instability, lack of protection, insecurity and social or economic vulnerability … what identifies precarious employment is a combination of these factors and the boundaries of the concept are inevitably arbitrary to some degree' (Rodgers 1989: 19). Rodgers outlines several dimensions within precariousness: the degree of uncertainty with respect to work continuity; control over work (working conditions, wages, work rhythm); protection at work, both from the point of view of social security benefits and from that of the fight against discrimination and for legal protection in employment conditions. Income is also included, since badly paid jobs must be considered as precarious if they are associated with poverty and with unstable social integration. In all these aspects, 'precarious' workers are particularly vulnerable, given their weak negotiating position in the labour market: their work permits are for brief periods ('A', 'B' and 'D'); their contracts of employment – when they have one – are also for short periods, and this does not depend on the fact that their work permits might be valid for only one year. Workers in this group often change job, they are frequently unemployed and they also frequently switch from regular to irregular situations. They are poorly qualified workers who work in sectors that have a higher degree of instability (catering, farming, construction, and so on). Spanish workers are not easily found in this particular labour market and the reason is not because they do not share sectors or even companies with foreign workers. It is rather that there is a great difference between the 'precariousness' that affects Spanish workers and the 'precariousness and discrimination' suffered by these peripheral immigrants. A large part of this immigrant segment is constituted by workers 'regularised' in the 1991 process and they are mainly Moroccans living in shared homes.

(c) 'Illegal' Immigrants

Those people who live in Spain with irregular residence and work permits and they compete for jobs with 'peripheral' immigrants. This latter group has the 'advantage' of being in a legal situation. They switch from frequent and long periods of unemployment to irregular jobs in the black market, where they are subjected to over-exploitation.[23] These workers' labour situations are particularly precarious, both because of the illegal character of their situation and because of their complete dependence on their employer, since their 'social negotiation power' is very low. They lack social security benefits and access to the health system, which means that in addition to the risk of losing their job they do not benefit from any social services in case of accident or illness. Their life standard is often at the threshold of poverty or below. They lack the right to family regrouping. Their accommodation is usually of a marginal type; indeed, most of the shanty towns in Spanish urban areas are occupied by these immigrants. All this makes isolation from the society they are working for, a much more likely prospect. Calvaruso (1987: 477) talking about the situation in Italy – which can also be applied to that of Spain – summarises the situation of these immigrants who work in the black market by saying that 'there is no social integration for illegal immigrants and there will never be if we take into account their structural situation.'

In order to have a deep knowledge of the different segments occupied by immigrants in the labour market we should quantify the groups, analyse the sectors and occupations where they work, their national origins and their personal characteristics. None of this is easy, because the available statistics do not take into consideration the accumulation of circumstances which give rise to these different types of situations or, quite simply, they just ignore the phenomenon of 'illegal' immigrants.

The main information available in Spain, for the purpose of analysing the presence of immigrants in the labour market, can be found in the statistical studies on work permits of the Ministry of Labour and Social Security (flow of granted work permits and estimation on the current work permit stock by the end of each year), together with the 'Labour Force Survey' (EPA) from the 'National Statistics Institute'. This survey shows the information obtained on a quarterly basis, from a sample of the population living in families, excluding those staying in hotels, hostels, and so on. The EPA underestimates in global terms, the foreign population and foreign workers in Spain, because it only reflects 'the population that has reached a certain degree of "stability", even if this accounts only for the fact that they have regular family housing' (Alvarez 1992: 3).

In the absence of a more specific instrument which will enable us to characterise adequately the three groups of immigrant workers proposed, we show in Table 10.2 a maximum and a minimum estimate of the volume of each of these segments. In the maximum estimate of the first two, we include as part of the 'settled' workers' group, those foreigners who appear in the EPA, since they live in family housing and this can be considered as a sign of integration in the host society. In the minimum estimate, we include the proportion of long-term work permit holders, out of

Table 10.2 Estimated number of non-EU immigrant workers for the three segments proposed (1993)

Types of Immigrants in the Spanish Labour Market	Estimated Number of Foreign Workers		Percentage Distribution		Proportion of Labour Force (%)	
	Max. (1)	Min. (2)	Max.	Min.	Max.	Min.
A. 'Settled'	58,873	41,557	22.2	21.8	0.38	0.27
B. 'Precarious'	73,880	56,564	38.8	21.3	0.48	0.37
SUB-TOTAL A + B	115,437		43.5/60.6		0.75	
C. 'Illegal' (3)	150,000	75,000	56.5	39.4	0.97	0.49
TOTAL A + B + C	265,437	190,437	100.0	100.0	1.72	1.24

Source: Own figures based on the following primary data sources.

(1) *Maximum column*: The proportion represented by foreigners according to the Labour Force Survey (fourth trimester 1993) on current work permits (31 December 1993).

(2) *Minimum column*: The proportion of work permits over three years duration, out of the total number of current work permits (31 December 1993).

(3) *'Illegal column'*: An estimate subject of four conditions: (1) number of irregular arrivals in 1990–1; (2) slight increase of flow of arrivals in the past two years; (3) non-legalised through the 1991 regularisation; and (4) unrenewed throughout the period 1992–3.

the total amount of current work permit holders, by the end of each year. In the case of 'illegal' workers, we have taken four points of reference which are specified in Table 10.2 and which reflect the reasoning process that the 'attractiveness' of being able to obtain employment is so strong for potential emigrants that it can be said that the immigration flows will still increase as long as there is a possibility of access to a job, no matter how precarious, undignified and irregular it might be (Aragón and Chozas 1993: 11).

In the maximum hypothesis, immigrant workers constitute by the end of 1993, 1.72 per cent of the Spanish economically active population. In the minimum one, 1.24 per cent. Since the total number of legal workers is fixed according to official statistics, the global variation between the two estimates depends on the number of 'illegal' workers considered (either 75,000 or 150,000). The two segments we distinguish in the group of legal workers are further divided into two halves in the maximum estimate, or include a higher number of 'precarious' workers in the lower estimate.

SECTORIAL CONCENTRATION OF 'SETTLED' AND 'PRECARIOUS' IMMIGRANTS

Most foreign workers with a work permit in Spain (65 per cent), that is, 'settled' or 'precarious' non-EU workers, are concentrated in five activity areas: 'domestic service' (18 per cent), 'catering' (13 per cent), 'construction' (13 per cent), 'retail trade' (11 per cent)[24] and 'farming' (10 per cent). These five branches together, constitute only 35 per cent of total employment in Spain, which gives us an initial impression of the degree of concentration of immigrant employment. If, on the whole, these workers constitute 1.1 per cent of employed workers in Spain, their relative presence is much higher in four of these branches: they represent 6.5 per cent of employment in 'domestic service', 2.9 per cent in 'catering' and slightly over 1.5 per cent in 'farming' and 'construction'. 'Domestic service' is occupied mainly by women (over 80 per cent), while 'farming' and 'construction' by men (98 per cent) (see Table 10.3).

Sectorial concentration coincides with 'specialisation' depending on the immigrants' country of origin: Morocco (75 per cent) and the rest of Africa concentrate over 95 per cent foreign workers in 'farming' and 78 per cent in 'construction' (among these, 70 per cent are Moroccans). In 'domestic service' we find Philippine and Dominican women and in 'catering' we find Moroccans, Latin Americans and Chinese (Cachón 1993b and Colectivo IOE 1991). Immigrant workers in these activity areas find themselves in the situations we have depicted above, though it is sometimes difficult to show a quantitative picture because of the lack of detailed statistical information. For example, in the area of domestic service, the figures from a survey among 424 immigrant women working in this sector in Madrid and Barcelona in 1990 (Marrodán 1991) show that 10 per cent had a permanent working contract, 10 per cent a temporary contract and 80 per cent had no contract at all. The differences according to national origin were also relevant: over 60 per cent of Filipino workers had working contracts, while only 16 per cent of the Latin Americans, 14 per cent of the Africans and 5 per cent of the Moroccans had a contract. Non-Filipino Asian workers had no contracts at all, in spite of the fact that they had legal residence permits. The presence of immigrant workers in farming is closely related to seasonal tasks such as the gathering of fruit and other products, except for some areas in the south where there is intensive agriculture. Here we find both regular and irregular workers, since they both attract the presence of the other group, though their conditions concerning employment and wages are very different. Peddling is another activity where we can find both regular and irregular workers. In the case of the latter group, they often work in situations of dependency towards other fellow countrymen.

Table 10.3   The 15 branches of productive activities with a larger relative number of non-EU, 'settled' and 'precarious' immigrant workers

Activity Branches	(1) Employed Population (000's)	(2) Foreign Workers (including EU workers)	(3) Foreigners (3)=(2)/(1) (%)	(4) Ranking	(5) Distribution of Foreigners (%)	(6) Ranking	(7) Female Foreigners (%)
1. Domestic help	383.9	24,870	6.5	1	17.8	1	81.0
2. Catering	637.9	18,541	2.9	2	13.3	2	27.9
3. Services to companies	390.1	10,523	2.7	3	7.5	6	32.7
4. Farming	786.2	13,191	1.7	4	9.5	5	2.0
5. Construction and civil engineering	1,164.4	18,537	1.6	5	13.3	3	1.8
6. Social, leisure and cultural services	294.0	4,439	1.5	6	3.2	7	31.4
7. Fishing	89.1	1,348	1.5	7	1.0	15	0.7
8. Silviculture and hunting	28.0	423	1.5	8	0.3	29	1.9
9. Extraction of solid fuels	27.5	366	1.3	9	0.3	31	0.5
10. Retail trade	1,365.9	14,862	1.1	10	10.7	4	13.1
11. Leather industry	28.9	304	1.1	11	0.2	34	11.8
12. Textile industry	125.2	1,294	1.0	12	0.9	16	19.8
13. Production and transformation of metals	61.7	628	1.0	13	0.5	26	4.3
14. Maritime and air transport	42.0	412	1.0	14	0.3	30	40.5
15. Other manufacturing industries	34.2	349	1.0	15	0.3	33	12.6
Subtotal 15 Branches	5,459.0	109,721	2.0	(15)	79.1	(15)	
Total	12,366.2	139,421	1.1	(44)	100.0	(44)	28.9

Source: (1) Fourth timestre 1992: Source: Instituto Nacional de Estadística, *Labour Force Survey.*
(2) Current work permits 31 December, 1992: Source: Ministry of Labour and Social Security, *Statistics of Work Permits for Foreigners 1992.*

NOTES

1. By migratory system we understand here 'the relationship that is established between an area which receives immigration and a group of countries from which emigration originates. This relationship will tend to be formed on a permanent basis and it will be accompanied by an intricate network of inter-relations of various types' (Arango 1993: 7).

2. In order to have an exact idea of the number of registered foreigners in Spain we would have to add to the number of foreigners with a current residence permit issued by the Home Office (210,350 in 1983 and 430,422 in 1993), a vast number of persons who are registered but who are not reflected in the official statistics (people under 18 and disabled living with their parents, Moroccans living in Ceuta and Melilla, persons who are granted political asylum, foreigners from EU countries with temporary residence permits, and so on). It has been calculated (Izquierdo 1992: 119–22) that the volume of this group is of about 20 per cent, which means that the total number of registered foreigners towards the end of 1991 would be about 517,000.

3. In the 1991 process of regularisation there were 132,934 applications: to this number we should add around 23,000 relatives who were estimated to have been living with the applicants during that period, which gives us a total of 156,000 unregistered residents in 1991.

   Before the 1991 regularisation process, several estimates had been made about the number of unregistered residents in Spain. The most well-known ones are those carried out by the 'Colectivo IOE' (1987), A. Izquierdo (1992) and the PASS group (Marcos and Rojo 1991). For 1989 the Colectivo IOE estimated around 300,000 illegal immigrants while Izquierdo calculated a figure ranging between 81,00 and 240,000. The PASS group drew a 'map of foreign immigrants in an irregular situation' with a volume of between 173,000 and 259,000. The applications during the regularisation process place the number of illegal residents well below the estimates of the 'Colectivo IOE' and the PASS group and slightly above A. Izquierdo's average hypothesis. Here, we have to take into account several factors: first, that these estimates are made for 1989 and that the regularisation process took place two years later; second, that all the evidence seems to show that the flow of immigrants during those two years was very important and on the increase; finally, that during the regularisation process, these flows were strengthened as a consequence of the 'appealing effect' of the ongoing process. Furthermore, we have to bear in mind the fact that regularisation was intended, initially, for 'workers' and only later for their relatives of whom only just over a quarter eventually applied for regularisation.

4. A special case is that of Portugal, whose number of immigrants has also risen considerably. There are several reasons that can account for this: the fact that Portugal is an EU country, which grants its population freedom of movement (though this was not effective until 1992); also, its long common frontier with Spain, the historical relationships between the two countries and the slightly lower degree of development in Portugal when compared with Spain. All these factors explain the intensity of Portuguese immigration to Spain, unlike immigration from other Community countries.

5. This 'problem' is highly dramatised by public opinion, a fact that is reflected in the evident lack of knowledge by a great number of Spaniards (over 30 per cent) who think that in Spain there are as many foreigners, or even more, than in France, Italy or Germany (C.I.S.). See Izquierdo 1994 for further reading on surveys about public opinion on immigrants.
6. See Martín, Gómez, Arranz and Gabilondo 1994.
7. These changes have not been studied in depth from the point of view of segmentation, nor has there been a proposal for a global vision of the different labour market segments before and after these transformation processes. However, there have been some attempts at carrying out studies of this kind (see Cachón 1994 and Recio 1988 and 1991).
8. By 'discrimination' we understand it to be, following the ILO (art. 1, Agreement 111, June 1958), 'any differentiation, exclusion or preference made on the grounds of race, colour, gender, religion, political opinion, national origin or social background, which will have as an effect the elimination or alteration of the right to equal opportunities and treatment in employment and occupation'. At present (second term of 1994) the ILO under the direction of R. Zegers de Beijl is carrying out an important research project among different countries – including Spain – in an attempt to collect evidence of the type of discrimination suffered by immigrants in their access to employment. For a more detailed idea of the approach followed in this research see Zegers de Beijl 1990 and 1991 and Bovenkerk 1992.
9. Organic Law 7/1985, 1 July, on the rights of foreigners in Spain (BOE, 3 July 1985).
10. The Parliamentary Act 119/1986, 26 May, establishes the regulations for the application of the Organic Law 7/1985, 1 July, on the rights of foreign residents in Spain (BOE, 12 July 1986), (art. 37.4.a).
11. A rough idea can be provided by comparing, at a national level, the number of unemployed workers registered at the National Institute for Unemployment (INEM, the Spanish public unemployment service) as an annual average for 1992, and the number of work permits granted in the five areas of activity with the highest number of work permits granted in that year. It is true that these figures cover neither the occupations nor the geographical location of the employment offers and demands, but some of the data are very significant:

Areas of Activity	Granted Work Permits (1992)	Registered Number of Unemployed (average for 1992)
Domestic services	16.261	23.600
Construction	13.497	279.600
Catering	11.693	167.900
Retail trade	10.250	206.100
Agricultural production	8.951	42.000

12. Resolution of 4 May 1993 of the Under-secretariat of the Ministry for Relations with Parliament and the Government Secretariat, establishes general and procedural instructions for the specification of a quota of allowed foreign workers for 1993 (BOE, 17 June 1993).

13. In Spain there have been two great immigration regularisation processes: the first one after the Immigration Law was passed in July 1985 and the second one after the Motion concerning the situation of foreigners in Spain was passed in March 1991. The differences between the two processes have been very significant, not only because of the number of applications for regularisation in each case (38.000 in the first one and 130.000 in the second one), but also because of the applicants' characteristics in the two processes ('illegal foreigners' in the first case and 'foreigners working irregularly in Spain' in the second one) and finally, because of the development of the processes as such and the direction taken by the immigration policy underlying these processes (see Aragón and Chozas, 1993 and Cachón, 1993b).

14. Resolution of 9 July 1992, of the Under-secretariat of the Ministry for Relations with Parliament and the Government Secretariat, which establishes the instructions for the renewal of work and residence permits negotiated as laid down in the Council of Ministers' Agreement of 7 June 1991 on the regularisation of foreign workers (BOE, 11 July 1992).

15. Here, we ignore the possible discriminatory effect of the application of this regulation towards workers regularised in 1991, since this regulation has more favourable effects than the general regulation derived from the Immigration Law (see Santos 1993: 39–40).

16. Preferences for granting work permits are established in Act 1119/1986 (art. 38 and following; the scope of the preferences can be modified 'when ... deemed advisable in view of the national employment situation' (art. 42). Certain aspects of the preferences are no longer valid as a consequence of EU stipulations, but in any case, in previous years they have had an effect on the structuring of the immigrant labour market.

17. Art. 22 of the Civil Law after the modification introduced by Law 51/1982 of 13 July (BOE, 30 July 1982).

18. This 'allocation' of specific groups (EU workers or others) to one of the proposed segments should be understood in terms of 'typical' tendencies: it is clear that we can also find certain EU workers in the 'precarious' segment, or even in the 'illegal' one (and sometimes in an unlawful one), but this is not the 'typical practice' we are trying to outline here.

19. Here, we could also include those who have acquired Spanish nationality and, consequently, do not need a work permit. In fact, their situation is so similar to that of the Spaniards in social and labour terms that they are legally Spanish. This means they are not reflected in the statistics as foreigners.

20. In the past two years (1992–3) type 'C' permits have increased to 11,000 from the 3,000 annual average in the previous five years and permits type 'E' to 2,000 from 1,500 in the previous period.

21. Among other reasons this is because non-EU immigrants can only be granted, at best, a five year work permit, even when the permit can be renewed almost automatically.

22. This phenomenon has been observed, for example, in the classical study by Rex and Moore (1967) for the United Kingdom and by Céu Esteves (1991) for Portugal.

23. In extreme cases we find situations that come close to 'slavery', for example, certain groups of Chinese workers recently found by the Madrid police (over 120 workers located across in 10 illegal textile workshops, between March and May 1994). These workers had been obliged to sell their freedom of movement – at least for a long period of time – to the persons who had 'facilitated' their trip from China to Spain, who kept the workers' personal papers and subjected them to constant threats. In addition to this, the workers were obliged to live in unhealthy conditions in enclosed quarters, suffered under-nourishment and had to work crammed together for extremely long periods.

24. Mostly peddling.

11 Refugee Care in Sweden: the Problems of Unemployment and anti-Discrimination Policies
Maritta Soininen

The chapter deals with the problem of refugee care and unemployment in Sweden. The official policies to integrate refugees in the Swedish society have met serious difficulties during the 1980s and 1990s. In an efficient way, the refugees are excluded from the Swedish labour market. The chapter provides a background by first describing how refugee care has been organised and then exemplifies some of the problems with how local care programmes work. Part of the explanation for the failure to integrate refugees in the labour market might be the lack of necessary skills, structural changes in the labour market and cutbacks in the public sector. Another kind of explanation deals with ethnic discrimination in the labour market, a particularly serious form of discrimination because it also undermines attempts to integrate refugees into society as a whole. Swedish legislation includes a law against ethnic discrimination in working life, passed by parliament as late as 1994. Attention is also paid to policies against ethnic discrimination in the labour market. These are examined in the context of the Swedish corporate model of administration, which has meant that Sweden chose to legislate against ethnic discrimination in the world of work as recently as 1994. According to this 'Swedish model' the state hands over responsibility for labour market questions to the labour market partners as far as this is feasible. Finally, it is proposed that a certain shift in perspective is vital in order to focus upon actors in the labour market and their more or less successful anti-discrimination policies. Otherwise there is a risk that studies which examine the existence of ethnic discrimination in working life will lead only to another 'victim' study, in which the experience and occurrence of discrimination are the main objects of analysis. A certain shift in perspective is therefore vital to focus upon actors in the labour market and their more or less successful anti-discrimination policies. When viewed as a problem in such a larger perspective, we are obliged to expand our field of interests to include questions of power and its structure within society.

During 1994, the levels of visible unemployment among immigrants and refugees in Sweden with non-Nordic citizenship climbed to 28 per cent and among those with non-European citizenship up to 37 per cent (AKU, SCB 1994). In round figures, six out of ten Africans and Iranians were without work in 1993 (AKU, SCB 1993). This chapter looks at the reform programmes of 1985 and 1991 which were intended to improve the possibility of integration into society and the world of work for refugees. The 1985 reform, which meant radical changes in the routines of the refugee reception programme, gave less than encouraging results when it came to getting refugees out into the labour market. The 1991 reform of the state grant system was intended to remove those barriers, which were seen as intrinsic to the refugee reception programme's attempts to prepare refugees for working life. A contributory factor to the reform's lack of success was the tenfold increase in the number of refugees who were accepted during the 1980s and sharp fall in employment at the end of the 1980s and beginning of the 1990s.

The regulation of refugee flows to both Sweden and Europe appears more and more as a challenge. European states are equipping themselves in order to meet the increasing stream of refugees from the Third World. A coordination of the differing European policies is seen by some as leading to the construction of 'Fortress Europe' where the harmonisation of refugee policies effectively excludes refugees and asylum-seekers from entering Europe. Economic stagnation, rising unemployment and elements of intensified xenophobia are seen as factors hastening this development (Brochman 1993; Hammar 1993).

In Sweden, the increase in the number of spontaneous refugee immigrants at the beginning of the 1970s coincided with the end of labour immigration. Once economic expansion and its demand for labour were replaced by stagnation, the attitude of the government became more restrictive. Labour migration from non-Nordic countries was regulated in 1967 and Nordic immigration was channelled through labour market services after 1973. During decades of economic growth after the Second World War, migration was viewed as a labour market question.

The question of refugees aroused scarcely any interest during the 1950s and 1960s. Sweden received a couple of thousand refugees annually from UN refugee camps. In the early 1970s, a turning point was reached when spontaneous streams of refugees began to reach the country's borders. Among some of the causes was the political instability in Latin America, which resulted in an increasing number of asylum-seekers attempting, by their own means, to come to Sweden, a process which intensified into the 1980s. During that decade the number of refugees and asylum-seekers placed in municipalities increased tenfold. In 1993, the government granted asylum to approximately 40,000 Bosnian refugees, the single largest group so far.

THE 1985 REFORM STRATEGY

Another watershed can be dated to the middle of the 1980s when the country's refugee reception programme was reorganised. The National Immigration Board (SIV-Statens invandrarverk) took over primary responsibility from the National Labour Market Board (AMS-Arbetsmarknadsstyrelsen). The 1985 reform, 'The Local Care of Refugees', was characterised by both significance and visibility. Hitherto, the annual reception of a few thousand refugees in need of asylum, accommodation and residency had affected only the larger conurbations. Now the country's municipalities were to become progressively involved following agreements between themselves and the National Immigration Board (Soininen 1992). An immediate result was a dramatic increase in the number of politicians and civil servants who, for the first time, came into contact with refugee issues during a short and intensive period of a few years. The regulation of refugees has become a highly visible issue in the Swedish mass media and has polarised public opinion during the transition to the 1990s. Questions about how much support is due to refugees and how much solidarity Sweden can afford, became burning issues and a new political party, espousing a policy hostile to refugees, took its place in the Riksdag during 1991–4.

Social questions, unemployment, education and general welfare are typical areas for public policy measures (Hall and Quinn 1983). In Sweden the refugee care policy also belongs to this category while in many other countries private, humanitarian and religious groups take on a much greater share of the burden.

NEW CARE FOR REFUGEES

The 1985 reform, 'The Local Care of Refugees', was initiated in 1980 by the National Working Group for Refugees' Responsibilities, AGFA (Ds A 1981: 11). However, it took four years before the government introduced its reform for Parliament and it was accepted in 1985.

The previous refugee reception programme, led by the National Labour Market Board, had been the object of much criticism, not least for the long and pacifying waiting period in refugee camps. This, it was believed, made it difficult, subsequently to integrate refugees into the labour market and society. As a result of the 1978 national investigation 'Sweden and Refugees', parliament had decided on special treatment for refugees. Given that refugees had been through difficult experiences before and during their exodus, the labour market perspective on immigration was not considered suitable in their case.

The criticisms directed at the National Labour Market Board were not entirely unwelcome as the Board was undergoing renewal and wished to hand more marginal tasks like refugee reception over to other government authorities. At the same time, even the larger conurbations had expressed a wish to see their share of the burden of spontaneous refugees lightened. Finally, the National Immigration Board was also affected. Previously, it had been responsible for the legal question of granting residence permits along with information and influencing public opinion. The reorganisation of the reception programme gave it the possibility to expand its sphere of operations. The wishes of both national authorities and the conurbations thus coincided in such way as to allow reconsideration of accepted routines. Mutual interests and complementary development needs had opened a policy window which brought the question onto the political agenda (Kingdon 1984).

The Social Services Law (SFS 1980-620, 1982) was chosen as the policy basis for the 'Local Care of Refugees', both as regards the design of the refugee care and the organisational solutions (Ds A 1981: 11). The Law's key paragraphs, flexibility, normalisation, continuity and the holistic view were to steer the municipal refugee work: refugees were to be given the opportunity to live in a normal environment as soon as possible after their arrival in Sweden. Local conditions and solutions adapted to their needs were to guide the work according to the flexibility principle while the holistic vision summarised the ideal of taking account of the individual's entire situation. 'That means that accommodation, work, education and the need for social support and services ought to be ascertained and taken care of in context' according to the report by the Working Group for Refugees' Responsibilities (Ds A 1981: 11). The need for therapeutic, psychological and social support was seen as great for many refugees and was to be met in a better way than had formerly been the case. It was thought that therapists, psychologists, psychiatrists and social workers who worked directly with refugees ought, preferably, to be bilingual. The National Immigration Board expressed a certain amount of concern over the municipalities' abilities to understand the special needs of refugees. However, the report had concluded that this competence would develop locally out of a social worker's ability to provide good care in a local environment (Soininen 1992).

The 1985 reform was characterised, to a great extent, by the general economic and political-administrative development in Sweden during the 1980s. The new notion of management by objectives, deriving from the programming–planning–budgeting system (PBBS) taken from the USA in the 1970s, provided the new framework. Together with the introduction of the framework legislation and the transition to management by objectives, the municipalities had gained a more central role in public sector administration. During the 1970s, an increasing proportion of public policy in Sweden was decided and administered by the municipalities. That they should also assume a greater responsibility for the implementation of the country's refugee programme can be seen as a natural consequence of this development.

PROGRAMME ORGANISATION

On account of costs, no significant organisational changes were suggested. Instead, the programme was to be implemented through the existing local social care services, thereby avoiding unnecessary parallel organisations and special solutions (Reg. prop. 1983/84: 124). Finally, the reform was based on the crucial assumption that refugee immigration to Sweden would continue to be of the same magnitude as during the previous years, that is 3,000–5,000 annually. The local care of refugees was to be carried out in a limited number of municipalities, hand-picked by the National Immigration Board, and consequently on a quite modest scale. The chosen municipalities were to have a certain amount of prior experience with immigrants and immigrant services. It was further assumed that 'the intended municipalities and surrounding regions have a labour market which will offer refugees prospects for eventual employment' (Ds A 1981: 11).

The reception municipalities could reapply for social grants from the state during the refugees' first 3–4 years in the municipality and also receive a once only compensation for each refugee received in order to cover extra costs thus incurred.

In its capacity as head of the refugee programme, the National Immigration Board had, for the first time, taken on responsibility for the direct implementation of a policy. Paradoxically, it was the new social services law which formed the basis for the reform work and not the principles of equality, freedom of choice and cooperation which inform the official immigration and minority policy as it stands in the 1974 Act. One of the Board's main tasks was to affect other authorities' actions in questions concerning immigrants and minorities. However, the Board now had responsibility for a refugee reception programme which rested upon premises enshrined in social services legislation. Without its own local organisational base it was obliged to work through local social services. Given its inability to exercise extensive control as a state authority over municipal affairs, it had only very limited possibilities to influence local refugee care.

Two distinct normative worlds met one another here. On the one hand, that of the social services and their ideas on the care of clients, and, on the other hand, the 1974 principles of the immigrant and minority policy with its strong emphasis on the meeting between two parties in a spirit of co-operation, equality and freedom of choice. These two normative systems then represented two different attitudes towards the problems and needs of refugees and how work with refugees ought to proceed.

The dichotomised organisation for implementing the reform, the Immigration Board at the national level and social services in the municipalities, formally under the control of another state authority, the National Social Welfare Board, had scarcely those qualities which are traditionally considered signs of a successful administration, namely, uniformity, good control, a minimal dependency upon other authorities, information, good communication and a limited number of links in the implementation chain (Hood 1976; Gunn 1980; Ham and Hill 1984). Neither could one speak of a process by which the centrally decided policy was translated into explicit instructions for those civil servants lower down the hierarchy who were to put them into practice. It was rather a question of a policy idea seen as an expression of the basic principles and aspirations, enshrined in the social services legislation now to be applied to refugees (Majone and Wildawsky 1978).

If several of the preconditions for a rational policy implementation were not fulfilled, the remainder fell away when it became time, in 1985, for the municipalities to receive their first refugees. During the interim period a 200–300 per cent increase in the numbers of refugees, compared with the planned totals, resulted in a shortage of time and lack of resources. This inevitably resulted in a delay in implementing the original goals of the reform, namely, the placement of refugees in municipalities with prior experience of immigrants where they would be able to reside and have access to education and employment. The Immigration Board, which did not have the necessary power, authority or legal back-up to control the municipalities, was effectively left to provide information, change attitudes through persuasion and recruit new municipalities. The Board, which had good previous experience of this kind of management (Jacobsson 1984), succeeded beyond all expectations in recruiting new municipalities to participate in the programme.

During the course of the negotiations between the Immigration Board and the municipalities, an increasing number of smaller municipalities were drawn into the programme. Those within the same county kept a watchful eye on one another and came to an agreement over their respective duties and responsibilities for the care of refugees. Group pressure played a part and an increasing number of municipalities shouldered their responsibilities. The Board was fairly innovative in its methods. By playing municipalities against one another a self-propelling recruitment system was built up by allowing them to demand solidarity from each other. The guiding ideology for the programme was now 'The Whole of Sweden Strategy', announced by the Board in the best 'muddling through' tone. It received extra help from pressure applied within the municipal collective which served to increase the pressure on municipalities with no, or only a very small, refugee quota. In the name of solidarity with others, everyone agreed to cooperate, even if the actual number of refugees received was very small, which was often the case.

The Board had, in effect, accepted that receiving refugees did not imply the immediate creation of preconditions for the long-term integration of refugees. In a large number of municipalities refugee reception was mainly a question of helping refugees onto some further destination. Municipalities with no previous experience of refugee matters or familiarity with the Board's immigrant policy principles were now responsible for the local care of refugees.

Shifts of this kind within a policy's goals and results, often caused by a shortage of time and resources during the introductory phase, are not uncommon. When the implementation of a policy is a matter of interaction between those responsible for the policy to be realised and the actual context where it is to be realised, it becomes a matter of continual negotiation where both the policy and its goals are successively renegotiated, transformed and modified so as to adapt it to the prevailing conditions (Barrett and Fudge 1981).

THE LOCAL CONTEXT

Local social services with their professional expertise were to be responsible for local care in most of the municipalities. Adaptation to local needs and conditions was to be primarily a matter of adapting to local professional and organisational structures, rather than to the target group of refugees (Soininen 1992). Due to lack of experience, the model for dealing with refugees was often one of pragmatism. Work with refugees became part of the on-going routines of the local social services.

Decisions are generally put into practice by those civil servants who have executive responsibility (Lipsky 1980). It is at this level that professional or semi-professional discourses enter the picture: they offer a somewhat concise and coherent interpretation of what is required for the programme's concrete implementation. In numerous municipalities, where only a handful of refugees were accepted, it was feasible in practice to have a very ambitious reception programme.

As for integration, what was required? The answer can be found in various reception programmes and job descriptions. The reception and care of refugees was divided into three stages in a manner not entirely typical, but none the less characteristic, of the way social services organised refugee care. The starting point for the work was the assumption that refugees were people 'in chaos' who were to pass through the phases 'introduction', 'attachment' and 'treatment' to become functioning members of society after about one and a half years (Soininen 1992).

The responsibility for this process of 'becoming' lay with the social workers. A kind of therapeutic relationship between the social worker and the refugee was to allow the latter to deal with his or her 'crises'. This is not an exaggerated interpretation as the terms 'weaned from social relations' with the social worker and 'preparation for separation' were used to describe the process.

The work was frequently permeated by the professional norms and practices of the social services department, designed to instruct families in the written and unwritten norms of raising children, family life and social behaviour in the community, as interpreted by the services themselves. The primary goal of the refugee programme was thus to remove any barriers to integration, put a roof over people's heads and even to act in questions such as 'the woman's role in the family'. In smaller communities, where social control was widespread and vital for social cohesion, any deviation from the norm would quickly attract attention and perhaps approbation. Pressure to integrate was applied to refugees and to those responsible for ensuring that integration proceeded as smoothly as possible.

In all its essential details, the reception policy thus followed the traditional working praxis of social services. Refugees and their needs were interpreted in accordance with the picture of the individual applied to 'ordinary' clients. That is those who, often for long periods, had got into a chaotic social and economic situation from which they could not extricate themselves. Working methods developed with clients, who usually had various problems such as drug or alcohol abuse, were used in one form or another with refugees. Social work consisted of listing problems, providing economic support, therapeutic intervention, in certain difficult cases, committing individuals to institutional care, and, finally, general social control (Soininen 1992; Similä 1992).

The prospects for success with such a programme were not always encouraging with the regular clientele, but were significantly better when it came to applying these socio-political ambitions in the refugee programme: the target group of refugees was comprised mainly of socially functioning and independent individuals who had been able to take care of themselves during a large part of their lives. The refugees, as a target group and unlike the social services' permanent clientele, were notable for having quite actively steered their own lives. In the majority of cases they had been politically active and had taken the initiative and fled from their homelands. However, the ascribed role of an incapable person subordinate to the control of the social services could arouse resistance in a number of refugees who wished to maintain control over their own lives and not passively accept the client role on offer.

THE 1991 REFORM: NEW ECONOMIC INCENTIVES

Policies can be described with reference to their basic elements, such as policy formulation, design, realisation and evaluation (Younis 1990). In a policy-cycle model the different phases succeed each other: initiation is followed by a policy decision, its realisation and evaluation and finally through feedback (Premfors 1989). Even if the policy process often deviates from this schematic model, the term policy cycle none the less indicates that policies are not once-and-for-all phenomena, but are best described in terms of an on-going process. Evaluation and feedback provide guidelines for future improvements.

In 1991, the time was ripe for a review of the 1985 care reform. It was also time for the municipalities to be given greater freedom in their working methods and organisation of local work with refugees (Reg. prop. 1989/90: 105). The greatest economic burden on the municipalities, the cost of social benefits, had been covered entirely by state grants during the first three to four years. The new state compensation system meant that the earlier earmarked state grants, compensation for social benefits, Swedish instruction and administrative costs, were replaced by a lump sum for each refugee received. In the government bill, it was stated that the reform aimed to promote measures which would get refugees out into the labour market and make them self-supporting as quickly as possible (Reg. prop. 1989/90: 105). The quicker refugees become self-supporting, the more profitable the deal for the municipality.

Why was there a need for further reform? The 1985 programme was believed to lead to a general pacification of both refugees and municipal praxis. The earmarked grant for social benefits, it was felt, gave the wrong signal. There was no incentive present to speed up the process of integration via the labour market. The measures taken in accordance with the 1985 reform (output), had resulted in unwanted effects (outcome) for refugees and the economy. Behind the final results it was possible to identify an exaggerated 'caring' orientation in the local social services' reception policy which tended to pacify the refugees. In fact, the effects of local care of refugees were all too reminiscent of the earlier much criticised reception programme administered by the National Labour Market Board at the end of the 1970s. Instead of pacification arising from long waits in refugee camps, the municipal programme had itself achieved the same unwelcome result.

Contradictory goals and a lack of resources and time often contribute to policy failure. Another important factor is the commitment and effort of those implementing the policy and how they can be utilised, without losing control of the direction in which they are working (Lippincott and Stoker 1992). One possible solution is to choose a policy design based on those values which are to be promoted and, thereafter, an organisational solution which best supports those values (Stoker 1989). The choice of local social services to take care of refugees had, quite logically, pushed the profession's traditional values of caring and clientalisation to the fore. Another kind of organisational solution would probably have promoted other values.

A totally different explanation for possible failure can be found in the criticism which has been directed at those theories which present public policies as exercises in 'means' and 'ends' rationality, based upon certain knowledge. According to the critics, that type of knowledge is unrealisable in the real world of policy processes (for example, Lindblom 1959, 1979; Van de Ven 1983; Gregory 1989). While the rational picture describes an ideal type, the incrementalist perspective is more attentive to, and perhaps a more adequate description of, the realities of actual policies (Gregory 1989). When these are initiated, decided and implemented, according to the incrementalist school of thought, the theoretical understanding of the different factors which go into the policy, and how they interact, is often low among those who actually make the decisions. Policy formulation and realisation are governed, so it is argued, by the tendency of decision-makers to note factors, values and consequences which are of immediate significance to themselves and which only marginally diverge from the status quo. Limited knowledge of alternatives often means that new policies are only marginal measures so that unintended and unforeseen consequences can easily be managed. As a result, the policy-makers' ability effectively to come up with, and analyse, alternative strategies, will be reduced. This can be said to have been the case with the 1985 refugee reception programme. It is obvious that, in practice, this reception policy only resulted in small shifts away from the earlier, excessively pacifying, policy.

The incrementalist perspective also points out that the decision process consists, in the main, of political and social integration, negotiation and bargaining between groups who protect their competing interests. Given the incrementalist conditions for a policy, the changes in a policy, and thus also in the refugee reception routines, ought not to be seen as a function of concrete policy goals (Gregory 1989). Perhaps it was a similar insight which lay behind the government's 1991 decision about the new state grant system. Instead of focusing upon new goals for the local work with refugees, the government took steps to change the economic interest structure between the state and the municipalities, an intervention which was supposed to be a more effective instrument for achieving the desired results, namely, to ensure that the municipalities were more effective in getting refugees into the labour market.

STRATEGIES AND FAILURES: THE 1991 REFORM

The 1991 reform actually resulted in a greater cost awareness in the municipalities (Bäck and Soininen 1993). As early as 1989, before the new government grant regulations of 1991 were introduced, the National Labour Market Board, The Swedish Association of Local Authorities and the National Immigration Board had reached an agreement on workplace training measures for refugees. The responsibility for acquiring practical work training lay with the local state employment exchange together with the municipal refugee reception services and local trade union organisations. The majority of municipalities had therefore initiated projects directed at the labour market. Co-operation between the refugee services and the state-run employment exchanges often involved offering courses where instruction in Swedish, work training and labour market orientation were combined with one another. Other activities included testing individuals abilities, work trials, drawing up a plan of action, information in the form of a study guide, labour market information and study visits. The refugee services contributed with advice on the educational requirements of specific refugee groups, and supported the labour market authorities whose earmarked state grants financed the study and training programmes.

Paradoxically, after 1991 the number of state-financed projects, often those measures specifically designed to help refugees into the labour market in the municipalities, decreased. In the spring of 1991, six out of ten municipalities with refugee quotas had some form of state financed project for the benefit of refugees. By 1992, the figure was down to four out of ten (Bäck and Soininen 1993). Also, by the spring of 1992, only a small minority (20 per cent) of refugees who had gone through the reception programme and were now ready to enter the labour market, had a regular job (Bäck and Soininen 1993).

Why then was the situation worsened when the 1991 reform was expressly designed to promote measures likely to make refugees self-supporting? The main reason lay in the fact that the opportunities available to local employment exchanges to carry out their key role, in the new reception programme, were inadequate. The state-run local exchanges were not integrated into the municipal infrastructure. Secondly, they were, at that time, also the object of other ongoing administrative changes. The National Labour Market Board had initiated an extensive programme of renewal at the beginning of 1991 with, among other things, consequences for the county council labour boards' guidelines and operations. New rules now applied for those resources intended to finance special measures to help refugees and immigrants. They were no longer to be earmarked. The Board's internal development towards greater management by objectives was followed by the delegation of prioritising decisions to the regional and local level. As a result of this, evident in plans for the period 1990/1 to 1992/3, the space devoted to refugees' and immigrants' needs had been significantly reduced after 1990/1 (Tunevall 1992).

It was obvious that regional and local employment authorities in 1991/92 had followed priorities in the matter of refugees other than those earlier derived from the central Board. Hence, there was a lack of resources for local employment exchanges to finance projects for refugees.

In general, it is the so-called 'social division of planning' between and within the relevant public and private actors which determines actual policy decisions and their realisation (Booth 1988). That coordination can sometimes be very insufficient is well illustrated by the 1991 reform. When the government sought to make the flow of refugees into the labour market more effective with the 1991 state grant reform, its policy was more or less obstructed by the new management policy of the Labour Market Board, which had abolished earmarking resources for immigrants and refugees, a step which can been seen as especially unfortunate at a time of high unemployment and stiffer competition for the Board's limited resources.

IMMIGRANTS AND THE LABOUR MARKET: PROBLEMATIC PRACTICES

In his study of the working careers of labour immigrants in Sweden from the 1950s and 1960s, Ekberg notes that they have tended to stay at the same level of pay, with poor working conditions and a high unemployment risk (Ekberg 1988). His study also shows that, while the position of these categories in the labour market is comparable to that of the population as a whole, those who arrived later, political refugees, experienced significantly higher levels of unemployment. Other studies also show that refugee ties to the labour market are weak (Andersson 1992). A study from 1993 by Ekberg investigates the social and geographic mobility of immigrants (Ekberg 1993). He notes that labour immigrants were concentrated in areas where service and industrial production were most expansive, and that the mobility of these immigrants has been limited to repatriation to the country of origin. A study of a car plant in southern Sweden was published 1994 in which the workings of an internal labour market, recruitment and promotion, access to training, job levels, education and the position of women were examined (Schierup and Paulson 1994). The results indicate that immigrants were systematically disadvantaged in virtually all aspects of working life in the plant.

Factors behind the exclusion of immigrants from the labour market are often divided into structural factors, including developments within the labour market and economic developments, and individual factors such as the cultural characteristics of immigrants themselves.

According to the estimations of municipal refugee coordinators, the employment situation is seen as decisive for refugees' chances to get a job and become self-supporting. In 90 per cent of municipalities during 1991/2, the labour market situation was judged to be the main cause of difficulty in finding work for refugees. Educational background and lack of skill in Swedish were also mentioned as important factors in a great number of municipalities. Even the attitude of employers is considered to play a significant role, with differences between the public and the private sector being noted. The attitudes of private employers were identified more often as a reason why refugees had difficulties in getting a job than those of public employers (Bäck and Soininen 1993).

Some of the causes behind the difficulties faced by refugees and immigrants when trying to get work concern their objective characteristics, such as lack of relevant skills or education, qualifications not suited to the Swedish labour market, and language difficulties. Another explanation points to ethnic discrimination in the labour market. Discrimination in the labour market is particularly serious because it not only makes it hard to find work or a job commensurate with one's qualifications, it also undermines attempts to integrate refugees and immigrants into society as a whole. Despite the existence of the ILO convention and legislation forbidding ethnic discrimination in many countries, numerous international studies testify to its existence.

In Sweden, ethnic discrimination in the labour market has usually been discussed in the context of more general national investigations concerning immigrants and employment. A 1984 national report lists the experience of discrimination at the hands of employers among immigrants (SOU 1984: 55; SOU 1983: 18). A later national report notes that immigrants encounter problems in the labour market linked to their ethnicity, that they feel themselves to be discriminated against and that the occurrence of ethnic discrimination cannot be excluded (SOU 1989: 14). Wadensjö has, among other things, paid attention to the question of highly educated immigrants in Sweden and their relatively low salaries, in his report 'Earning of Immigrants with Higher Education In Sweden' (Wadensjö 1992).

Swedish legislation includes the protection afforded by the 1974 constitution which recognises that all people are equal regardless of race or ethnic identity. The law against ethnic discrimination in working life was taken by the parliament as late as 1994. The first part of the law follows the previous law from 1986 against ethnic discrimination, and has been expanded to include a second part governing employment and the sanctions against unjustified negative special treatment of both employees and job applicants. The law is part of civil law, in keeping with the existing regulation of the labour market. According to the law, the Office of the Discrimination Ombudsman (DO) is supposed to prosecute in cases which are likely to have significant consequences for developing legal praxis, or cases which are significant for other special reasons. Otherwise, the goal is to reach agreement between the two sides in the dispute.

The 1994 law is not without its problems. One difficulty is finding cases that can be taken up by the work tribunal so that legal praxis can be developed. Given the way that law is formulated, it is extremely difficult. During the first year of the law, the DO received some 75 written complaints about suspected ethnic discrimination, but neither the DO, or an employee organisation were able to use the law to press charges and have the case tried in a work tribunal (Arbetsdomstol) (Soininen and Graham 1995, 1997).

However, there have existed for some time a number of other laws and regulations which implicitly forbid ethnic discrimination. For example, we can mention the DO, which was founded in 1986, whose role is noted in an ILO report from 1991 (Zegers de Beijl 1991). There is also the handbook for workplace relations and discrimination which has been available since 1987 due to the initiative of the labour market organisations and SIV, and the National Immigration Board.

The ILO attaches particular importance to legislation, but also accords certain authorities, such as ombudsmen, an important role in attempting to tackle the problem. It is not difficult to agree with the point made by Zegers de Beijl (1991) that 'By enacting rigorous anti-discrimination laws the legislator can define, promote and enforce a society's goal of ensuring effective equality of opportunity and treatment ... which will serve as a last remedy for victims of discrimination.' The 'Joint Declaration on the Prevention of Racial Discrimination and Xenophobia and the Promotion of Equal Treatment at the Workplace', issued by the European social partners at the Social Dialogue Summit in Florence in 1995, also makes a contribution to preventing and combating ethnic discrimination at the workplace. In several countries, legislation against ethnic discrimination in the labour market has existed for some considerable time. Before 1994, however, Sweden had chosen to go down another road. There are several reasons for this.

LEVELS OF CONFLICT AND CORPORATISM

The likelihood of conflict surrounding a proposed policy may influence its content. Classifying policies into separate typologies has been questioned, among other reasons, because most policies are multidimensional. In addition, it has been argued that it is ultimately the perspective of those who finally implement the policy which determines its character and not some form of objective categorisation of its content (May 1986). The level of conflict, which varies between policy questions and areas has, however, been shown to have an effect on both the policy formulation process and policy content (Lowi 1972).

Perhaps the Swedish delay in legislating against ethnic discrimination in the labour market can partly be explained by the fact that the issue is, potentially, one of high levels of conflict. The issues which are usually characterised by high conflict levels include the distribution of resources where both the winner and loser can be identified. Low conflict issues include, for example, the creation of new bodies or regulation policies. So, measures like the creation of the new state authority, the DO in 1986, is a low conflict way of trying to solve the problem of discrimination. However, given that it is possible to identify a winner and a loser when one legislates to prevent negative special treatment, then it ought to increase the element of conflict involved.

A different explanation for an absence of Swedish legislation can be found in the special character of Swedish state administration. If one stresses the role of the state behind anti-discrimination policies, one is likely to give a misleading picture of the Swedish context. Unlike most other countries, it is the labour market partners, represented by their organisations, especially the LO (Swedish Trade Union Confederation), TCO (Confederation of Professional Employees) and SAF (Swedish Employers' Confederation), which, in practice, are responsible for essential parts of the labour market and work environment policy. This Swedish tradition, of the state handing over responsibility to the labour market partners, as far as this is feasible, is grounded in the special circumstances usually associated with the Swedish model. By international standards the trade union movement is very well organised and 80–90 per cent of employees are organised in two large unions. This has made it possible for these organisations to influence the initiation of legislation, the drawing up of legislation in government committees, the making of decisions and the realisation and evaluation of labour market and employment policies. Responsibility for the formulation and execution of anti-discrimination policies in Sweden is also located at the level of the labour market partners, rather than that of the state. And finally, even these government decisions which affect the concrete realities of the workplace are, to a significant extent, implemented through, by and together with the labour market partners.

The Swedish model has clear corporate characteristics, where labour market organisations are important actors along with the State. Internationally, this is a rather unique arrangement, that is, those who are the subject of legislation are allowed a major say in how it is formed and implemented. Instead of civil servants in bureaucracies or professional agents, it is representatives or ombudsmen for these organisations who are the central actors in this model (Rothstein 1991). In particular, measures that affect the work environment and the labour market, and which require adjustment to local conditions are not considered suitable for the classic legal-bureaucratic model. The corporate organisational model influences both the content of public discourse and policy decisions. The agenda-setting of questions related to anti-discrimination policies and the position of refugees and immigrants in the labour market is therefore affected by the division of labour and relations between the labour market authorities and organisations.

Discrimination in the workplace is also a clear example of a question situated in the 'grey zone', between the state and the private sphere. When attention is directed solely to legislation, it misses the fact that the policy area is structured by the division of labour between private and public bodies. Generally, public policies are often realised in increasingly multi-organisational contexts where national and local, as well as public and private goals, work together and where responsibility is shared by a number of representatives of different private and public actors (Hanf and Scharf 1978). This is, of course, especially true in the case of anti-discrimination policies. Here are to be found the determinants of public discourse and practice. But even if labour market organisations are central actors alongside the authorities they are, of course, also subjects of state policies. In part, they are governed by national laws and recommendations dealing with discrimination in the world of work and, in part, they are the subjects of the national management policies which allow them a central role and responsibility for the formulation and realisation of policies in this area.

The central role of the trade unions in formulating policy may be unique for Sweden. But even in the international context, the willingness of labour market organisations to adopt and implement anti-discrimination policies in everyday contexts is of crucial importance for controlling ethnic discrimination. There is a need to involve private and state actors to combat the problem. A focus upon the initiation, formulation and implementation of policies within the corporate policy-making and implementation context is therefore of international interest.

In most other countries, the trade union movement – not least for religious reasons – is often too fragmented and lacks the necessary organisation to perform the role it does in Sweden. Although it is said that the Swedish model is currently being dismantled, the corporate organisational model still helps us to understand policy design. The argument for not legislating against ethnic discrimination was, especially, that it was a matter for the labour market partners, rather than for direct state intervention in the form of legislation (SOU 1983: 18).

In organisational contexts it is often a question of having to deal in parallel with conflicting and mutually exclusive demands where resources are scarce. A popular strategy is to stress common values and ideologies in order to bring different interests into line with each other. Giving priority to ideological management, rather than other forms, has become increasingly common in society (Czarniawska-Joerges 1988). For example, structurally determined ethnic discrimination can be redefined and transformed into a question of personal relations in the workplace and a common concern for all without threatening the interests of any specific group. One possible alternative is to mobilise power and authority or sequentially deal with demands made by members in an organisation (Jacobson 1989). Thus, for example, questions of ethnic discrimination might receive attention during a certain period, only to be replaced by other members' interests, like gender discrimination, at a later date. In other words, trade union and state anti-discrimination policies ought not to be seen as isolated phenomena, but must be seen in the context of overarching demands and interests. It is especially important, given that the trade union movement in contemporary Sweden is becoming increasingly heterogeneous as regards the interests and groups it represents (Micheletti 1988).

Partly due to the corporate organisational model, the rather narrow, traditional trade union questions have given way to a much broader range of issues in Sweden (Rothstein 1991). As organisations have grown larger and stronger, membership has become more heterogeneous with ever more specific interests, and a consequent expansion of the organisational field of interest. The fact that a number of today's trade union members have an immigrant background has also contributed to this trend. While most of their interests coincide with other employees, they do have their own special demands. One of these is an effective anti-discrimination policy covering recruitment, training and education, promotion, working relations and working environment.

A study of anti-discrimination policies of labour market organisations and authorities from initiation to evaluation, and how these policies are related to each other, is needed in order to give an adequate account of the relationship between the incidence of ethnic discrimination and the policies directed against it, as well as the support such policies enjoy in everyday contexts. The occurrence of discrimination ought not, then, to be seen only in the light of direct state measures – their extent and efficiency – or lack thereof. At best, such measures can have a presumptive effect or function as a last resort for victims of discrimination.

So far, Swedish studies of ethnic discrimination in the labour market have, to a large extent, focused upon knowledge of actual discrimination and the experiences immigrants have of such discrimination. Less attention has then been paid to the actor-oriented questions about mechanisms and policies which make discrimination possible. The processes which result in discrimination are poorly understood and should receive more attention. The focus ought to be upon the social actor's routine – conscious and unconscious – reproduction of discriminatory practices, in the structured contexts of working life, to a greater extent than before. The social networks of immigrants and of private and public employers, as well as recruitment practices and organisational cultures, ought to be related to the position of refugees and immigrants in society and to the anti-discrimination policies which labour market organisations represent and implement (Graham 1994).

Without closer ties to a more overarching policy analysis there is a risk that establishing the existence of discrimination will be no more than a 'victim' study in which the experience and occurrence of discrimination are the main objects of analysis. A shift in perspective on to actors in the labour market and their more or less successful anti-discrimination policies is needed. When viewed as a problem in a wider perspective, we are obliged to expand our field of interests to include questions of power and its structure within society.

A policy does not only include active measures but also 'the action and non-action of the system in response to the demands made on it ...' (Jenkins 1978). This includes non-decisions and non-policies which are answers to demands raised by society's members. In theory, there are questions and needs which can clearly be seen by many as problems, but which are never allowed to appear on the political agenda or become the focus for political decisions. Alternatively, policies which have been decided on are never implemented (Crenson 1971; Jenkins 1978).

In general, policies can be said to consist of both an explicit declaration and non-decisions. Policies designed to combat ethnic discrimination are no exception. Non-decisions can be seen as the result of a decision but a decision whose result is difficult to discover (Bachrach and Baratz 1971). Hence questions which might threaten the decision-makers' interests or values, for example the interests of the majority of union members, are prevented from appearing in the decision-making arena. Politicisation of a potential conflict can be blocked with the help of a non-decisions strategy, especially when certain groups and their demands are excluded from the decision-making centre, which is to a large extent the case with refugees and immigrants in Sweden. Potential conflicts due to their interests are thus avoided. Whether we focus on political representation or representation within labour market organisations these groups are poorly represented, if they are represented at all (Bäck and Soininen 1996). Such a lack of representation can easily lead to a distortion of questions in public discourse and debate, which are of direct interest to these groups (see, for example, Grillo 1985). Possible explanations for the absence of issues on the decision-making agenda can therefore be found in the policy-area's power structure.

Power structures can suppress questions and prevent them from being aired in the first place. Even a pluralistic system, whether political or organisational, can, in practice, exclude certain groups and their demands. Policies which are built upon non-decisions can be tracked down in several ways (Jenkins 1978). One way to identify the kinds of questions which are the subject of non-decisions is to locate areas of conflict and the need for controls. In addition, one can identify demands which have been branded illegal or irrelevant and have thereby been eliminated from the system. A not unusual method for neutralising the object of a non-decision is to set up an investigation. More visible strategies are the use of threats or sanctions, whether positive or negative.

But only when power struggles between actors give observable results can non-decisions be studied (Lukes 1974). In cases where both parties accept the status quo, and no demands are made, conflict itself cannot be identified. The prevailing ideology together with the conscious striving by decision-makers to maintain the status quo can then explain why certain types of demand are never formulated. One can then speak of power's third dimension, the power over thought, as a possible explanation of non-questions and non-policies.

CONCLUDING REMARKS

Atkin (1993), in a study of the consumer perspective within British public services seen through the eyes of minorities, provides us with an example of power's third dimension. The relation between minorities and society in Britain is often seen exclusively in terms of the problematic cultural practices of Black people. Similarly, ethnic discrimination in the labour market can also be seen, at first glance, as a question of the problematic cultural practices of immigrants and refugees, rather than as a result of public policies that reproduce the power structures which give sustenance to problem definitions of this type in the first place.

Consequently, a central question must be the design and implementation of public policies against ethnic discrimination in the world of work, which both the labour market authorities and organisations actually support. How, for example, does the internal policy-making process within the trade unions work and what role, if any, do immigrant trade unionists and their interests play in this process? To what extent does the internal power structure of the organisation mean that the special interests of immigrants are transformed into non-questions once decisions have to be made and the general policy direction formulated?

Another central question concerns the eventual implementation of anti-discrimination policies. In what circumstances and how are these realised both when it comes to the coordination of different private and state actors and in concrete situations in the workplace where discrimination can arise in contexts of recruitment, promotion and further training?

Within an international perspective, an interesting question is that of the labour market organisation's relative power vis-à-vis relations with the state. What special implications does the Swedish corporate model have for tackling ethnic discrimination compared with other countries?

The traditional Swedish labour market policy of full employment with training and retraining has been the way to address the problem of ethnic minority unemployment, but it can be said to have failed to tackle the kind of structural problems which have been identified here. In the mid-1990s, the effectiveness of the traditional Swedish labour market policy has been called into question. Even if some of the criticisms are clearly motivated by political ideologies which oppose state measures, they do point to a realisation that some of the tried-and-tested methods for dealing with unemployment are no longer adequate. Based on what has been said here, this would seem to be even more true of the problems facing immigrants and refugees as they attempt to find work.

More attention therefore needs to be paid to policies and non-policies as well as the institutional actors and mechanisms which allow ethnic discrimination in the labour market to arise and persist, rather than a mere stock-taking of discrimination's frequency and the immigrant experience of it.

REFERENCES

SCB, 'Arbetskraftsundersökningar 1993, 1994'.
Ds A (1978) 'Sverige och flyktingarna'.
Ds A (1981: 11) 'Ett lokalt omhändertagande av flyktingar'.
Ds A (1991) 'Invandrar- och flyktingpolitik'.
SfU (1983/84: 27) 'Socialförsäkringsutskottets betänkande om mottagandet av flyktingar och asylsökanden'.
SOU (1967: 18) 'Invandringen. Problematik och handläggning'. Stockholm: Allmänna förlaget.
SOU (1983: 18) 'Lag mot etnisk diskriminering i arbetslivet. Delbetänkande av diskrimineringsutredningen'. Stockholm: Allmänna förlaget.
SOU (1984: 55) 'I rätt riktning. Etniska relationer i Sverige'. Stockholm: Liber.
SOU (1989: 14) 'Mångfald mot enfald. Stockholm', Allmänna förlaget.

SOU (1992: 69) 'Förbud mot etnisk diskriminering i arbetslivet', Stockholm: Allmänna förlaget.

Regeringens proposition (1983/84: 124) 'Mottagandet av flyktingar och asylsökande m.m.'.

Regeringens proposition (1983/84: 144) 'Invandrings- och flyktingpolitiken'.

Regeringens proposition (1989/90: 105) 'Samordnat flyktingmottagande och nytt system fär ersättning till kommunen, m.m.'.

III
Responses and Implications

12 Migratory Movements: the Position, the Outlook. Charting a Theory and Practice for Trade Unions[1]

Albert Martens

Immigration, the presence of foreigners or workers who are considered not to belong to the 'traditional national or native' community, has always constituted a challenge for organised workers and their unions. Confronting this challenge, the labour organisations have developed – or must develop – several different strategies. They have different objectives and are implemented at different times. The result is that these strategies can appear incoherent or even contradictory. In this chapter, we will try to see to what extent they are or are not incoherent or contradictory. The dimension of 'time and moment' is a strategic variable in understanding the coherence of these strategies.

In considering trade union strategies for combating racism and xenophobia – which is, in fact, a matter of trade union action or practice – two matters must be taken into account, namely, a theory or doctrine and the organisation of (or ability to organise, mobilise and provide guidance to) workers. To be of practical use, any strategy must be based on a policy agenda that analyses and maps out prospects and aims and on the machinery that puts the actions decided upon into effect.

The trade union movement cannot, therefore, any more than any other social movement, dispense with a trade union analysis and theory of immigration or migratory movements as a basis for a trade union strategy (in the present instance, one with which to combat racism and xenophobia).

CONTROLLING NUMBERS AND EQUAL TREATMENT [STRATEGIES I & II]

It might, understandably, come as no small surprise to find this question under consideration as either particularly new or pressing. From the very outset, industrial capitalism sought to impose its own approach, its 'vision'

219

of the world, by reducing work to a commodity, a factor of production to
be bought and sold in a market (euphemistically termed the 'labour market' for the purpose!). The logic of the system, then, made it 'obvious' that
success in business would depend on the ability to locate and hire this
'commodity' at the lowest price. Exploitation of the best and cheapest
'labour reservoirs' was thus encapsulated in the logic of the system.
Where fixed capital was 'tied up' or 'locked in', it was up to labour to
move to it. Where it was less so, however, the company was able to locate
wherever the labour production or reproduction costs were lowest. There
followed unprecedented movements of human beings (daily, weekly, seasonal and semi-permanent), first, within towns, then from the countryside
to towns, and finally between regions, countries and continents.

   In response to this strategy of the capitalist class – and in an effort to
keep the price of labour from falling below labour force reproduction costs
– workers strove to enforce a two-pronged strategy: first, to limit the
labour supply, and second, to demand and impose equal conditions, rules,
and prices (wages). This strategy, which forms part of the theory of union
action, was called by Sidney and Beatrice Webb: 'the device of restriction
of numbers and the device of the common rule' (Webb and Webb 1897).[2]
The trade union aim, then, was to achieve a position in which it could
restrict the number of workers in order to ensure that they enjoyed equal
working conditions. Or, to put it another way, the idea was to acquire a
monopoly over the representation of the labour force.

   The success of this twin strategy depends on a union's ability to organise workers and its ability to impose rules on each and every one of them
and on the employers. To that extent, trade unionism is essentially 'corpo-
ratist' in its intention to protect workers as a collective body against the
continual lowering of labour costs through deregulation.

   In their efforts to secure a high(er) price for labour power, the unions
have not always successfully prevented employers from drawing on new
pools of labour. The aftermath of World War II witnessed a massive influx
of foreign workers into the industrialised countries of Western Europe.
Having failed to stem the flow of immigration (which was vast in certain
industries like coal mining [except in some countries such as the United
Kingdom, for example], engineering, automobile manufacturing, building
and civil engineering, personal services, cleaning, the hotel and catering
trades, and so on), the unions were left with no alternative but to demand
equal treatment and equal pay ('equal pay for equal work').

   The pursuit of these two aims (restriction of numbers and equal conditions) is neither easy nor straightforward for the unions. The strategy has
to be a two-stage one. First, the aim is to prevent employers recruiting

from 'elsewhere' [Strategy I]. (All European countries regulate recruitment of workers from other countries through a system of prohibitions and licenses such as prior employment authorisation, work permits, quotas, and so on.) Should this strategy fail, however, then equal treatment has to be demanded for the newcomers without delay [Strategy II]. It is thus a question of reconstituting the 'labour community' by solidarity with the workers who have come from somewhere else.

That indigenous employed workers should find the transition from one strategy to the other difficult to comprehend, let alone to accept is not in question. Probably, it may even be seen as a partial defeat (or partial victory?). Within the organised labour movement, workers find it hard to understand how and why they should first be mobilised to prevent cheap labour being hired – 'against that of imported foreign labour' – only to find thereafter, when that strategy has failed, they have to welcome those same workers with open arms and prevent them being singled out for exploitation, segregation, and victimisation. Impeccably logical and reasonable as these succeeding strategies may seem, they tend to stick in the throats of the rank and file. The second strategy comes into play only after a defeat, namely, a failure to prevent foreign recruitment, or recruitment of 'foreigners'. Aware as trade union officers may be of the need for such a reversal, few are willing to advertise it in public, or even to admit it. This makes it very hard – failing what might be dubbed the 'psychoanalysis of such collective amnesia' – to get over to trade union members the reasons for campaigning against discrimination, which the newcomers must inevitably suffer.

It is, however, a reversal of the utmost importance and one on which the future of trade unionism depends. It gives perspective and sequence to two distinct stages – first opposition, then imposition, saying to the employers 'we are against this type of recruitment, but if you ignore us and force us to work with these people, then it has to be on equal terms'. Equal treatment thus becomes the condition for acceptance of 'foreigners'. Equality, therefore, conditions acceptance.

HOW FAR DOES THE PRINCIPLE OF EQUALITY GO? [STRATEGY III]
(Introduction of variables: space, time, scope, flow and 'stocks' in the preceding model.)

It can well be imagined that this twin strategy (opposition–imposition) could be developed relatively easily within a given company or branch of industry. It can be put in place and controlled by company or industry trade union officials. It is also found that the 'threat' of wholesale recruitment of foreign or significantly underpaid workers is lower where workers are well organised (where unionisation rates and the ability to mobilise organised action is great) than in poorly unionised industries. Some sectors – such as the civil service, posts and telecommunications, water/gas/electricity – which are veritable 'bastions of trade unionism' have in many countries managed virtually to pull up the drawbridge on employment of foreign workers, while other fiercely competitive ones (coal mining, engineering, motor manufacturing, building and civil engineering, personal services, cleaning, the hotel and catering trades, and so on) have been forced to accept them in large numbers.

There is no doubt that where union presence is strong the working conditions of immigrants or nationals are clearly more 'equal' and better than where the union presence is weak. This is the case, for example, in the coal, iron and steel, and non-ferrous metal industries, where union presence is strong and long-established.

The number and proportion of foreign workers employed in a business or an industry thus becomes an indicator of relatively poor pay, working conditions and unionisation. Note that this is true not only for foreign workers. The changing sex balance in jobs and industries paints a similar picture. A significant presence (in percentage or absolute terms) of women or immigrants in an occupation or industry is a pointer to inadequate working conditions in that occupation or branch (Rubery and Fagan 1993).

This raises the question of labour market segmentation – that is, the systematic allocation of 'low-grade' jobs to the 'weaker' categories of workers – women, immigrants, young people, the chronically unemployed – and the equally systematic preservation of 'high-grade' jobs for the 'strong' categories: men, adults, nationals, those with good quality training or extensive employment experience (Rubery and Fagan 1993: 133).[3]

These questions only become critical, however, when the newcomers have become numerous, geographically widespread and long-term. In other words, where changes in scope become apparent in terms of number, space, and time. These temporo-spatial changes in scope, in turn, give rise to a qualitative leap in the expression of, and solutions to, the problem. For the repeated application of the 'opposition–imposition' strategy (or, if you will, the restriction of numbers and the common rule) may in the long term lead to a wholesale, across-the-board spread in the employment of such workers. This is what happened with Italian workers in the 1950s, with workers from Spain, Greece, Portugal, the Maghreb and Turkey at the end of the 1960s, and with refugees from Africa and the South East in the

1980s. It is now happening again with those from Central and Eastern Europe.

The qualitative, that is, structural, changes brought about in the 'givens' of the problem by this incremental build-up and extension in space and time, necessitating a profound and radical re-assessment of the problem, should neither be under-rated nor ignored.

1. Extended stays and large populations of 'immigrants' – who have not been so for several generations! – makes it increasingly difficult to continue operating the 'opposition–imposition' strategy on a piecemeal basis.
2. Demands for equality (equal treatment, but also a proportional presence in the different occupations and industry branches, access to different levels of responsibility, and so on), are becoming increasingly strident, and it is becoming increasingly difficult to ignore them.
3. This is compounded by EU provisions on free movement and equal treatment, which are increasingly undermining the idea of 'nationals only' jobs, positions, or industries.
4. EU provisions are also creating new rifts between 'foreign' workers – especially between those from other EU member states and those from non-EU countries. The former enjoy advantages that should ultimately place them on par with national workers. The latter enjoy such advantages only if they become naturalised citizens of the host country.
5. Cross-influences between the status of worker and that of nationality also raises the question of citizenship, which may or may not be granted to long-time residents in countries where they are not nationals.

The emancipation of workers within the organised labour movement was not directed solely to improved social and economic conditions but was also concerned with political and cultural emancipation. But many trade union organisations seem to be having a particularly hard time incorporating these areas into the trade union struggle.

For example, the type of institutional framework that should be given to the creed and practices of Islam in Western European countries is a question that trade unions are doing their level best to side-step. And yet it is very important to several million workers.

The permanent and definitive presence of these workers in the production system – which involves a structural change in the job market – is then expressed by new demands that encompass and surpass the union actions in companies and sectors of industry and services. These are more general demands that are intended by the term 'equal opportunity'

[Strategy III]. In other words, it is now a matter of guaranteeing access, advancement, training, pay and the like for all jobs in all sectors without restrictions or limitations for all immigrants or foreigners who already reside, for a specific period of time, in the host country.

POLICY OBJECTIVES AND OUTLOOK [STRATEGY IV]

Given past, present (and future?) migratory flows, what are the possible policy objectives and outlooks for trade union action? An attempt will be made here to outline a selected few here.

(a) Take Account of the Problem as a Complex Whole

The world-wide growth of the capitalist production system (globalisation), and its efforts to shake off the constraints of time and space, continually call into question precisely those measures that must be applied in time and space, especially those connected to migratory movements, which, by their very nature, occur in time and space. The playing field is, therefore, far from level from the outset. The outcome will depend on the ability of the unions to impose global constraints of time and space on capitalist systems. They are far from having a global strategy in this respect, and yet that is precisely what must be built, alongside whatever specific measures may be taken.

(b) Establish Appropriate Strategies in Firms and Industries

That strategies to 'restrict numbers and impose equality' remain effective with regard to new immigration is not in question. Unions must pursue such strategies, therefore, however difficult it may be to put them into practice. Imposing equal treatment seems to me to be an absolute priority and more effective than ever in securing a restriction of numbers. It must be said, however, that trade unions seem to have difficulty in coming to grips with equal treatment:

– What is the object of equal treatment? (fair play or fair scores):
  - Procedures (recruitment, selection, promotion, dismissal, and so on) or
  - Results (actual number of immigrants recruited or employed in different jobs, industry branches, and so on)
– Within what time frame, and for whom and how, is equal treatment to be secured? How is it to be measured, evaluated, controlled?

– Can proactive remedial measures be taken? Will they be contested on the grounds of equal treatment to perpetuate inequality in the status quo? (Discrimination, segregation, concentration, and so on)
– Such proactive remedial measures (equal opportunities policies) must not be confined to combating segregation but must also lead to improved organisation and working conditions in the jobs concerned.

(c) Organise the Struggle for Equal Treatment Jointly with Others

Alliances with other groups engaged in the struggle for equality (women, native minorities, nationals, and so on) must be considered and can be forged. The setting up of permanent monitoring centres to supply aggregate comparative data can be valuable (cf. Employment, Equity Act in Canada, US, UK, and others).

(d) Global Action to Impose Acceptable Working Conditions in All Countries (social clause) [Strategy IV]

The objective of achieving these objectives cannot be confined to a single company, industry or region (country). Actions directed to that end must be pursued in conjunction with international and continental actions (international labour standards, jobs, wages, recruitment, dismissal, working time, protection of minors, women, and so on). Support could be given, for instance, to the inclusion of social clauses designed to limit or prevent goods being imported from countries that deny freedom of association and trade union rights, that tolerate discrimination (on grounds of race, sex, religious or political belief), that do not prohibit child labour and starvation wages. There are at present on the international level several conventions and recommendations of the International Labour Organisation (ILO) or of the United Nations, which, if they were ratified by every state, would constitute a solid social basis for combating social dumping. Unifying equal working conditions world-wide would remove much of the point of migratory movements.

We are, however, aware that, today, the strategy of the 'social clause' is not devoid of a degree of ambiguity (Misplon 1993; see also Delarue 1993; De Smedt 1993). In more economically developed countries, new alliances can arise between employers and unions in order to combat imports from low-wage countries because there the rights of workers are not recognised. This national 'neo-corporatism' of the wealthier countries is challenged by the low-wage countries. Because of it, they contend, their development is hindered and therefore also the possibilities for their workers to acquire better pay and working conditions in the future. The 'social clause' would thus miss its mark. What it is intended to achieve it makes impossible. This criticism is certainly correct. The content of the 'social clause' is largely dependent on the growth of social rights in the welfare state. And this growth occurred over the long history of organised labour. Ultimately, the position adopted by unions in the rich countries will depend on the attitude of organised workers in the low-wage countries themselves. The debate on the subject is certainly not closed. Neo-nationalism and neo-corporatism overshadow the struggle for socio-economic emancipation.

CONCLUSION

From the outset, but also over the course of the years in which massive recourse to the importation of manpower was used by employers, the unions developed, or were compelled to develop, a series of different strategies with respect to employers and 'newly arrived' workers. These strategies, as they have been described above, appeared at different times and can be represented as in Figure 12.1.

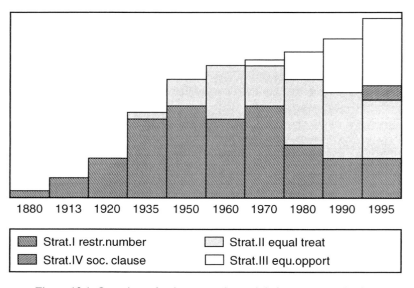

Figure 12.1 Overview of union strategies and their appearance in time.

The first two strategies (I & II), 'opposition–imposition', flow from the very essence of unionism: the collective defence of workers by means of the restriction and control of numbers and the imposition of equality of treatment on all those who are employed in an enterprise or sector. These strategies appear when unionism is a force that cannot be evaded. In Great Britain, these strategies had already appeared around 1850.

When it is no longer possible to prevent the entrance of 'others', one must make sure that the occupation, the employment, operates under equal conditions. The imposition of equality of treatment, then, appears to be a useful way of limiting this kind of recruitment in specific companies or sectors. Nevertheless, the repetition over time of these two strategies could not prevent a structural change in the labour market, the definitive arrival of immigrants, and the constitution of major communities of foreigners in the countries of Western Europe in the 'Golden Sixties'. The members of these communities, then, enter a subsequent phase, demanding for themselves not only equality of treatment when they are employed, but also equal opportunity (including equivalent, proportional representation) (Strategy III). This is a significant generalisation of equality of treatment within, but also outside, the firm. Again, the unions feel challenged, but this time on a much larger scale across all sectors, even for the sectors where this manpower is not or is not yet employed. This third strategy was 'superimposed', in a way, on the two others in the course of the 1970s.

Finally, the generalised globalisation of the production and consumption of goods and services requires unions to demand and impose minimal working conditions and respect for human rights for all production output that would subsequently be exported to countries where unionism is a real force. This is the imposition of the social clause (Strategy IV) on exporting countries and sectors. This strategy is, in a way, the extension and the global generalisation of the demand for equality of treatment and, consequently, is situated between Strategies II and III in the 1990s.

Unionism is thus pressured to develop together (but sometimes also at different moments) four different strategies. It cannot, a priori, omit any of them lest it fail to achieve its final objective, the defence of organised workers.

We find that distinguishing these different fields of application of union action is important to better understanding the degree to which these strategies can become contradictory or complementary. However, it is even more important that they be able to contribute to effectively combating racism and xenophobia.

NOTES

1. This text was presented to the 'Conference on Trade Union Strategies to combat Racism and Xenophobia' organised by the European Trade Union Confederation on 3 and 4 of December 1993, in Brussels. It was revised somewhat, in reaction to the comments and remarks it generated. The theoretical reflection on labour union strategies has been restructured and systematised.
2. 'For the improvement of the conditions of employment, whether in respect of wages, hours, health, safety or comfort, the Trade Unions have, with all their multiplicity of regulations, really two expedients, which we term, respectively, the Device of the Common Rule, and the Device of the Restriction of Numbers' (Webb and Webb 1897: Vol. II (560–1) Chapter XIII – 'The Assumptions of Trade Unionism'). This rule, which is crucial to the future of trade unions, is at the present being dangerously and very insidiously turned on its head, the reasoning being that 'equal treatment will be possible only if the influx of newcomers can be restricted (stemmed)'. Trade unions cannot accept that equal treatment should be made dependent on the successful restriction of migratory flows without imperilling their own action. Restricting migratory movements is, for a series of reasons, being seen to be an increasingly complex not to say impossible proposition. In making this a priority, unions are likely to forfeit their ability to impose equality for a long time to come. In my view, imposing the obligation of equal treatment is beyond all doubt the more effective way of restricting migratory flows.
3. An 'instrument' for measuring the labour market position of minority groups in the labour market is found in Rosvelds et al. 1993, Appendix 2.

13 Employers and anti-Discrimination Measures in Europe: Good Practice and Bad Faith

John Wrench

The evidence presented in many of the chapters in this book is that discrimination and exclusion affect the employment opportunities of migrant workers and their descendants in various European countries in ways still not acknowledged by politicians, employers' organisations, trade unions and others. For many observers, this points to the necessity of strengthening legislation against employment discrimination at a national level in each member state (although some believe that this is not going to happen without the encouragement which comes from an EU Directive against racial and ethnic discrimination, along the lines of that on sex discrimination). In recent years there has been a number of comparisons of national anti-discrimination legislation in European countries (Zegers de Beijl 1991; Forbes and Mead 1992; MacEwen 1995; Wrench 1996). However, this concluding chapter looks not at national measures against discrimination, but at measures at an organisational level. It first presents some examples of 'good practice' in various European countries. Then, given that such examples are still relatively rare in a European context, it sets out evidence which reveals the hostility, misunderstandings and conceptual confusions that frequently underlie resistance to the introduction of anti-discrimination measures in organisations by European employers.[1] Next it explains some of the key differences in national context which help us to understand the contrasting ways that 'anti-discrimination' is perceived and effected in different countries. Finally, it considers whether the business case for such measures is adequate to stimulate their greater introduction, or whether there is an argument for less 'voluntarism' and more compulsion as a means to getting employers to do more.

EQUAL OPPORTUNITY AND ANTI-DISCRIMINATION POLICIES

It has been argued elsewhere that legislation at national level against employment discrimination is an indispensable first step in combating racist exclusion in the labour market. However, it is also clear that legislation alone is not adequate, and alongside this must operate other measures at the level of the organisation. Experience in the United States shows that anti-discrimination legislation is a necessary but not sufficient means of reducing racial discrimination in employment. The effect of such legislation is often that racism becomes more subtle, and that indirect, institutional or unintentional discrimination becomes more important. Therefore, as well as laws against discrimination, there is a need for the stimulation of a range of social policy initiatives against racism and discrimination, including equal opportunities programmes, codes of practice, positive action, education and information provision, and training. The law can be used not just to prohibit, but to allow, to encourage and to facilitate. It can provide a stimulus for employers to undertake 'voluntary' action, such as adopting equal opportunity policies. Such policies are 'voluntary', in that they go beyond legal minimum requirements on employers, although they are perhaps not entirely 'voluntary' in countries where they are introduced by an employer to avoid possible trouble with anti-discrimination legislation.

An equal opportunity policy consists of a set of aims and procedures adopted by an organisation which can be summarised in a public statement and made known to all employees. An equal opportunity policy could include several or all of the following measures:

- measures to avoid discrimination in recruitment, selection, dismissals and redundancies;
- procedures against racial harassment;
- measures to allow for cultural and religious difference;
- the ethnic monitoring of job applicants and employees;
- positive action measures to stimulate ethnic minority applications;
- equality targets for recruitment;
- anti-discrimination training.

Thus equal opportunity practices are not the same thing as integration measures. Generally speaking, the activities we are concerned with here do not include integration measures such as the provision of language training to migrants, nor measures to improve service delivery to minority populations by, for example, social work agencies or voluntary organisations. The emphasis is instead on the practices within organisations that are designed to facilitate equal access of migrant and ethnic minority workers to jobs, training, promotion, and, so on, and to reduce discrimination, prejudice and xenophobia in the workplace. In this sense the targets of such policies are more likely to be employees from the white or national majority, rather than migrants or ethnic minorities themselves.

EXAMPLES OF EMPLOYERS' POLICIES IN EUROPE

There are examples to be found of equal opportunity and anti-discrimination measures in various European countries. For example, the Netherlands has long experience of private and public sector equal opportunity measures, and also has codes of practice for different sectors: for employment agencies, for labour exchanges and for the Ministry of the Interior. Research by the Association of Dutch Municipalities (Vereniging Nederlandse Gemeenten) (Mulder 1991), demonstrated that of all 672 local municipalities in the Netherlands, 116 (20.7 per cent) of them were taking positive action measures for non-natives, either for non-natives in general, or for specific groups, in particular Surinamese, Antilleans, Moluccans, Turks and Moroccans. Over 80 per cent of the municipalities that were taking positive action measures operated a preference policy in the selection of employees. For most of these, this implied a preference for a non-native in the case of equally qualified applicants. Targets were being used by a quarter of the municipalities that were taking positive action measures. Over 40 per cent of them found that the relative number of non-natives in their employment had increased, although this increase was to be found mainly in the lowest salary scales. In 1988 Amsterdam adopted a policy to strive for a proportional representation of ethnic minorities in the municipal workforce, related to the composition of the Amsterdam population (21 per cent). In 1992 the total contribution of non-natives in the workforce had risen to 10.1 per cent, of whom the larger part consisted of Surinamese. A number of municipalities stipulated that grants or licences to institutions or private persons would not be granted, or would be withdrawn, if the institution or private person was found to be guilty of racial discrimination (Gras and Bovenkerk 1995).

In Sweden, examples of positive policies are found in the public sector. For example, Stockholm County Council (SLL) is the largest employer of immigrants in the country and maintains a recruitment policy within which the bilingualism of immigrants is weighted as a positive advantage in job applications. An SLL action plan 'Immigrants in Work and Education' (1991) sets out a number of goals, including recruiting employees with 'language and cultural skills', ensuring that the competence of highly educated immigrants is utilised in work which matches their qualifications, educating personnel in the prevention of ethnic discrimination, and ensuring that cases of discrimination are dealt with effectively. In the private sector, however, such initiatives are almost unknown, being in the most part in the form of information and persuasion rather than practical anti-discrimination measures (Soininen and Graham 1995). One exception has been Telia, formerly Sweden's public telecommunications service. This company has introduced a plan for ethnic equality couched in terms of business efficiency, with advertisements encouraging immigrants with a knowledge of foreign languages to apply, and a group set up to monitor issues of equal opportunity for women and employees from an ethnic minority background.

The UK has many examples of equal opportunity and anti-discrimination policies. Although generally speaking it is the public sector which has embraced these most strongly, many sectors of private sector employment in the UK also exhibit an acceptance of equal opportunity measures, with some even positively enthusiastic about them, particularly in the retail sector. The WH Smith retail group, the Midland Bank, the John Laing construction company, Tate & Lyle Ltd and British Gas are all organisations cited as case studies of good practice in a 1995 campaign by the Commission for Racial Equality (CRE). Many were taking an audit of their employees and working actively to goals of recruiting a greater proportion of their staff from ethnic minority communities. Employers have been encouraged in this field by both the Department for Education and Employment's Race Relations Employment Advisory Service, and the CRE, which introduced in 1984 the 'Code of Practice for the Elimination of Racial Discrimination and the Promotion of Equal Opportunity in Employment'. In autumn 1992 a UK publication, *Equal Opportunities Review* (EOR), carried out a survey of its subscribers to identify which initiatives are being undertaken by employers to promote equal opportunities for ethnic minorites. The most popular initiatives were the provision of guidance on race equality to recruiters and selectors, and recruitment initiatives to encourage ethnic minority applicants.

Evidence from other European countries is much more patchy. In Belgium, long-standing resistance to special measures is beginning to change, and there have recently been positive action schemes initiated with the collaboration of the Fondation Roi Baudouin to encourage employers to adopt such measures (Martens 1995). In Denmark a national retail chain store and a public transport employer in the Århus region have implemented recent initiatives on the employment of migrants. These are characteristic of the somewhat isolated cases to be found in many other countries, and there are some countries where such examples seem to be difficult to find at all (Wrench 1996). Across the EU as a whole, more common than a willingness to embrace anti-discrimination measures is a general resistance to them.

EVIDENCE OF RESISTANCE TO EQUAL OPPORTUNITY MEASURES

In 1994 the European Foundation for the Improvement of Living and Working Conditions (EFILWC) launched a project 'Preventing Racism at the Workplace in the European Union'. It commissioned a report from each of the 15 member states (plus Norway) on, amongst other things, measures against racism and discrimination in employment in each country. Whilst some of these national reports could identify the sorts of 'good practice' examples set out above, in the context of the EU as a whole such cases still constitute a relatively insignificant body of activity. More notably, there was found to be a widespread resistance by employers to the ideas of anti-racist and anti-discrimination initiatives. Resistance could be rooted in different things, such as arguments of opposition to constraints on the free market operations of business, philosophies about the principle of racially or ethnically specific policies as opposed to universalistic measures, or confusion, ignorance or misapprehension about the true nature of such measures.

Amongst employers and their associations across Europe the conviction is common that state encouragement of anti-discrimination practices is an unwarranted interference in the operation of the free-market, and that equal opportunity measures constitute a totally unnecessary shackling of industry with unworkable restrictions. For example, one study conducted in 1992 in the Brussels region, covering 30 import/export companies, 20 banks and 20 insurance companies (Van Roost and Buyse 1992), revealed that employers were quite hostile to the introduction of even basic equal opportunities measures, rejected the idea of any intervention by the public authorities that may restrict their freedom in the selection process, and even rejected the suggestion that certain phrases should be added to job advertisements to encourage immigrants to apply. The resistance to special policies on discrimination is backed up by a battery of arguments which collectively conclude that such devices are at best unnecessary, at worst counter-productive and that there is 'no problem anyway'.

The various arguments and ideologies of resistance commonly expressed by employers in Europe can be categorised under a number of headings.

1. 'No Problem Here'

The assumption which most commonly categorises the arguments of resistance is that there is 'no problem here'. In general, in societies with egalitarian ideologies and where racism and discrimination are viewed as objectionable, there is a tendency to deny that a problem exists. The 'denial of racism' is found at many levels, from whole nations to individuals. National politicians often emphasise how in their respective countries the word 'racism' cannot be applied in the context of their laws, their traditions and their populations (van Dijk 1993). In different countries there are often different arguments as to why racism is not endemic in their society. For example, where a country has no history of major colonial oppression of non-white people, this is seen to be the reason for an 'absence of racism' in society. In traditional countries of emigration it is often stated that people are sympathetic to the experiences of migrants. These and other reasons are used as explanations as to why there is 'no racism here'.

A national lack of awareness on the issue can be reflected lower down in the institutional culture of organisations. In France, the Central Services of the Paris Labour Inspectorate told researchers in 1994 that they had never undertaken any research on racial discrimination and, accordingly, were unable to provide any information whatsoever on the subject. One labour inspector pointed out that racism and racial discrimination at places of recruitment and employment are 'not part of our working culture. Discrimination on grounds of trade union activity and sex, yes, but racism and racial discrimination, no' (De Rudder et al. 1995). Employers readily subscribe to this view. An employee of a French public employment agency told the same research team:

> In the 25 years I have worked [in this department], I have never heard anybody say 'I don't want anybody from another race'. I have my doubts as to what happens in reality. It is the foreign workers themselves who are most worried about it … They are afraid of being rejected. If they are turned down for a job, they reassure themselves by putting it down to the colour of their skin, though in fact, if they are not taken on, it is because they are not profitable.

In Germany, research suggests that equal opportunity or positive action policies are generally absent, because there is thought to be 'no problem'. Employers tend to think that such policies are unnecessary, because everybody already has equal opportunities – every worker is treated in the same way, everybody has the same access to training and further qualifications

(Räthzel and Saricca 1994). The term 'discrimination' is a contested one in Germany – the view is common that one can only talk about discrimination when migrant workers are paid less in the same job as an indigenous worker (see Baker and Lenhardt 1991). Räthzel (1995) argues that in Germany, both at national and company level, one of the main obstacles to preventing racism and discrimination is the lack of awareness about the existence of everyday racism and discrimination at the workplace. In her research, management representatives all claimed there were no conflicts between migrant and indigenous workers. This is also the official opinion of the employers' federation (Arbeitgeberverband). In an issue of their journal they assured the public: 'In companies, integration of migrant fellow-citizens is a reality and social equality is realised. The pragmatic relationship between colleagues who work together towards a common goal and depend on each other does not know of any resentment against aliens' (*Der Arbeitgeber*, No. 20/45, 1993, p. 721). The same thing is said by works council representatives and indigenous shop stewards. Correspondingly, German companies were found to have very few measures for preventing racism, reflecting the general view in Germany that anti-discrimination policy is unnecessary, because there is no general discrimination against the migrant population.

Of course, in theory it is quite possible that a 'no problem here' opinion could indeed largely reflect reality. The problem arises when such opinions are expressed in a context where there is at least *prima facie* evidence from other sources that racial or ethnic discrimination exists, and where there is an absence of research or other investigation into the circumstances and experiences of migrants.

2. 'Colour-blindness'

Individual employers will often declare an emphatic 'colour-blindness' along with a corresponding assumption that notions of 'equal treatment' means that they cannot countenance any special measures for migrants. Employers will say, 'I don't care what colour they are – white, black or blue – we treat them all the same' (see Lee and Wrench 1983; Jenkins 1986; van Dijk 1993). This (often mistaken) view that minorities are always treated the same as everyone else leads to a refusal to concede that there could be any special policy needs. The problem is that as racism and discrimination affect only the visible minorities within a workforce, then certain measures to address the resulting inequality will often apply only to those groups. However, many employers are strongly opposed to any measures which do not apply equally to all workers. For example, the policy of the Danish Employers' Association (Dansk Arbejdsgiverforening) is that refugees and immigrants should not be regarded as a special group. The rights and obligations of foreign nationals, they argue, are regulated by the same laws and regulations as apply to Danish citizens. The fact that foreign nationals are guaranteed equal conditions of employment, pay, vacation and unemployment insurance as Danes means that there is no need for any special measures (Hjarnø 1995). Martens (1995) describes how in the early 1980s the reason for not including protection against discrimination in employment in Belgian law was that such protection would be seen by other workers as a privilege 'and might therefore reinforce rather than combat xenophobia'. A study of employers in Hamburg, Germany (Haugg 1994) found an under-representation of migrant apprentices, but also that interviewing panels rejected the idea of encouraging migrants to apply. They even felt that including the sentence 'We welcome applications by young people of migrant origin' in an advertisement would contravene the principle of equal treatment. 'Equal treatment' by this logic is seen solely as migrant workers getting the same pay for the same work. The fact that there are hardly any other German workers doing the same work is not seen to be a problem, and the factors which have led to this segregation at work, and the channelling of migrants into the least desirable, lowest paid and most unhealthy work, are not critically examined (Räthzel 1995; see also in this volume).

3. Blaming the Victim

'Blaming the victim' is very common in public discourse and in the literature on the origins of racism. Discriminatory practices are often rationalised or legitimated by the perpetrators, and a common device is to explain it away in terms of the character of those who are discriminated against. There are different versions of the 'blaming the victim' syndrome. One is to see the major problem to lie within a lack of education, qualifications, language or experience on the part of the migrant workers. The other is to emphasise the factor of 'cultural difference' to explain patterns of inequality.

In the UK, a noticeably higher rate of industrial injuries for ethnic minority workers was assumed to be the result of factors to do with the 'newness' of a migrant population: for example, rural migrant workers might be unfamiliar with industrial work; language difficulties might lead to problems in understanding safety instructions; or injuries may reflect a syndrome of maladjustment and stress from the social disruption of the migration process. There was even the idea that a 'cultural proneness' might exist for those ethnic minority groups which exhibited a cultural 'fatalism' towards the occurrence of injuries. In fact, a study of 4,000 accidents in the Midlands demonstrated that the apparent predisposition to suffer injuries was entirely attributable to the fact that migrant and ethnic minority workers were over-represented in the more dangerous jobs. The commonsense 'blaming the victim' explanations had been entirely inappropriate (Lee and Wrench 1980).

French researchers encountered the view that if discrimination occurs, it is probably due to differences in levels of qualification, language comprehension, or physical aptitude of migrants. Thus complaints of racism can be dismissed as advanced by people who do not have the cultural and behavioural attributes that fit naturally into the openings provided by the labour market (De Rudder et al. 1995; see also Vourc'h et al. in this volume). Differences *between* individual foreign population groups are also seen as deriving from their respective 'cultural characteristics': some are seen as experiencing more difficulty in 'integrating within the firm', whilst others are seen to show more 'dynamism' (De Rudder et al.). Similarly, Räthzel (1995) found in Germany that migrant workers were seen as a problem because of their assumed lack of qualifications or poor command of the German language. The unequal distribution of migrant workers within a company's hierarchy is not seen to be an effect of direct or indirect discrimination (if unequal distribution is acknowledged at all) but rather as a consequence of migrants' lack of skills, language and qualifications. The 'cultural' argument is also current in Germany, with the idea that migrants have an 'alien culture' and do not fit well into German society. There is a widespread assumption that the more 'distant' the culture of the migrant is from the culture of the host country, the more problems there will be (Räthzel 1995). Hjarnø (1995) writes that a comparable 'blaming the victim' discourse has evolved in Denmark, in which the alleged lack of knowledge of the refugees and immigrants of the language and culture of the majority, and their insistence on maintaining their own cultural and religious traditions, are seen as the cause of all their problems.

4. Misconceptions about Racism and Discrimination

It is often the case that politicians and policy-makers are willing to condemn racism if it is seen as the activity of unrepresentative right-wing extremists. They are less willing to undertake action which would imply that racism in both its ideological and practical manifestations forms part of the structure of their society, operating routinely in the allocation of services, housing and jobs. There is therefore a readily accepted view that racism should be defined only as the sort of untypical behaviour exhibited by extremists, a marginal problem originating from deprived youth or right-wing fringe groups. Sometimes only direct, overt violence is regarded as racism. It is true that, in Germany, for example, racism or 'hostility towards foreigners' has only become a serious object of concern for companies and trade unions since violent racist attacks against people of migrant origin have substantially increased. But precisely because of this, the problem has mostly been located outside the factories (neo-Nazis, right-wing extremists) or within individuals (prejudices). Structural and individual discrimination inside their own organisations has not yet become a main focus of concern for German employers.

Another misconception commonly revealed in interviews with employers is that racism is due to an 'information deficit'. Because racism is mainly seen as an individual problem of prejudice due to false information, a logical emphasis of anti-racist activities should therefore consist in providing correct information. Hjarnø (1995) discovered the view amongst Danish employers that if racism plays a part in marginalising immigrants and refugees, then more information on the circumstances of migrants and refugees is required in order to eradicate this discrimination. Consistent with this view is the response of several German companies surveyed by Räthzel and Saricca (1994). These companies argued that because of their international character, and the fact that many of their German employees had also worked for periods abroad, they had no problems with discrimination. These arguments presume that discrimination and racism are due to a lack of knowledge of 'another culture'. In some European countries there are training initiatives in employment which work from this assumption: programmes to encourage 'inter-cultural awareness' and promote better communication and understanding, which provide demographic facts and figures on migrants, their countries of origin, their current employment patterns, and cultural information on migrant and ethnic minority communities. Implicit in this approach is the idea that the provision of correct information and raising trainees' cultural awareness is enough to reduce discriminatory behaviour (see Wrench and Taylor 1993).

5. A Confusion over Concepts

A 1989 survey of employers in Britain revealed ignorance and misconceptions on the part of many employers on some of the basic concepts of the Race Relations Act. For example, when asked to state what they understood by indirect discrimination, about half of respondents gave incorrect answers. Some respondents appeared to believe that intention to discriminate was necessary for there to be indirect discrimination. Others thought that it referred to a willingness to recruit but not to promote; or to unconscious prejudice or reverse discrimination. Just 15 per cent of employers gave correct replies (CRE 1989). A 1991 project revealed that major UK employers still confuse equal opportunities – and more specifically, positive action – with positive discrimination and giving an unfair advantage to ethnic minorities. Some employers argued that there was no need for an equal opportunities policy in their organisation because they didn't want to 'give preference to anybody or any group' (Wrench et al. 1993).

This confusion of equal opportunities initiatives with positive discrimination or quotas is found amongst employers in many other European countries. For example, it is reported that in Denmark one reason why employers are generally resistant to positive action policies is that they sometimes confuse 'positive action' with 'positive discrimination' (Hjarnø 1995). The Danish Employers' Association was reported to be against equal opportunities measures because it did not believe that the high rate of unemployment among immigrants and refugees could be solved by introducing 'positive discrimination' or 'quotas'. With regard to recruitment, it is felt that it is the employer's right to employ whomever is needed, and recruitment should be carried out in any way chosen by the employer.

6. A Confusion of 'Multicultural' with anti-Discrimination Policies

Related to the above misconceptions and confusions is a lack of understanding of what anti-discrimination measures entail. For example, German employers, when asked about their measures against discrimination, replied in terms of their 'social' or 'education' policy (Räthzel 1995). Strategies included organising the seminars on 'knowledge of different cultures' and 'encouraging people to get to know each other'. Companies in Germany will often have some kind of social or education policy on combating racism in general, especially right extremism, by, for example, making public declarations against 'hostility towards foreigners' in advertisements in the most popular national newspapers. Companies will occasionally finance projects which worked for integration or seminars for their training staff on right extremism and the experiences of migrants in Germany. Recent years in Germany have seen an abundance of 'joint action weeks', declarations and information initiatives against racial prejudice from the employers and trade unions, from individual companies up to national level with trade union umbrella organisations. Whilst all the above initiatives continue to be important, necessary and valuable, there is one aspect which remains neglected, and that is the area of company policies designed specifically to counter discrimination towards migrants within the workplace itself. Whilst cultural, educational and political initiatives are important, they are not a substitute for more specifically directed anti-discrimination measures.

Similarly in France, a number of educational programmes have been devised for police officers, magistrates, teachers and social workers, with the general aim of instilling a professional awareness of the diversity of population groups and cultural origins represented among those they have to deal with. With the same aim in mind, specialised agencies have been set up, such as the Agence pour le Développement des Relations Interculturelles (Agency for the Promotion of Inter-cultural Relations). However, the above-mentioned programmes are all concerned with making service delivery more culturally sensitive, rather than combating discrimination.

The above material shows that there is a long way to go before equal opportunities activities at the organisational level achieve a proper legitimacy amongst employers in the European Union. It is clear that the first hurdle is frequently ideological or conceptual. The next section of this chapter first sets out in greater detail some of the specific conceptual problems which remain a barrier to progress in this field. It then looks at some of the differences between national contexts which render difficult a common approach across Europe.

VARIATION IN NATIONAL CONTEXTS FOR EQUAL OPPORTUNITIES

1. Differences in the Meaning of Equal Opportunity

Despite the fact that there has been an established discourse on equal opportunities issues and a history of practice on this subject in some countries for many years, there remains some disagreement even within these countries about what exactly constitutes effective equal opportunities activity. In an international context, there is inevitably going to be an even greater problem in defining the subject area. Some of the different perspectives on what constitutes broader equal opportunities activity can be categorised under the following headings (MacEwen 1995):

- The *equal treatment approach*. With this approach, it is believed that equal opportunities follows on from making sure that all are treated the same, regardless of ethnicity or colour.

- The *'level playing field'* approach. This recognises the need to remove some unfair barriers which operate in the labour market by special action, such as training gatekeepers, advertising in the migrant/ethnic minority press, and so on.
- The *equal opportunities approach*. This aims for longer-term proportional representation of minorities by a range of organisational measures, such as ethnic monitoring and targets. It will probably include ethnic record-keeping, and might include training to change the attitudes or practices of staff.
- The *equal outcome approach*. This uses quotas and 'positive discrimination' to achieve a much shorter-term proportional representation of minorities. It is the most controversial type, seen by many to be in breach of natural justice.

Examples of several of these different approaches can be found simultaneously within one country, including the UK or the Netherlands, where there are many examples of the third 'equal opportunities' approach as well as the first two. In countries where there is no tradition of an 'equal opportunities' approach, it is probably the case that most employers subscribe implicitly to the 'equal treatment' approach (Forbes and Mead 1992; MacEwen 1995). They will state that they are being fair because they treat all employees the same, regardless of ethnicity or colour. If formal equality exists, there can be no problem. In Germany, for example, unions fought hard to ensure that migrant workers were covered by the same regulations as German workers, that they received equal pay for equal work, that they had equal rights to be represented by or elected to works councils, and so on. Therefore, for employers and unions there is 'no discrimination'. In France the republican tradition of universalism means that special policies regarding ethnic minorities are regarded with suspicion. Although there have been some elements of the fourth 'equal outcome' approach in the US, with selective use of numerical goals and targets, this radical type is probably unknown in practice in Europe. Probably the strongest policy in Europe is found in the Netherlands, where a positive action programme allows a minority candidate to be favoured in the case of equal qualification with another applicant.

In many European countries there has been no history of organisationally based policies and no tradition of discourse on equal opportunities issues, and in some countries policies in, for example, the forms found in the UK or the Netherlands, would not be seen to make any sense. Nevertheless, in some of these countries activities take place which would be labelled by their instigators as 'policies to prevent racial discrimination and xenophobia' or 'activities to promote equal treatment in the work-place'. In order to be able properly to comprehend these different approaches they must be understood within their own national contexts. There are other national differences which will be relevant to how equal opportunities/anti-discrimination activities are defined and opera-tionalised. Further examples of national differences which will have major implications for the character of such policies are.

2. Differences in National Responses to Migration and Ethnic Diversity

Castles (1995) categorises the major policy responses to immigration and ethnic diversity found in different countries. These include:

- *Differential exclusion*: immigrants are seen as guestworkers with-out full social and political rights (for example, Germany, Austria, Switzerland, Belgium).
- *Assimilation*: immigrants are awarded full rights, but are expected to become like everyone else (for example, France, the UK in the 1960s).
- *Pluralism/multi-culturalism*: immigrants have full rights but maintain some cultural differences (for example, Canada, Australia, Sweden, the UK more recently).

These are 'ideal' types, and in reality there have been some tensions within them. The *differential exclusion* model was based on the desire to prevent permanent settlement, and has proved hard to maintain because it leads to social tension and contradicts the democratic principle of including all members of civil society in the nation-state. The case of Germany fits this model, although there has been a shift to assimilation policies in some areas, and some multicultural policies in education. In France, probably the best example of the *assimilation* model with its republican tradition of 'equal treatment for all', there has been a move to some elements of the pluralist model, and this has led to some difficulties because of contradictions between explicit goals and actual policies. In the UK, in the 1950s and 1960s, there was a sort of *laissez-faire* assimilation which moved to *pluralist* and *multicultural* models in the 1970s. There is now a mixture of assimilationist and pluralist policies, without a clear overall objective (Castles 1995).

These contrasting national approaches provide very different contexts for equal opportunities activities. Often, the ideologies relating to these 'ideal types' remain in official discourse, and are directly reflected in how policies on the treatment of migrants and ethnic minorities are expressed. In Britain, for example, debates on the forms that 'multiculturalism' might take are a regular part of public debate in some sectors, and equal opportunities policies recognise ethnic difference. In France, the emphasis is on broader 'equal rights' policies as a means of avoiding discrimination for all citizens and workers, and initiatives to encourage the recruitment of migrants have been phrased not in terms of 'anti-discrimination' or 'anti-racism' policies for migrants, but as egalitarian approaches guided by a universalistic ideology.

3. Differences in the Recording of Data by Ethnic Minority Status

This leads us directly to another very important and practical national difference: the recording of data by ethnic minority status. Between European countries there are wide differences in the readiness to record and use data according to ethnic minority background. This ranges from the UK, where a question on ethnic background forms part of the official Census, and where ethnic monitoring within organisations is often used to evaluate the progress of policies, to France and Denmark, where the recording of 'racial' or ethnic origin in official or private registration is legally restricted. In the Netherlands, ethnic record keeping is officially encouraged through the workings of the new law on the proportionate employment of minorities, but still encounters some resistance in practice through memories of its misuse in the Netherlands by the Nazis during the second world war. As ethnic monitoring is a key component of some models of equal opportunity practice, all these differences must be allowed for in understanding international differences.

4. Differences in the Legal Status of Migrants

The working population of the EU can be divided into five main categories in terms of legal status (Wrench 1996: 3). These reflect formal status, and a continuum of rights ranging from full rights and privileges of citizenship in category 1 to relatively few rights in category 5.

1. Citizens living and working within their own country of citizenship.
2. Citizens of an EU member state who work in another country within the Union (EU denizens).
3. Third country nationals who have full rights to residency and work in a member state (non-EU denizens).

4. Third country nationals who have leave to stay on the basis of a revocable work permit for a fixed period of time.
5. Undocumented or 'illegal' workers.

It is clear that the problem of discrimination in the labour market of countries in the EU differs according to which categories most of its migrant and minority ethnic workers fall in to. This will have corresponding implications for employers' policies and practices on discrimination and equality.

In countries of Northern Europe, migrants and ethnic minorities are more likely to be skewed towards the top groups of the five legal categories of worker. Here, migrants are longer established and issues of the 'second generation' are important, concern over the unjustified exclusion of young people of migrant descent from employment opportunities by informal discrimination on 'racial' or ethnic grounds, and their over-representation in unemployment. In the UK, for example, most migrants and their descendants are found in group 1; the legal status of migrant workers is generally not a problem, and a major part of equal opportunities activity concerns tackling the informal discrimination which in practice reduces the opportunities of minority ethnic workers, either at the workplace or within a trade union. In other countries of northern Europe, a higher proportion of workers fall into group 3, suffering not only 'informal' racial discrimination, but also formal legal discrimination. Here, the first stage of any initiatives is generally concerned with the sorts of exclusion related to naturalisation and citizenship issues. This has implications for the overtones of the concept of discrimination itself. In the UK there is an acceptance of a broad definition of 'discrimination' which allows for measures which tackle indirect, institutional or unintentional discrimination. In other countries of northern Europe such as Germany, avoiding discrimination is more likely to be seen more narrowly as working to ensure equal employment rights, and paying equal wages for equal work, through formal agreements between the social partners.

In countries of southern Europe immigrants are likely to be over-represented towards the bottom of the five groups. Groups 4 and 5 workers are actively preferred and recruited because they are cheaper, more vulnerable and more pliable – they are less able to resist over-exploitation in terms of work intensity or working hours, in conditions which indigenous workers would not tolerate (see Cachón, and Campani and Carchedi in this volume). 'Anti-discrimination' activities in these circumstances are initially more likely to emphasise measures to empower such workers and reduce their vulnerability to exploitation, with, for example, initiatives to unionise, regularise and train them.

Thus a practice within one context might carry different overtones to the same practice in another: for example, in a sector within a southern European country where migrants are severely exploited in illegal work because they don't have the power to resist or to seek alternative employment, providing language training for them in the national language might be seen to be part of 'anti-discrimination' activity because it empowers them and enables them to resist such discrimination. In a country of northern Europe where migrants are longer established, including a 'second generation', the provision of language training is less likely to be seen as countering discrimination, and might even be interpreted as an 'alibi' for the absence of stronger measures.

5. Differences in Legal Measures against Discrimination

The strength of the law against employment discrimination provides an important context for the introduction of policies at an organisational level on equal opportunity. Although such policies are generally defined as 'voluntary', in practice some will be introduced through the latent pressure of legislation, and the fear by some organisations of the bad publicity which might ensue from a court or tribunal case on discrimination. In some European countries there is very little such legal pressure; in others there is recently enacted legislation against racial discrimination in employment, the effects of which cannot yet be properly judged. Even when strong law exists in theory, there can be problems in practice. The case of France is an example where a number of problems are experienced with the use of the criminal law against racism and discrimination. Cases of employment discrimination are seldom brought to court for lack of concrete evidence, and in practice employers are free to take on whomever they like, provided they do not openly show that the decision was based on criteria prohibited by law (see Vourc'h et al. in this volume). Similarly in Sweden, from more than 100 cases of alleged discrimination in employment reported to the Ombudsman after the introduction of the law against discrimination in employment, none found its way to court. In the Netherlands a recent law commits companies with more than 35 employees to aim for the proportional representation of 'non-natives' in their workforces, and this puts pressure on them to formulate policies to achieve this. In theory, therefore, there is now more legal pressure in the Netherlands to institute such policies than in any other EU member state. There is thus a great deal of variety between different EU countries on the degree of 'background pressure' to introduce policies for the prevention of racial discrimination and the promotion of equal treatment.

This fifth point leads us to the question of whether more legal compulsion at EU level is necessary to get national laws into shape. The obligations of the Equal Treatment Directive led to every EU country introducing legislation to guarantee equal treatment between men and women in the labour market (Forbes and Mead 1992). The same might be done for racial and ethnic discrimination. An EU Directive sets out certain goals which have to be met by a given deadline. Each member state must then pass the necessary laws.

> Protection against discrimination in the member states needs to include elements that are common to the whole Community – so that there is some uniform protection throughout the EC. But complete uniformity would be impossible, given the different legal systems and conditions in the 12 countries. A directive is therefore the ideal instrument laying down a common basis in firm goals to be achieved through legislation but allowing each national government the flexibility to deal with its own particular problems. (Dummett 1994: 14)

THE BALANCE BETWEEN VOLUNTARISM AND COMPULSION

Employers are generally against the idea of such legally-based pressure to introduce equal opportunity policies. Michael Banton writes:

> One of the reasons for resisting equal opportunities measures is that they entail changes to traditional assumptions … and introduce external rules into what have previously been self-regulating processes. They extend the sphere of public control and diminish that of private arrangement. (Banton 1994: 67)

This constitutes another example of the moving boundary between the private and the public sphere: once car drivers thought that drinking alcohol was a private concern, smokers thought they could smoke anywhere and motorcyclists thought that it was entirely their own business as to whether or not they wore a crash helmet. 'Such things are now regarded as a matter of public concern and there are vigorous debates as to where the line between private and public should be drawn' (Banton 1994: 68). Early in industrialisation an employer thought that employing whom he liked was his decision, later labour legislation introduced state control into the labour relationship. The exact degree of this remains an issue of contention: the American philosopher Robert Nozick argues that the right of employers to hire is just the same as the right of individuals to marry.

Individuals should marry whom they please and private employers hire whom they please, and the government has no right to interfere in either of these decisions (Nozick 1974, cited in Ezorsky 1991: 81). Whilst few European employers today would go that far, most remain intrinsically and temperamentally opposed to legal constraint in this field.

Discussion on the possibility of further legal measures was probably one of the factors which pushed European employers and trade union representatives towards agreement on the Joint Declaration on the Prevention of Racial Discrimination and Xenophobia and Promotion of Equal Treatment at the Workplace, agreed by the European social partners in Florence in October 1995. The aim of this Declaration is to encourage the voluntary adoption of measures designed to facilitate equal treatment in recruitment and selection, work allocation and promotion, training and development, and dismissal and redundancies, as well as dealing with discrimination, and showing respect for cultural and religious differences. It also calls for a Compendium of Good Practice to be compiled as part of a series of measures to follow up the Joint Declaration. This would identify examples of good practice in the different member states, and disseminate the information gathered, contributing to a broader exchange of experiences amongst the members of the European Union regarding the promotion of equal treatment and the combating of racial discrimination at the workplace. Significantly, it declares that the Compendium should also 'promote the notion that it is in the interests of business to implement equal opportunities policies'.

THE BUSINESS CASE FOR EQUAL OPPORTUNITIES

Given the varied and widespread ideologies of resistance to such measures exhibited by European employers, it seems that the Joint Declaration will have to operate in an unsympathetic environment. The task would be therefore greatly assisted if reluctant employers could be convinced that there is a 'business advantage' in equal opportunity practices. This is the kind of argument stressed by the UK's Commission for Racial Equality in its 1995 campaign 'Racial Equality Means Business'.

There may be a number of reasons why an individual employer might decide to introduce specific measures to counter discrimination and to further equal opportunities at the workplace, over and above the desire to reduce the likelihood of unlawful behaviour occurring within the organisation in countries where there is legislation against discrimination. There may be a calculation of commercial advantage by making the company more attractive to ethnic minority clients, or improving the company image in a culturally diverse area. It may form part of an internal labour market policy to maximise the potential of existing valued employees, avoiding, for example, the poor motivation and low productivity that stems from workers employed below their capacity. Or it may be motivated by broader moral and social concerns over the divisions in the social fabric which may result from unwarranted exclusion from opportunities of one section of the community. Furthermore, the introduction of a well-managed equal opportunities programme which includes the accurate monitoring of both the existing workforce and new applicants can give new and helpful insights into aspects of the organisation's human resource management.

It is true that there can be identifiable advantages for an employer in the introduction of equal opportunity measures, and that in some EU member states some individual employers have embraced them willingly. However, the 'business' argument can be overstated. Michael Rubenstein, writing in *Equal Opportunities Review* (November/December 1987), calls the argument that equal opportunities makes good business sense a 'modern myth and misconception'. He argues that if this really were the case, then profit-maximising employers would have rushed to adopt policies years ago. The problem is that, far from being irrational, under some circumstances racial discrimination can be quite rational behaviour. Equal opportunities procedures cost time and money, and taking on a black employee instead of a white employee might impose a cost in terms of customer behaviour. Mark Gould, writing in the US, argues that although institutional racism may well be a characteristic of an inefficient system, organisations manifesting racism can nevertheless be competitive within the current institutional context because it lowers wages and reduces costs, even though alternative institutional arrangements would enhance the efficiency of production. Thus institutional racism can be profitable and sustainable for individual employers even though its elimination would lead to a more efficient and prosperous economy (Gould 1991). Rubenstein concludes that although equal opportunities is morally, socially and politically right, most employers will continue to discriminate until it costs them more to discriminate than not to discriminate, whether through financial sanction, the threat of law or loss of commercial contract. Something similar was concluded after a major study of employers' equal opportunities practice, financed by the UK Department of Employment. The researchers concluded that a successful policy needed to have the commitment of organisational power holders such as senior directors, but that this commitment was unlikely to be 'voluntarily' secured without some sort of pressure.

They argued that there were a number of ways in which this might be felt, such as moral pressure and example from government; financial incentives, such as those entailed in contract compliance; legal sanctions and penalties; and the emergence of perceived business advantage. Most of the initiatives they encountered in their research had their origins in outside pressures, such as urban disturbances or accusations of malpractice. A significant number of managers also told the researchers that as equal opportunities were costly of time and resources, they would be inclined to do more if there were a business advantage, or, more frequently, a discernible price to be paid for inaction (Jewson et al. 1992, 1995).

The conclusion has to be that little progress is to be made if the major thrust of policy development in this area is left to factors of 'equal opportunities is good for business'. Where a 'business pay-off' is not immediately obvious, some extra pressure will need to be applied via the legal framework.

CONCLUSION

This chapter has shown that specific initiatives and measures by employers to counter racism, discrimination and the exclusion of migrants and their descendants are still not accorded the legitimacy they deserve in member states of the EU. Although examples of positive practices exist, demonstrating the sorts of measures that might be adopted by others, when these are set in a broader EU context they remain untypical. As we have seen, one problem is that, on the whole, employers and their organisations remain ideologically unsympathetic to equal opportunities measures. Receptivity to them seems to be greater in the public sector, and in the retail part of the private sector where a pay-off in terms of broader customer appeal is recognised. Although a major hurdle to change is ideological resistance, we have also seen that differences between countries in the readiness of employers to adopt such measures lie deeper than this. There are national differences of context which mean that ideas and practices seen as quite normal in one country are perceived to be quite alien in another, and this contributes to a view that 'while such policies are sensible in your country, they are irrelevant in ours'.

The danger is that a recognition of genuine difference in national context can be turned into a position of complete cultural relativity on this issue, denying the possibility of coming to any judgement that practices current in one country might be more desirable than those in another. Whilst recognising that national practices can only fully be comprehended and evaluated in a context of a knowledge of the historical, cultural, political and socio-economic environment of that country, it is also important to recognise the principle that all parties can benefit from an exposure to the ideas and practices of others. For example, we cannot assume that because a particular practice is associated with the ideology of 'assimilation' it is therefore irrelevant to a location where 'multi-culturalism' is dominant, or vice versa. There are already conflicts, internal tensions and inconsistencies of practice in all of these 'ideal types' of approach within one country. Sometimes the ideology of one particular dominant national discourse can lead to 'blind spots', which only become apparent in international comparison. Sometimes the social, economic or legal environment which helped to determine the original policy traditions has changed, meaning that policies are no longer so relevant or effective in that form. There may be changes in national or European law, or changes in the legal or ethnic character of migration. Therefore, despite the different ways that anti-discrimination activities find practical expression, there are grounds for thinking that in the light of new pressures and developments, organisations in very different countries may benefit from the application of some common principles.

For example, taking some of the approaches listed earlier, we might come to the conclusion that it is unlikely that a simple 'equal treatment' approach by an employer in any country is going to be adequate, for the simple reason that migrants and ethnic minorities do not start from an equal position in relation to white national workers. Their current circumstances may reflect a legacy of past discrimination, or they may still be experiencing discrimination in ways which render their condition very different from white peers or co-workers. Nor is it likely that an employer in any country who, for example, simply provides information on different ethnic cultures to aid 'inter-cultural understanding' is going to be seen as adequately working to counter racism and discrimination.

In countries where previous legal discrimination against migrant workers has been removed, the institution of formal equality has blinded people to the recognition of the operation of informal discrimination. The extent of the 'no problem here' view, and the refusal to recognise the legitimacy of special policies to counter the processes of exclusion and informal, indirect and institutional discrimination, contrast sharply with the evidence on discrimination and exclusion set out in the various chapters in this volume. Although within different national contexts the particular practical expression of anti-discrimination activities is likely to vary, the need for them remains a constant. As things stand, there must be a question mark over the possibility of significant numbers of employers instituting changes voluntarily without the application of some forms of external pressure.

NOTE

1. The chapter does not include trade unions, even though trade unions themselves are employers. Consideration of European trade union policies regarding migrant and ethnic minority workers can be found in Penninx and Roosblad forthcoming, CES 1997 and Wrench 1997.

Bibliography

Abou Saada, G. and Zeroulou, Z. (1993) 'L'insertion sociale et professionnelle des jeunes diplômés issus de l'immigration', *Critique Régionale*, 19: 7–38

Aku (1981; 1988; 1991) *Årsmedeltal. Råtabeller* (Annual Averages Raw Tables), Stockholm, Statistics Sweden

Ålund, A. (1989) 'The Power of Definitions: Immigrant Women and Problem-Centered Ideologies', *Migration*, 4: 37–55

Ålund, A. (1991) *"Lilla Juga'. Etnicitet, familj och kvinnliga nåtverk'* ('Little Juga'. Ethnicity, Family and Female Networks), Stockholm, Carlssons

Ålund, A. and Schierup, C.U. (1991) *Paradoxes of Multiculturalism: Essays on Swedish Society*, Research on Ethnic Relations Series, Aldershot, Avebury

Alvarez, F. (1992) *La inmigración americana en España*, Ponencia presentada en la Conferencia de la Unión internacional para el estudio de la población sobre 'El poblamiento de las Américas', Veracruz, May

AMS (1991) *Arbetsförmedling som informationskanal bland arbetsökande*, Rapport från Utredningsenheten, Stockholm, AMS

Anderson, B. (1983) *Imagined Communities*, New York, Verso

Andersson, L. (1992) 'Det tar tid att bli svensk. En enkät och intervju-undersökning av flyktingar och företags beteenden pä den svensk arbetsmarknanden', Högskolan i Växjö

Angel de Prada, M., W. Actis, C. Pereda and R. Pérez Molina (1996) *Labour Market Discrimination against Migrant Workers in Spain*, Geneva, ILO

Aragón, R. and Chozas, J. (1993) *La regularización de inmigrantes durante 1991–1992*, Madrid, Ministerio de Trabajo y Seguridad Social

Arango, J. (1993) 'El 'Sur' en el sistema migratorio europeo. Evolución reciente y perspectivas', *Política y sociedad*, 12: 7–20

Atkin, K. (1991) 'Community Care in a Multi-Racial Society: Incorporating the User View', *Policy and Politics*, 19, 3: 159–66

Bachrach, P. and Baratz, M. (1971) *Power and Poverty: Theory and Practice*, New York, Oxford University Press

Bäck, H. and Soininen, M. (1993) *Flyktingmottagande i förändring*, Svenska kommunförbundet, Upplands Väsby

Bäck, H. and Soininen, M. (1996) 'Invandrana, deokratin och samhället. Om invandranas politiska deletagande i dagens Sverige', Förvaltningshögskolans rapporter, No. 2, Göteborgs universitet

Baker, D. and Lenhardt, G. (1991) 'Nationalismus und Arbeitsmarkintegration in der BRD (alt)' *Zeitschrift für Soziologie*, 20, 6: 463–78

Balazs, G. (1983) 'Les facteurs et les formes du chômage', *Actes de la recherche en sciences sociales*, 50: 69–83

Banton, M. (1994) *Discrimination*, Buckingham, Open University Press

Banton, M. (1997) 'The Ethics of Practice-Testing', *New Community*, 23, 7, July

Bardet-Blochet, A., Bolzmann, C. et al. (1988) *Les associations d'immigrés: repli ou participation sociale? L'exemple de Genève*, Genève, Centre de Contact Suisses-Immigrés et groupe de recherche Migrations

Barrett, S. and Fudge, C. (eds.) (1981) *Policy and Action*, London, Methuen

Bastenier, A. and Dassetto, F. (1981) 'La deuxième génération d'immigrés en Belgique', *Courrier hebdomadaire*, 907–08

Bastenier, A. and Dassetto, F. (1985) *Étude des facteurs susceptibles d'être responsables de la morbidité des travailleurs migrants*, Louvain-La-Neuve, GREM, UCL

Bastenier, A. and Dassetto, F. (1986) *La situation de formation professionnelle des étrangers en Belgique*, Luxembourg, CEDEFOP

Bastenier, A. and Dassetto, F. (1987) 'Work and the Indeterminate Status of Young North Africans and Turks in Belgium: Integration into the Working Class or the Formation of a Sub-proletariat?', in Wilpert, C. (ed.) *Entering the Working World*, Aldershot, Gower

Beauftragte der Bundesregierung für die Belange der Ausländer (ed.) (1994) *Bericht der Beauftragten der Bundesregierung für die Belange der Ausländer über die Lage der Ausländer in der Bundesrepublik Deutschland 1993*, Bonn, Mitteilungen der Beauftragten der Bundesregierung für die Belange der Ausländer

Beek, K. van (1993) *To be Hired or Not to be Hired, the Employer Decides*, Amsterdam, University of Amsterdam

Berghuys, R.E. and Zegers de Beijl, R. (1993) 'Wie echt wil, die kan ... Integratie-en discriminatie beleid ten behoeve van migranten op de arbeidsmarkt', *LBR-bulletin*, 6: 3–15

Biegel, C., Becker, A. and Tjoen-Tak-Sen, K. (1987) *Rassendiscriminatie ... Tenslotte is het verboden bij de wet*, Zwolle, Tjeenk-Willink

Bigo, D. (1996) *Polices en réseaux*, Paris, Presses de Sciences Politiques

Biller, M. (1989) *Arbeitsmarktsegmentation und Ausländerbeschäftigung*. *Frankfurt-Main*, New York, Campus

Bolzmann, C., Fibbi, R. et Garcia, C. (1987) 'La deuxième génération d'immigrés en Suisse: catégorie ou acteur social', *Revue Européenne des Migrations Internationales*, Poitiers, Université de Poitiers, 3, 1–2: 1–3

Booth, T. (1988) *Developing Policy Research*, Aldershot, Gower

Borkowski, J.L. (1990) 'L'insertion sociale des immigrés et de leurs enfants', *Données Sociales*, INSEE

Bourdieu, P. (1979) *La distinction*, Paris, Ed. de Minuit

Bouvier, P. (1989) *Le travail au quotidien*, Paris, Presses Universitaires de France

Bouw, C. and Nelissen, C. (1988) *Gevoelige kwesties. Ervaringen van migranten met discriminatie*, Leiden, Centrum voor Onderzoek van Maatschappelijke Tegenstellingen, University of Leiden

Bovenkerk, F. (1992) *A Manual for International Comparative Research on Discrimination on the Grounds of 'Race' and Ethnic Origin*, Geneva, ILO

Bovenkerk, F. and Breunig-van Leeuwen, E. (1978) 'Rasdiscriminatie en rasvoorordeel op de Amsterdamse arbeidsmarkt', in Bovenkerk, F. (ed.) *Omdat zij anders zijn; patronen van rasdiscriminatie in Nederland*, Boom, Meppel

Bovenkerk, F., Gras, M.J.I. and Ramsoedh, D. (1995) *Discrimination against Migrant Workers and Ethnic Minorities in Access to Employment: The Netherlands*, Geneva, ILO

Boyd, M. (1990) *Migrant Women and Integration Policies*, Paris, OECD

Brassé, P. and Sikking, E. (1988) 'Discriminatie van migranten binnen arbeidsorganisaties', *Migrantenstudies*, 2: 13–24

Brettell, C. and Simon, R.J. (1986) 'Immigrant Women: An Introduction', in Simon, R.J. and Brettell, C. (eds.) *International Migration: the Female Experience*, Totowa, N.J., Rowman and Allanheld

Bridges, L. (1994) 'Tory Education: Exclusion and the Black Child', *Race and Class* 36, 1

Brochmann, G. (1993) *Immigration Control, The Welfare State and Xenophobia, Towards an Integrated Europe*, Brussels, Paper presented at *COST A2* meeting

Bruschi, C. (1989) 'La politique migratoire: ruptures et continuités', *Migrations-Société*, 1, 3

Burstein, P. (1992) 'Affirmative Action, Jobs and American Democracy: What Has Happened to the Quest for Equal Opportunity', *Law and Society Review*, 26, 4

Büyükbozkoyum, O., Stamatiou, M. and Stolk, M. (1991) 'Turkse HTS'ers zoeken werk; Verslag van een sollicitatie experiment', *Sociologische Gids*, 38: 187–92

C.I.S. (1993) 'Actitudes ante la inmigración (Estudio 2.051)', Madrid

Cachón, L. (1993a) 'Population, education et marché du travail: les changements sociaux des années 80 (en Espagne)', *ENA mensuel*, 232, June: 38–40

Cachón, L. (1993b): *Informe sobre la inmigración en España*, Brussels, Organización Internacional del Trabajo-Confederación Europea de Sindicatos

Cachón, L. (1994) 'La contratación temporal en España: mercado de trabajo y prácticas empresariales', *Ekonomiaz*, 31–32: 208–35

Cachón, L. (1995) *Preventing Racism at the Workplace: Report on Spain*, Dublin, European Foundation for the Improvement of Living and Working Conditions

Calvanese, F. (1983) 'Gli immigrati stranieri in Italia', *Inchiesta*

Calvanese, F. and Pugliese, E. (ed.) (1991) *La presenza straniera in Italia. Il caso della Campania*, Milan, Franco Angeli

Calvo, T. (1990) *¿España racista? Voces payas sobre los gitanos*, Barcelona, Anthropos

Carchedi, F. (1994) 'La presenza immigrata nella provincia di Siracusa', CGIL, CISL and UIL, Progress intermedio, Syracuse, September

Carchedi, F. and Ranuzzi, G. (1987) 'Tra collocazione nel mercato del lavoro secondario ed esclusione dal sistema di cittadinanza' Sergi, N. (ed.) *L'immigrazione straniera in Italia*, Rome, Edizioni Lavoro

Carchedi, F. and Ricci, P. (1995) 'La presenza immigrata nella provincia di Latina. Accoglienza e mercato del lavoro', Todisco, E. (ed.) *Immigrazione: dai bisogni ai diritti, dall'emarginazione all'integrazione*, Latina, Università degli Studi La Sapienza, Facoltà di Economia, sede di latina

Caritas di Roma (1995) *Immigrazione*, Rome, Dossier statistico 94, Anterem

Carlos, M.L.P. and Borges, G.C. (1995) *Preventing Racism at the Workplace in Portugal*, Dublin, European Foundation for the Improvement of Living and Working Conditions

CASI (1990) *Entre souvenir et avenir. Enquête sur les jeunes italiens de Bruxelles*, Bruxelles, CASI-UO

Castles, S. (1995) 'How Nation-states Respond to Immigration and Ethnic Diversity', *New Community*, 21, 3, July

Castles, S. and Kosak (1973) *Immigrant Workers and the Class Structure in Western Europe*, London, Oxford University Press

Cavalruso, C. (1989) 'La inmigración ilegal en Italia', en O.C.D.E., *El futuro de las migraciones*, Madrid, Ministerio de trabajo y Seguridad Social

CEFA-UO (1989) *Les jeunes espagnols en question*, Bruxelles, CEFA-UO

Censis (1979) *I lavoratori stranieri in Italia*, Rome, Istituto Poligrafico e Zecca dello Stato

Centlivres, P. and Centlivres-Demont, M. (1991) *Devenir suisse: adhésion et diversité culturelle des étrangers en Suisse*, Genève, Institut universitaire d'études européennes

CES (1997) *Les Syndicats contre le Racisme, la Xenophobie et la Discrimination sur le Lieu de Travail*, Bruxelles, Confédération Européenne des Syndicats

Céu Esteves, M. de (coor.) (1991) *Portugal, país de imigraçao*, Lisboa, Instituto de Estudos para o Desenvolvimento

Chiapparugi, M. (1983) 'L'immigrazione straniera in Italia: quadro di riferimento teorico', *Studi Emigrazione*, 71, September

Colectivo IOE (1987) 'Los inmigrantes en España', *Documentación social*, 66

Colectivo IOE (1991) *Foreign Women in Domestic Service in Madrid, Spain*, Geneva, ILO

Commissariat Général au Plan (1988) *Immigrations: le devoir d'insertion*, Paris

Commissariat Royal à la Politique des Immigrés (1990) *Pour une cohabitation harmonieuse*, Bruxelles, INBEL

Cornioley, C. (1994) 'La situation des jeunes au chômage', *La vie économique*, Paris, A. Colin, 1, 94

Costa-Lascoux, J. (1991) 'Assimiler, Insérer, Intégrer', *Projets*, 227, Autumn

CRE (1989) *Are Employers Complying?* London, Commission for Racial Equality

Crenson, M. (1971) *The Unpolitics of Air Pollution*, Baltimore, Johns Hopkins University Press

Cross, M., Wrench, J. and Barnett, S. (1990) *Ethnic Minorities and the Careers Service: an Investigation into Processes of Assessment and Placement*, London, Department of Employment Research Paper No. 73

Cross, M. and Wrench, J. (1990) 'Racial Inequality on YTS: Careers Service or Disservice?', *British Journal of Education and Work* 4, 3

Czarniawska-Joerges, B. (1988) *Att handla med ord*, Stockholm, Carlssons

De Certeau, M. (1985) 'L'actif et le passif des appartenances', *Esprit, Français et immigrés*, Paris, 6, juin: 115–71

De Rudder, V., Tripier, M. and Vourc'h, F. (1995) *Prevention of Racism at the Workplace in France*, Dublin, European Foundation for the Improvement of Living and Working Conditions

De Smedt, J. (1993) *Sociale clausules als bijdrage tot sociale ontwikkeling*, Brussels, Wereldsolidariteit

de Troy, C. (1987) *Migrant Women and Employment*, Brussels, Commission of the European Communities

Delarue, R. (1993) 'Sociale clausules: een stimulans voor de wereldhandel' *De Gids op Maatschappelijk Gebied* 84, 12: 1018–24

Derriche, O., Franck, D., Hecq, F. et Plateau, N. (1992) *L'école au féminin*, Bruxelles, Ed. Maison des Femmes

Desplanques, G. and Tabart, N. (1991) 'La localisation de la population étrangère'. *Economie et Statistiques*; No. 242

Dijk, T. van (1993) 'Denying Racism: Elite Discourse and Racism', in Wrench, J. and Solomos, J. (eds.) *Racism and Migration in Western Europe*, Berg, Oxford

Drew, D., Gray, J. and Sime, N. (1992) *Against the Odds: The Education and Labour Market Experiences of Black Young People*, Employment Department Research and Development Paper No. 68, Sheffield

DS (1981) *Invandrarkvinnor och jämställdhet* (Immigrant Women and Equality), Stockholm, Ministry of Labour, 2

DS (1990) *År de nya jobben bra eller dåliga?* (Are the new jobs good or bad?), Stockholm, The Ministry of Labour), 35

Dubar, C. (1991) *La socialisation, construction des identités sociales et profession-nelles*, Paris, Armand Colin

Dubet, F. (1989) *Immigrations: qu'en savons-nous? Un bilan des connaissances*, Paris, La Documentation française

Dummett, A. (1994) *Citizens, Minorities and Foreigners: a Guide to the EC*, London, Commission for Racial Equality

Echardour, A. and Maurin, E. (1993) *Données Sociales*, Paris, INSEE

Eckmann-Saillant, M., Bolzmann, C. and De Rham, G. (1994) *Jeunes sans qualification: trajectoires, situations et stratégies*, Genève, Les Editions IES

Ekberg, J. (1988) 'Arbetskarriär för en invandringskohort', Report Yrkeskarriär och yrkessegregering bland invandrare, Högskolan i Växjö, ser. 1, *Ekonomi och Politik* 15, April

Ekberg, J. (1990) *Invandrare och arbetsmarknaden.* (Immigrants in the labour market) in DS, Stockholm, Ministry of Labour, 35

Ekberg, J. (1993) 'Geografisk och socioekonomisk rörlighet bland invandrare', Stockholm, Gotab, ERU rapport 78

Ekholm, E. and Pitkänen, M. (1995) *Preventing Racism at the Workplace in Finland*, Dublin, European Foundation for the Improvement of Living and Working Conditions

Esmail, A. and Everington, S. (1993) 'Racial Discrimination against Doctors from Ethnic Minorities', *British Medical Journal* 306, March

Essed, Ph. (1984) *Alledaags racisme*, Amsterdam, Feministische uitgeverij Sara

Essed, Ph. (1991) *Understanding Everyday Racism. An Interdisciplinary Theory*, Newbury Park/London/New Delhi, Sage Publications

Ezorsky, G. (1991) *Racism and Justice: The Case for Affirmative Action*, New York, Cornell University Press

Fijalkowski, J. (ed.) (1990) *Transnationale Migranten in der Arbeitswelt*, Bonn, Edition sigma

Fix, M. and Struyk, R.J. (eds.) (1992) *Clear and Convincing Evidence*, Washington, DC, Urban Institute Press

Fleischer, H. (1990) 'Entwicklung der Einbürgerung seit 1986', in Sieveking, K., *Ausländerrecht und Ausländerpolitik 1990*, Bremen, ZERP-DP, 4

Flückiger, Y. (1992) 'La politique suisse en matière d'immigration', in Burgenmeier, B. *Main-d'oeuvre étrangère, une analyse de l'économie suisse*, Paris, Economica

FoB (1985) *Immigrants in the 1985 Population Census*, National Figures, Örebro, Statistics Sweden

Forbes, I. and Mead, G. (1992) *Measure for Measure*, London, Employment Department Research Series No. 1

Freyssinet, J. (1984) *Le chômage*, Paris, La Decouverte

Fürst, G. (1985) *Reträtten från mansjobben* (The Retreat from Male Jobs), Göteborg, Department of Sociology

G.I.S.T.I. (1993) *Légiférer pour mieux tuer les droits*, Paris, G.I.S.T.I

G.I.S.T.I. (1994) *Les discriminations dans l'emploi*, Contribution to European Guidelines to good employment practice to combat discrimination', Paris, G.I.S.T.I

Gallissont, R., Boumaza, N. and Clément, G. (1994) *Ces migrants qui font le pro-létariat*, Paris, Ed. Méridiens-Klincksieck

Gillmeister, H., Fijalkowski, J. and Kurthen, H. (1989) *Ausländerbeschäftigung in der Krise? Die Beschäftigungschancen ausländischer Arbeitnehmer am Beispiel der West-Berliner Industrie*, Berlin, edition sigma

Giraud, M. and Marie, C.V. (1990) *Les stratégies socio-politiques de la communauté antillaise dans son processus d'insertion en France métropolitaine*, Paris, Rapport de recherche, Ministère de la Recherche

Goldberg, A., Mourinho, D. and Kulke, U. (1995) *Labour Market Discrimination against Foreign Workers in Germany*, Geneva, ILO

Gould, M. (1991) 'The Reproduction of Labour-Market Discrimination in Competitive Capitalism' in Zegeye, A., Harris, L. and Maxted, J. (eds.) *Exploitation and Exclusion: Race and Class in Contemporary US Society*, London, Hans Zell

Graham, M. (1994) *Handlingar, organisationer och diskriminering: några teoretiska funderingar. I Invandring, forskning och politik*, Edsbruk, Akademitryck AB, CEIFO

Gras, M. and Bovenkerk, F. (1995) *Fighting Discrimination and Ethnic Disadvantage on the Dutch Labour Market*, Dublin, European Foundation for the Improvement of Living and Working Conditions

Gregory, R. (1989) 'Political Rationality or Incrementalism?', *Policy and Politics*, 17, 2: 135–53

Grell, P. (1985) *Etude du chômage et de ses conséquences: les catégories sociales touchées par le non-travail. Histoires de vie et modes de débrouillardise*, Montréal, Groupe d'analyse des politiques sociales, Université de Montréal

Grillo, R.D. (1985) *Ideologies and Institutions in France*, Cambridge, Cambridge University Press

Groenendijk, K. and Hampsink, R. (1995) *Temporary Employment of Migrants in Europe*, Nijmegen, Reeks Recht and Samenleving No. 10, Katholieke Universiteit Nijmegen

Guillaumin, C. (1992) 'Une société en ordre. De quelques-unes des formes de l'idéologie raciste', *Sociologie et Société*, XXIV, 2

Gunn, L. (1980) 'Implementation: problems and approaches', in Younis, T. (ed.) (1990) *Implementation in Public Policy*, Worcester, Billings & Sons

Haavio-Mannila, E. (1981) 'The Level of Living of Immigrants in Sweden: A Comparison of Male and Female Immigrants from Finland and Yugoslavia with Swedes of Same Age and Occupational Groups', in Municio (ed.) *Family and Position in the Swedish Society*, Stockholm, Split-Report Vol. II, Commission for Immigration Research

Hagendoorn, L. and Hraba, J. (1987) 'Social Distance Toward Holland's Minorities; Discrimination against and amongst Ethnic Groups', *Ethnic and Racial Studies*, 120: 317–33

Hall, R.H. and Quinn, R.E. (eds.) (1983) *Organizational Theory and Public Policy*, London, Sage

Hall, S., Critcher, C., Jefferson, T., Clarke, J. and Roberts, B. (1978) *Policing the Crisis: Mugging, the State and Law and Order*, London, Macmillan

Ham, C. and Hill, M. (eds.) (1984) *The Policy Process in the Modern Capitalist State*, Brighton, Harvester Wheatsheaf

Hammar, T. (1993) 'The Costs of Immigration Control System', Paper presented at the Planning Session on 28 September, Bergen

Hanf, K. and Scharpf, F. (eds.) (1978) *Interorganizational Policy Making. Limits to Coordination and Central Control*, London, Sage

Hannerz, U. (1981) 'Sweden as an Immigrant Society', in Municio, I. (ed.) *Family and Position in Swedish Society*, Stockholm, Split-Report Vol. II, Commission for Immigration Research

Harzig, C. (1994) 'Analyse des veröffentlichten Diskures über Fremde anhand des Weserkuriers 1945–1955', Unpublished Manuscript

Haugg, S. (1994) *Wir vertreten die, die hier im Hause sind*, Hamburg, Landeszentrale für politische Bildung

Heath, A. and McMahon, D. (1995) *Educational and Occupational Attainments: The Impact of Ethnic Origins*, Paper 34, Centre for Research into Elections and Social Trends, February

Heisler, B.S. (1991) 'A Comparative Perspective on the Underclass: Questions of Urban Poverty, Race and Citizenship', *Theory and Society*, 20, 4

Hjarnø, J. (1995) *Preventing Racism at the Workplace: The Danish National Report*, Dublin, European Foundation for the Improvement of Living and Working Conditions

Hjarnø, J. and Jensen, T. (1997) 'Diskrimineringen af unge med invandrerbaggrund ved jobsøgning', *Migration papers No. 21*, Esbjerg, South Jutland University Press

Hood, C.C. (1976) *The Limits of Administration*, London, Wiley

Hooghiemstra, E. (1991) 'Gelijke kansen voor allochtonen op een baan? Wervings- en selectieprocessen op de arbeidsmarkt voor on- en laaggeschoolden', *Migrantenstudies*, 1: 15–23

Hubbuck, J. and Carter, S. (1980) *Half a Chance? A Report on Job Discrimination against Young Blacks in Nottingham*, Commission for Racial Equality, London

Hutton, W. (1995) *The State We're in*, London, Jonathan Cape

I.R.F.E.C.D (1985) *Les discriminations pour l'emploi des femmes étrangères*, Bruxelles, Rapport pour la Commission européenne

ILO (1992) *Discrimination of Migrant Workers in Western Europe*, Geneva, ILO

ISOPLAN (coor.) (1991) 'Immigration of citizens from third countries into the southern member states of the EEC. A Comparative Survey of the Situation in Greece, Italy, Spain and Portugal', *Europe sociale*, Supplement 1, 91

Izquierdo, A. and Muñoz-Pérez, F. (1989) 'L'Espagne, pays d'immigration', *Population*, 2, 257–89

Izquierdo, A. (1992) *La inmigración en España 1980–1990*, Madrid, Ministerio de Trabajo y Seguridad Social

Izquierdo, A. (1994) 'Las encuestas contra la inmigración', in Martín, L., Gómez, C., Arranz, F. and Gabilondo, A. *Hablar y dejar hablar (Sobre racismo y xenofobia)*, Madrid, Ed. Uni. Autónoma de Madrid, 165–76

Jacobsson, B. (1984) *Hur styrs förvaltningen*, Lund, Studentlitteratur

Jacobsson, B. (1989) *Beslut och styrning mellan organisationer*, Sjöblom & Ståhlberg (eds.), Den mångtydiga styrningen

Jenkins, R. (1986) *Racism and Recruitment*, Cambridge, Cambridge University Press

Jenkins, W.I. (1978) *Policy Analysis. A Political and Organizational Perspective*, New York, St. Martin's Press

Jenson, J. and Mahon, R. (1992) 'Representing Solidarity: Class, Gender and the Crisis of Social-Democratic Sweden', Paper prepared for the *Eighth International Conference of Europeanists*, Chicago, IL

Jewson, N., Mason, D., Lambkin, C. and Taylor, F. (1992) *Ethnic Monitoring Policy and Practice: A Study of Employers' Experiences*, London, Department of Employment Research Paper No. 89

Jewson, N., Mason, D., Drewett, A. and Rossiter, W. (1995) *Formal Equal Opportunities Policies and Employment Best Practice*, London, Department for Education and Employment, Research Series No. 69

Jonung, Ch. (1982) *Migrant Women in the Swedish Labour Market*, Stockholm, Commission for Immigration Research

Kartaram, S. (1992) *Final report on legislation against racism and xenophobia in the Netherlands*, Utrecht, Landelijk Bureau Racismebestrijding

Keith, M. (1995) 'Making the Street Visible: Placing Racial Violence in Context', *New Community* 21, 4, October

Kingdon, J. (1984) *Agendas, Alternatives and Public Policies*, Boston, Little, Brown & Co

Kloek, W. (1992) *De positie van allochtonen op de arbeidsmarkt*, Heerlen, Centraal bureau voor de statistiek

Knocke, W. (1983) *Invandrade kvinnor möter facket. Förstudie och projektplan. (Immigrant Women's Encounter with the Trade Unions) Pilot Study and Project Plan*, Stockholm, Arbetslivscentrum (unpublished manuscript)

Knocke, W. (1986) *Invandrade kvinnor i lönearbete och fack. (Immigrant Women in Wage Work and the Unions)*, Stockholm, Arbetslivscentrum

Knocke, W. (1991) 'Immigrant Women – What is the Problem?', *Economic and Industrial Democracy*, 12, 4

Knocke, W. (1994) 'Gender, Ethnicity and Technological Change', *Economic and Industrial Democracy*, 15, 1

Köhler, C. und Preisendörfer, P. (1988) 'Innerbetriebliche Arbeitsmarktsegregation' in Form von Stamm und Randbelegschaften, *MittAB*, 2: 268–77

Kompetensutredningen (1992) 'Invandrare och kompetensutveckling i svenskt arbetsliv' (Immigrants and Skills Development in Swedish Working Life), in Pettersson, Å., Knocke, W. and Marking, Ch. (eds.) *Kompetens i arbete. En Antologi*, Stockholm, Publica

Kremer, M. und Spangenberg, H. unter von Lothar Jäger, M. und Schnitzler, S. (1980) *Assimilation ausländischer Arbeitnehmer in der Bundesrepublik Deutschland. Forschungsbericht*, Königstein/Ts, Peter Hanstein Verlag

Lalive D'Epinay, C. et Garcia, C. (1988) *Le mythe du travail en Suisse, splendeur et déclin au cours du XXème siècle*, Genève, Georg

Lalive D'Epinay, C. et Sue, R. (1987) *Chômage, marginalité et créativité*, Genève, Actes du colloque de Genève, Université de Genève, juin 1986

Lapeyronnie, D. (1993) *L'individu et les minorités. La France et la Grande-Bretagne face à leurs immigrés*, Paris, PUF

Lebon, A. (1986) 'Les jeunes et l'emploi', in Abou Saada, G. et Milet, H., *Générations issues de l'immigration: mémoires et devenirs*, Paris, Ed. Arcantière

Lebon, A. (1993) *Immigration et présence étrangère en France. Le bilan de l'année 1992–1993*, DPM, Ministère des Affaires sociales de la santé et de la ville

Ledrut, R. (1986) *Sociologie du chômage*, Paris, PUF

Lee, G. and Wrench, J. (1980) 'Accident-Prone Immigrants: An Assumption Challenged' *Sociology*, 14, 4

Lee, G. and Wrench. J. (1983) *Skill Seekers – Black Youth, Apprenticeships and Disadvantage*, Leicester, National Youth Bureau

Leiniö, T.-L. (1980) *Städarnas arbetssituation.* (*The Work Situation of Cleaners*), Stockholm, Arbetslivscentrum

Leiniö, T.-L. (1986) 'Köns-och etnisk segregering på den svenska arbetsmark-naden 1980', (Gender and Ethnic Segregation in the Swedish Labour Market 1980), in *Immigrant Women's Situation in Working Life*, Stockholm, JÄMFO and CEIFO

Lindblom, C. (1959) 'The Science of Muddling Through', *Public Administration Review*, 19, 2: 79–88

Lindblom, C. (1979) 'Still Muddling, not yet Through', *Public Administration Review*, 39, 6: 517–26

Lindblom, C. and Cohen, P. (1979) *Usable Knowledge*, New Haven, Yale University Press

Lippincott, R.C. and Stoker, R.P. (1992) 'Policy Design and Implementation Effectiveness: Structural Change in a County Court System', *Policy Studies Journal*, 20, 3: 376–87

Lipsky, M. (1980) *Street-level Bureaucracy*, New York, Russel Sage Foundation

Lochak, D. (1987) 'Réflexions sur la notion de discrimination', *Droit Social*, 11

Lochak, D. (1990) 'Les discriminations frappant les étrangers sont-elles licites?', *Droit Social*, 1

Lochak, D. (1991) 'Conseil National des Populations Immigrées. Groupe 'Egalité des droits': Rapport, *Actualités-Migrations*, 363

Lochak, D. (1992) 'Discrimination against Foreigners under French Law', Horowitz, D.L. and Noiriel, G. (eds.) *Immigrants in two Democracies: the French and American Experience*, New York, University Press

López, B. et al. (1993) *Inmigración magrebí en España. El retorno de los moriscos*, Madrid, MAPFRE

Lowi, A. (1972) 'Four Systems of Policy, Politics and Choice', *Public Administration Review*, 32: 298–310

Lukes, S. (1974) *Power: A Radical View*, London, Macmillan

Lyon-Caen, A. (1990) 'L'Egalité et la loi en droit du travail', *Droit Social*, 1

MacEwen, M. (ed.) (1997) *Anti-Discrimination Law Enforcement: A Comparative Perspective*, Avebury, Aldershot

MacEwen, M. (1995) *Tackling Racism in Europe*, Oxford, Berg

Majone, G. and Wildavsky, A. (1978) 'Implementation as Evolution', *Policy Studies Review Annual*, 103–17

Manço, U. and Manço, A. (1990) *Enquête auprès des jeunes issus de l'immigra-tion sur l'insertion aux structures de formation et au marché du travail*, Liège, Université de Liège, GRESP

Marchand, O. (1991) 'Autant d'actifs étrangers en 1990 qu'en 1980', *Economie et Statistiques*, 242

Marcos, R. and Rojo, J. (1991) 'Trabajadores extranjeros en España', *Revista de economía y sociología del trabajo*, 11, March: 8–17

Marrodán, M.D. et al. (1991) *Mujeres del tercer mundo en España. Modelo migra-torio y caracterización sociodemográfica*, Madrid, Fund, CIPIE

Martens, A. (1976) *Les immigrés. Flux et reflux d'une main-d'oeuvre d'appoint*, Louvain, EVO-PUL

Martens, A. (1990) 'L'insertion des immigrés dans l'emploi', in Bastenier, A. and Dassetto, F. (eds.), *Immigration et nouveaux pluralismes*, Bruxelles, Ed. de Boeck

Martens, A. (1995) *Preventing Racism at the Workplace in Belgium*, Dublin, European Foundation for the Improvement of Living and Working Conditions

Martín, L., Gómez, C., Arranz, F. and Gabilondo, A. (1994) *Hablar y dejar hablar (Sobre racismo y xenofobia)*, Madrid, Ed. Uni. Autónoma de Madrid

Martinelli, D. (1990) 'Le chômage des immigrés en Île-de-France', *Lettre d'information Île-de-France*, 16, June

Martiniello, M. (1993) *Minorités ethniques dans l'espace européen*, Bruxelles, De Boeck

Martiniello, M. (ed.) (1995) *Migration, Citizenship and Ethno-National Identities in the European Union*, Aldershot, Avebury

Mason, D. and Jewson, N. (1992) "Race", Equal Opportunities and Employment Practice: Reflections on the 1980s, Prospects for the 1990s', *New Community*, 19, 1

Maurin, E. (1991) 'Les étrangers: une main-d'oeuvre à part?', *Economie et Statistiques*, 242, April

May, P.J. (1986) 'Politics and Policy Analysis', *Political Science Quarterly*, 101, 1: 109–25

Mayer, D. (1992) 'L'appréhension du racisme par le Code pénal', *Mots*, 33

Meillassoux, C. (1976) *Femmes, greniers et capitaux*, Paris, Ed. Maspero

Micheletti, M. (1988) 'De svenska intresseorganisationerna – i går, i dag och i morgon'. *Statsvetenskaplig tidskrift*, 91, 1

Michon, F. (1987) 'Flexibilité et marché du travail', *Cahiers français*, La Documentation, 232, May/June

Miles, R. (1993) *After Race Relations*, London, Routlege

Mingione, E. (1983) 'Gli immigrati in Italia', *Inchiesta*, 62, October/December

Mingione, E. (1985) 'Gli immigrati in Italia: mercato del lavoro, marginalità e povertà', paper, Messina

Misplon, F. (1993) 'Sociale clausule. Bedenkingen en praktische Voorstellen', *De Morgen*, 2 November

Modood, T., Berthoud, R., Lakey, J., Nazroo, J., Smith, P., Virdee, S. and Beishon, S. (1997) *Ethnic Minorities in Britain: Diversity and Disadvantage*, London, Policy Studies Institute

Morokvasic, M. (1983) 'Women in Migration: Beyond the Reductionist Outlook,' in Phizacklea, A. (ed.) *One-Way Ticket: Migration and Female Labour*, London, Routledge and Kegan Paul

Mottura, G. (1992) 'Forme della presenza extracomunitaria nell'agricoltura italiana. Risultati di una prima esplorazione', *Quaderni di Economia del lavoro*, 143

Mulder, F.E. (red.) (1991) *Positieve Actie; Een kwestie van beleid, Handreiking om de positie van vrouwen en allochtonen in de gemeentelijke organisatie te verbeteren*, Den Haag, VNG-uitgeverij

Nozick, R. (1974) *Anarchy, the State and Utopia*, New York, Basic Books

Nys, M. et Beauchesne, M.N. (1992) *La discrimination des travailleurs étrangers et d'origine étrangère dans l'entreprise*, Courrier Hebdomadaire, CRISP, 1381–2

OECD (1985) *The Integration of Women into the Economy*, Paris, OECD

Office Fédéral de la Statistique (1993) *Recensement fédéral de la population 1990*, 3, Emploi et vie active

Office Fédéral des Etrangers (1993) *Les étrangers en Suisse*, 1 & 3, December

Ouali, N. and Rea, A. (1993) *Les jeunes d'origine étrangère. Contribution à l'étude de l'insertion socio-professionelle de la population bruxelloise*, Bruxelles, Université Libre de Bruxelles, CSER

Owen, D. and Green, A. (1992) 'Labour Market Experience and Change among Ethnic Groups in Great Britain', *New Community* 19, 1

Paulson, S. (1991) *Utvecklingsbehov för framtidens arbetskraft. En studie om invandrare på Göteborgs arbetsmarknad*, Göteborg, Göteborgs Näringslivssekrateriat

Paulson, S. (1994) 'Långtidssjukfrånvaro och arbetsmiljö' (Long-term Sick Leave and the Working Environment), in Schierup, C.U. and Paulson, S. (eds) *Arbetets etniska delning. Studier från en svensk bilfabrik*, Stockholm, Carlssons

Penninx, R. and Roosblad, J. (eds) (forthcoming) *Trade Unions, Immigration and Immigrants in Europe 1960–1993*, Berg, Oxford

Phizacklea, A. (ed.) (1983) *One Way Ticket. Migration and Female Labour*, London, Routledge and Kegan Paul

Poglia, F. (1993) 'Il concetto di immigrato: referente di identità e sfida sociale', in Di Nicola, G. and Py, B., *Alterità al quotidiano, migrazioni Abruzzo-Neuchâtel*, Teramo, Collana del Dipartimento di Teoria dei Sistemi e delle Organizzazioni, Università Gabriele d'Annunzio

Poglia, F. (forthcoming), 'Le concept d'immigré: référent identitaire et enjeu social, perception des notions d'immigré et d'immigré de deuxième génération par une population immigrante', in Di Nicola, G. and Py, B., *Altérité au quotidien – Migrations Abruzzes-Neuchâtel*, Lausanne, L'Age d'Homme

Premfors, R. (1989) *Policyanalys*, Lund, Studentlitteratur

Pugliese, E. (1985) 'Quale lavoro per gli stranieri in Italia', *Politica economica*, September

Pugliese, E. (1990) 'Gli immigrati nel mercato del lavoro', *Polis*, IV, 1 April

Pugliese, E. (1993) *La sociologia della disoccupazione*, Bologne, Il Mulino

Pugliese, E. (1995) *Gli immigrati extra-comunitari in Campania. Inserimento lavorativo ed entità delle presenze regolari ed irregolari*, Rapporto intermedio di ricerca, Naples, Università degli Studi di Napoli, Department of Sociology of Work

Pugliese, E. and Macioti, M.I. (1990) *Gli immigrati stranieri in Italia*, Bari, laterza

Rath, J. (1993) 'La construction des minorités ethniques aux Pays-Bas et ses effets pervers', in Martiniello, M. (ed.), *Minorités ethniques dans l'espace européen*, Bruxelles, De Boeck

Räthzel, N. (1995) *Preventing Racism at the Workplace in Germany*, Dublin, European Foundation for the Improvement of Living and Working Conditions

Räthzel, N. and Sarica, Ü. (1994) *Migration und Diskriminierung in der Arbeit. Das Beispiel Hamburg*, Hamburg-Berlin, Argument-Verlag

Ray, J.E. (1990) 'L'égalité et la décision patronale', *Droit Social*, 1

Rea, A. (1995) 'Social Citizenship and Ethnic Minorities in the European Union', in Martiniello, M. (ed.), *Migration, Citizenship and Ethno-National Identities in the European Union*, Aldershot, Avebury

Recio, A. (1988) *Capitalismo y formas de contratación laboral*, Madrid, Ministerio de Trabajo y Seguridad Social

Recio, A. (1991) 'La segmentación del mercado de trabajo en España', in F. Miguelez and C. Prieto, (eds.) *Las relaciones laborales en España*, Madrid, XXI: 96–115

Rex, J. and Moore, R. (1967) *Race, Community and Conflict*, Oxford, Oxford University Press

Roberts, K., Connolly M. and Parsell, G. (1992) 'Black Youth in the Liverpool Labour Market', *New Community* 18, 2

Rodgers, G. and Rodgers, J. (1989) *El mercado precario en la regulación del mercado laboral. Crecimiento del empleo atípico en europa Occidental*, Madrid, Ministerio de Trabajo y Seguridad Social

Roelandt, Th. J.A. (1994) *Verscheidenheid in ongelijkheid, Een studie naar etnische stratificatie in de Nederlandse samenleving*, Amsterdam, Thesis Publishers

Roelandt, Th., Roijen, J.H.M. and Veenman, J. (1992) *Statistisch Vademecum 1992*, SDU uitgeverij, The Hague

Rosvelds, S., Martens, A., Ben abdeljelil, Y. and Arryn, P. (1993) *Zelfde zweet, ander brood. Onderzoek naar de arbeidsmarktpositie van Belgen en migranten op twee lokale arbeidsmarkten: Antwerpen en Gent*, Brussels, Diensten voor Programmatie van het Wetenschapsbeleid

Rothstein, B. (ed.) (1991) *Politik som organisation*, Stockholm, SNS Förlag

Rubery, J. and Fagan, C. (1993) *Occupational Segregation of Women and Men in the European Community*, Synthesis report, Social Europe, Supplement 3

Sales, R. and Gregory, J. (1995) *Employment, Citizenship and European Integration: the Implications for Migrant and Refugee Women*, paper presented at the Annual Conference of the British Sociological Association

Salt, J. (1992) *Current and Future International Migration Trends Affecting Europe*, Strasbourg, Council of Europe, Report to the Council of Europe, Fifth Conference of Ministers Responsible for Immigration Affairs in Athens

Santos, L. (1993) *De nuevo sobre el trabajador extranjero y la regularización de 1991*, Itínera Cuadernos No. 5, Barcelona, Fund. Torras Domènech

Sassen, S. (1996) *Transnational Economies and National Immigration Policies*, Amsterdam, IMES, University of Amsterdam

Sayad, A. (1991) *L'immigration ou les paradoxes de l'altérité*, Bruxelles, De Boeck

Schaub, G. (1993) *Rekrutierungsstrategien und Selektionsmechanismen für die Ausbildung und die Beschäftigung junger Ausländer*, Berlin, BIBB

Schierup, C.U. and Paulson, S. (eds.) (1994) *Arbetets etniska delning. Studier från en svensk bilfabrik*, Stockholm, Carlssons

Schierup, C.U. et al. (1994) 'Den interna arbetsmarknaden. Etniska skiktningar och dekvalificering' (The Internal Labour Market. Ethnic Stratification and dequalification), in Schierup, C.U. and Paulson, S. (eds.) *Arbetets etniska delning. Studier från en svensk bilfabrik*, Stockholm, Carlssons

Schnapper, D. (1981) *L'épreuve du chômage*, Paris, Gallimard

Seifert, W. (1994) 'Berufliche und ökonomische Mobilität ausländischer Arbeitnehmer – Längsschnittanalysen mit dem Sozio-Ökonomischen Panel', in Werner, H. and Wolfgang S., *Die Integration ausländischer Arbeitnehmer in den Arbeitsmarkt. Beiträge zur Arbeitsmarktforschung*, Nürnberg, Institut für Arbeitsmarktforschung der Bundesanstalt für Arbeit

Sengenberger, W. (1988) 'Dinámica de la segmantación del mercado de trabajo', in Sengenberger, W. (ed.), *Lecturas sobre el mercado de trabajo en la república federal de Alemania (I). Mercado de trabajo, ocupación y desempleo*, Madrid, Ministerio de Trabajo y Seguridad Social

Similä, M. (1992) *Det kommunala flyktingmottagandet. Konflikter och roller*, Stockholm, universitet Stockholm, CEIFO

Simon, P. (1993) 'Nommer pour agir', *Le Monde*, 28, 4
Simpson, A. and Stevenson, J. (1994) *Half a Chance, Still?* Nottingham, Nottingham and District Racial Equality Council
SIV (1992) *Kvinna och invandrare. Rapport om invandrade kvinnors ställning i det svenska samhället med förslag till åtgärder* (Women and Immigrants. A Report on the status of immigrant women in Swedish Society with Recommended measures), Norrköping
Sjöblom, S. and Ståhlberg, K. (eds.) (1989) *Den mångtydiga styrningen*, Åbo Akademins förlag
Smith D.J. (1977) *Racial Disadvantage in Britain: the PEP report*. Harmondsworth, Penguin
Soininen, M. (1992) *Det kommunala flyktingmottagandet: Genomförande och organisation*, Stockholm, universitet Stockholm, CEIFO
Soininen, M. and Graham, M. (1995) *Persuasion contra Legislation: Preventing Racism at the Workplace*, Dublin, European Foundation for Improvement of Living and Working Conditions
Soininen, M. and Graham, M. (1997) *Case Studies of Good Practice for the Prevention of Racial Discrimination and Xenophobia and the Promotion of Equal Treatment in the Workplace – Sweden*, Dublin, European Foundation for the Improvement of Living and Working Conditions
Solomos, J. (1993) 'Races, politiques et société dans la Grande-Bretagne contemporaine', in Martiniello, M. *Minorités ethniques dans l'espace européen*, Bruxelles, De Boeck
SOU (1979) *Kvinnors arbete. En rapport från Jämställdhetskommittén.* (Women's Work. A Report from the Commission on Equality), Stockholm, Ministry of Labour
SOU (1981) *Svenskundervisning för vuxna invandrare. Kartläggning av nuläget.* (Swedish Language Training for Adult Immigrants. An Overview of the Current Position), Stockholm, Ministry of Labour
SOU (1981) *Svenskundervisning för vuxna invandrare. Överväganden och förslag.* (Swedish Language Training for Adult Immigrants. Deliberations and Recommendations), Stockholm, Ministry of Labour
SOU (1989) *Invandrare i Storstad.* (Immigrants in the Big City), Stockholm, Statsrådsberedningen
Statistics Sweden (1977) *Invandrarnas levnadsförhållanden 1975.* (The Living Conditions of Immigrants 1975), Stockholm, rapport 9
Statistics Sweden (1984) *Tema Invandrare. Levnadsförhållanden* (Theme Immigrants. Living Conditions), Stockholm, Örebro, rapport 38
Statistics Sweden (1991) *Tema Invandrare. Levnadsförhållanden* (Theme Immigrants. Living Conditions), Stockholm, rapport 69
Stoker, R.P. (1989) 'A Regime Framework for Implementation Analysis: Cooperation and Reconciliation of Federalist Imperatives', *Policy Studies Review*, 9, 1: 29–49
Sv. Metallindustriarbetareförbundet (1989) *Solidarisk Arbetspolitik för det Goda Arbetet.* (A Solidaristic Labour Policy for Good Jobs), Stockholm, Congress 1989
Thala, L. (1989) *Le salariat immigré dans la crise*, Paris, Editions du CNRS
The Swedish National Insurance Audit Office (1992) *Att värdera utländsk kompetens – ett regeringsuppdrag.* (Evaluating Foreign Qualifications – a Government Commissioned Study), Stockholm

The Swedish National Insurance Audit Office (1992) *Utländsk kompetens – ett resurstillskott till arbetsmarknaden.* (Foreign Qualifications – an Additional Resource in the Labour Market), Stockholm

The Swedish National Insurance Office (1990) *Den med sjukpenning ersatta frånvaron år 1988 efter medborgarskap.* (Absenteeism Qualifying for Sickness Benefit in 1988 by Citizenship), Stockholm, The Swedish National Audit Bureau – Analysis Department

Toksöz, G. (1990) 'Arbeitsbedingungn und betriebliche Interessenvertretung der Arbeiterinnen aus der Türkei in der Bundesrepublik Deutschland', in Fijalkowski, J. (ed.) *Transnationale Migranten in der Arbeitswelt*, Bonn

Tribalat, M. (1989) 'Immigrés, étrangers, Français: l'imbroglio statistique', *Population et Société*, 241

Tribalat, M. (ed.) (1991) *Cent ans d'immigration. Etrangers d'hier, Français d'aujourd'hui*, Paris, PUF-INED, Travaux et Documents No. 131

Tribalat, M. and Simon, P. (1993) 'Présentation de l'enquête 'mobilité géographique et insertion sociale', *Population*, 1, February

Tripier, M. (1972) 'Concurrence et différence, les problèmes posés au syndicalisme ouvrier par les travailleurs immigrés', *Sociologie du travail*, 3

Tripier, M. (1990) *L'immigration dans la classe ouvrière en France*, Paris, CIEMI-L'Harmattan

Tunevall, C.M. (1993) *AMVs medverkan i det samordnade flyktingmottagandet*, Stockholm, Lägesrapport, AMV

Uyl, R. den, Choenni Ch. and Bovenkerk, F. (1986) *Mag het ook een buitenlander wezen?*, Utrecht, LBR-reeks 2

Van de Ven, A. (1983) 'Three R's of Administrative Behavior. Rational, Random and Reasonable', in Hall R.H. and Quinn R.E. (eds), *Organizational Theory and Public Policy*, London, Sage

Van Roost and Buyse, (1992) *Les Immigrés et l'Emploi. L'intégration des immigrés par la valorisation du potentiel économique des forces de travail étrangères dans la région de Bruxelles-Capitale*, Brussels, Mens & Ruimte

Vanhoren, I. and Bracke, S. (1992) *Entrepreneuriat ethnique dans la région Bruxelles-Capitale*, Leuven, HIVA

Veenman, J. (ed.) (1990) *Ver van huis: achterstand en achterstelling bij allochtonen*, Groningen, Wolters-Noordhoff

Villa, P. (1990) *La estructuración de los mercados de trabajo. La siderurgia y la construcción en Italia*, Madrid, Ministerio de Trabajo y Seguridad Social

Virdee, S. (1997) *Cases of Good Practice for the Prevention of Racial Discrimination and Xenophobia and the Promotion of Equal Treatment in the Workplace: The UK*, Working Paper WP/97/48/EN, Dublin, European Foundation for the Improvement of Living and Working Conditions

Wadensjö, E. (1992) *Earnings of Immigrants with Higher Education in Sweden*, Paper presented to the Fourth EALE Conference in Warwick, England

Webb, B. and Webb, S. (1987) *Industrial Democracy*, New York, Longmans, Green and Co.

Wihtol de Wenden, C. and Tanguy, A. (1995) *L'Europe et toutes ses migrations*, Bruxelles, Ed. Complexes

Wrench, J. (1990) 'New Vocationalism, Old Racism and the Careers Service', *New Community* 16, 3

Wrench, J. (1995) 'Racism and the Labour Market in Post-War Britain: The "Second Generation" and the Continuance of Discrimination', in M. van den Linden and J. Lucassen (eds.) *Racism and the Labour Market: Historical Studies*, Bern, Peter Lang

Wrench, J. (1996) *Preventing Racism at the Workplace: A Report on 16 European Countries*, Dublin, European Foundation for the Improvement of Living and Working Conditions

Wrench, J. (1997) *Trade Unions, Migrants and Ethnic Minorities in the European Union: National Differences and Common Dilemmas*, Esbjerg, Migration Papers No. 20, South Jutland University Centre

Wrench, J. and Solomos, J. (1993) 'The Politics and Processes of Racial Discrimination in Britain', in Wrench, J. and Solomos, J. (eds.) *Racism and Migration in Western Europe*, Oxford, Berg

Wrench, J. and Taylor, P. (1993) *A Research Manual on the Evaluation of Anti-Discrimination Training Activities*, Geneva, ILO

Wrench, J., Brah, H. and Martin, P. (1993) *Invisible Minorities: Racism in New Towns and New Contexts*, Monographs in Ethnic Relations No. 6, University of Warwick

Wrench, J. and Hassan, E. (1996) *Ambition and Marginalisation: A Qualitative Study of Under-achieving Young Men of Afro-Caribbean Origin*, London, Research Studies RS31, Department for Education and Employment

Wrench, J. and Qureshi, T. (1996) *Higher Horizons: A Qualitative Study of Young Men of Bangladeshi Origin*, Research Studies RS30, London, Department for Education and Employment

Yamgnane, K. (1992) *Droits, Devoirs et Crocodile*, Paris, Ed. Robert Laffont

Younis, T. (ed.) (1990) *Implementation in Public Policy*, Worcester, Billings & Sons

Zander, E. and Höglund, S. (1992) *Tomtebodaundersökningen. Anledningar till sjukfrånvaro bland den underställda personalen vid Tomteboda, Mariehäll, Kista och Täby.* (The Tomteboda investigation. Causes of Sick Leave Among Subordinate Staff at Tomteboda, Mariehäll, Kista and Täby) Umeå., Dept. of Sociology, Stockholm, The National Post Administration

Zegers de Beijl, R. (1990) 'Discrimination of Migrant Workers in Western Europe', Working Paper, *International Migration for Employment*, Geneva, ILO

Zegers de Beijl, R. (1991) *Although Equal before the Law ... The Scope of anti-Discrimination Legislation and its Effects on Labour Market Discrimination against Migrant Workers in the United Kingdom, the Netherlands and Sweden*, Geneva, ILO

Zegers de Beijl, R. (1995) 'Labour Market Integration and Legislative Measures to Combat Discrimination against Migrant Workers', in Böhning, W.R. and Zegers de Beijl, R. *The Integration of Migrant Workers in the Labour Market: Policies and their Impact*, Geneva, ILO.

Subject Index

acceptability, criteria in recruitment, 15
affirmative action, 231
Africa, immigrants from, 1
Afro-Caribbeans, in UK, 61, 62, 64
Algerians
 in Belgium, 30
 in France, 77
anti-discrimination legislation, 12, 13, 245
 France, 79–80, 89
 Netherlands, 94
 Sweden, 208, 210
 Switzerland, 134
 UK, 59
anti-discrimination measures, 229ff
Asia, immigrants from, 1
assimilation, 242
 France, 73
 Switzerland, 142
asylum-seekers, 1, 6, 13
 in Netherlands, 96
 in Switzerland, 134
au pairs 6

Bangladeshis, in UK, 60–1, 65–6
Belgium, 4, 21ff
 access to first job, 31
 CPAS, 24
 feminisation of immigrant labour force,
  28
 minimex, 24
 Royal Commission on Immigration
  Policy, 24, 27
 social security benefits, 24
 urban riots, 33
blaming the victim, 236–7
brain drain, 16

census data, 243
citizenship, see naturalisation
colour-blindness, 235–6
Combating Social Exclusion Conference, 16
communication skills, 15; see also
 language, problems of acquisition
contract work, 14
cultural awareness training, 12
cultural integration
 Belgium, 33
 France, 73
 Switzerland, 132

denial of racism, 234
Denmark, 3, 23, 236
discrimination, 4, 21
 Belgium, 33
 France, 80–1
 Germany, 46ff
 Netherlands, 93–4, 99–107
 Sweden, 208
 Switzerland, 135
 UK, 58
 see also xenophobia
discrimination testing, 9–10
 UK, 55, 56–7
Dublin Convention, 16
Dutch Antilles migrants, in Netherlands, 95

East European migrants, in Sweden, 110
economic restructuring, 1, 8, 14
 Belgium, 22
 France, 75–6
 Spain, 178
 UK, 55
EFILWC, 233
egalitarianism, 234
employers' policies, 231–3
employment rights, 2, 14
endemic racism, 237–8
equal conditions, 220
equal opportunities, 4, 5, 223–5, 229–31
 business case for, 247–9
 differences in meaning, 240–2
 policies, 11–14
 resistance to, 233–40
equality, principle of, 73, 221–4
ethno-stratification
 Belgium, 26, 31
EU member states
 accession of Spain, 175
 as immigration countries, 1
 immigrants from, 28, 31, 73, 96
 migratory flows into, 15
EU migration control policies, 16
European identity, 4
European Monitoring Centre on Racism and
 Xenophobia, 17–18
exclusion, 5, 10
 differential, 242
executive/skilled immigrants
 in Belgium, 24

executive/skilled immigrants – *continued*
in Germany, 42
exploitation, 13, 220

family reunions, as reason for migration, 2, 6
France, 79
Netherlands, 96
Spain, 183
Sweden, 116
Finnish migrants, in Sweden, 110, 112, 116, 121
Fortress Europe, 16
France, 4, 21, 28, 72ff, 234, 237, 240, 245
collective and social rights, 81–3
Conciliation Boards, 82
cultural distance/proximity, 78
DOM-TOM immigrants, 74
exclusion from employment categories, 80
French by acquisition, 73, 75
illegal discrimination, 80–1
job refusals, 81
RAP, 81
Nationality Code, 74
native French, 75
racial categories, 72
short-term visas, 79
socio-national integration, 73
solidarity allowances, 83
territoriality principle, 83
wage discrimination, 81

gender discrimination, Belgium, 32, 33
gender equality, Sweden, 111
gender subordination, 11
Germany, 3, 35ff, 234–5, 237, 238, 239–40
aliens law, 37
Ausländer, 37
biculturalism, 47
bilingualism, 47
Constitution, 35
disadvantage, 45
East/West migration, 35
ethnic Germans, 36
Federal Office of Statistics, 38
guestworkers, 36
metal industry, 40
National Employment Bureau, 38, 39
nationality by descent, 35
nationality, criteria for, 35
globalisation, 17, 224
Greece, 3, 42
Greeks, in Sweden, 114

illegal labour market/workers, 4, 6–7, 244
France, 79
Spain, 179, 186–8
indirect discrimination, 10
Belgium, 33
UK, 58, 70
Indonesians, in Netherlands, 95
informal economy, 14
Italy, 157
integration
Belgium, 25, 30
Germany, 44
Sweden, 195, 204
Switzerland, 142
intercultural competence, 17
International Convention on the Elimination of all Forms of Racial Discrimination, 8
International Labour Organisation, 9, 209
invisibility, 113, 141
Italians
in Belgium, 30
in Germany, 36
in Switzerland, 132, 135, 139, 142–50
Italy, 3, 7, 42, 13, 155ff
immigrant legislation, 155
indigenous workers, 158
seasonal work, 158ff
labour flexibility, 159–61
commuting, 162
agricultural sector, 164
construction sector, 164
Martelli Law, 169
seasonal labour, requirements of, 165–6
seasonal work, regulation of, 169–71

'Joint Declaration on the Prevention of Racial Discrimination and Xenophobia …' (EU), 17

labour flexibility, 14
labour market
analysis, 21
Belgian, 22
deregulation, 13
exclusion, 5
segmentation
in Germany, 44–5
in Spain, 176–9
in Sweden, 195, 197, 198, 205, 206, 210
labour mobility, 162
labour supply, 220
language, problems of acquisition, 8
France, 78
UK, 61

language policies
  Netherlands, 98
  Sweden, 110, 121, 128–9
legal status, 243–4

Maastricht Treaty, 16
manual/unskilled work
  in Belgium, 24, 27–8
  in France, 77
  in Germany, 39
  temporary, 1
mass immigration to Europe, 95
migration flows, 1
migration policies, 15
  Belgium, 24, 27
minorities, terminology to describe, 3
Moroccans
  in Belgium, 24, 30, 33
  in France, 77
  in Germany, 36
  in Netherlands, 96, 97, 100–3
motivation, 15
multi-skilling, 15
multiculturalism, 239–40
  Sweden, 111
  UK, 60
multilingualism, 17

naming and labelling, 110
national migration policies, 1
naturalisation
  Belgium, 22, 33
  France, 75
  Germany, 37
  restrictions on, 8
  Sweden, 110, 116
  Switzerland, 134, 135
  Netherlands, 3, 93ff, 231, 241
    Dutch Constitution, 93
    Equal Treatment Act, 94
    National Bureau for Combating Racism, 94
    Promotion of Proportional Labour Participation of Immigrants Act, 98
    STAR agreement, 98
    work discrimination, 93–4, 99–107
new migration, 6

occupational mobility, Belgium, 30
outsiders, 4

Pakistanis, in UK, 55
pendulum migration, from Central Europe, 1
pluralism, 242

Polish migrants, in Sweden, 115, 117
Portugal, 3
Portuguese
  in Belgium, 30
  in Germany, 36
  in Switzerland, 132, 136, 139, 142–50
postwar migration, 1
poverty, 6
  UK, 61
'Preventing Racism in the Workplace in the European Union', 233

qualifications and employment
  Belgium, 31–2
  Sweden, 207, 208
  UK, 57, 61

race, as social construction, 3–4
racial discrimination, 2
  definition, 8
  evidence of, 8–9
racism, euphemisation of, 88
recruitment procedures and practices, 10
  Belgium, 22–3
  France, 76, 86–7
  Germany, 39–41, 44
  Netherlands, 93–4, 98
  Spain, 181–3
  Sweden, 205–6
  UK, 57, 58, 59, 64–5
  see also sectoral stratification; qualifications; seasonal work; short-term/temporary contracts; unemployment
refugee care, 195ff
  reform, 203–4
refugees, 1, 6–7
  Netherlands, 96
  Sweden, 195ff
  refugee flows, 196
regularisation, 175, 182
reliability, 15
residence permits, 23
  Italy, 163, 171
  Spain, 180–1

Scandinavia, 3
Schengen Agreements, 16
seasonal work, 6, 155ff
  regulation of, 171
seasonal, workers, 2
second-generation migrants, 1, 2, 5
  Belgium, 26
  France, 74

second-generation migrants – *continued*
　Germany, 43
　Netherlands, 95
　Switzerland, 139–42
　UK, 56
sectoral concentration/stratification
　Germany, 39–41
　Spain, 189–90
　Sweden, 120
　UK, 55, 65
sécuritaire logic, 1
segmentation theory, 45
self-employment
　Belgium, 23
　France, 76
　Germany, 44
short-term/temporary contracts
　Germany, 48
　Spain 185
　see also Italy, seasonal work
situation testing, Netherlands data, 93, 99–100
social citizenship, 1
social competence, 15
social exclusion, 16
　Sweden, 207
social integration
　Belgium, 24
　France, 73
　Spain, 185
social mobility
　Belgium, 28–9
　France, 74
Southern Europe, 13
Spain, 3, 7, 13, 174ff
　black economy, 179
　emigration, 174
　Immigration Law, 175, 180
　immigration policies, 179–83
　Latin American immigrants in, 175
　North African immigrants in, 175
　precarious immigrants, 186
　settled immigrants, 184–5
Spanish
　in Belgium, 28
　in Germany, 36
　in Switzerland, 132, 139, 142–50
stereotyping, 58, 127–8
subcontracting, 14
Surinamese, in Netherlands, 97, 103
sweatshops, 14
Sweden, 3, 108ff, 19ff, 231–2, 245
　'Local Care of Refugees', 197, 198
　National Immigration Board, 197, 199, 200–1

National Labour Market Board, 197, 198, 205, 206
　Office of the Discrimination Ombudsman, 208–9
Switzerland, 132ff
　French-speaking cantons, 133
　German-speaking cantons, 133
　immigration sphere, 145–8
　national identity, 133
　referendums, 133–4
　spheres of insertion, 143

team working, 15
temporary labour migration, 6
terminology, 3, 21
trade unions, 17, 219ff
　France, 88
　Germany, 50, 52
　Sweden, 119
training in the workplace, Sweden, 124–8, 205–6
Treaty of Amsterdam, 16, 17
Treaty of Rome, 22
Tunisians
　in Belgium, 24
　in France, 77
　in Germany, 36
Turks, 3
　in Belgium, 27
　in Germany, 36, 37, 42, 44
　in Netherlands, 97
　in Sweden, 115, 119

UK 3, 12, 54ff, 232, 236–7, 241, 244
　Commission for Racial Equality, 55 57, 59
　National Survey of Ethnic Minorities, 60
　Policy Studies Institute, 60
　postwar migrants, 54
　protective channelling, 59
　Race Relations Act, 59
　racialisation of areas, 67–8
　school experiences, 61–3
　Social and Community Planning
　　Research, 60
　Youth Cohort Study, 68
underclass, 5–6
　Belgium, 26
underqualification, 26, 31; *see also*
　qualifications and employment
undocumented workers, 2, 13; *see also*
　illegal labour market
unemployment of immigrants, 5
　in Belgium, 22, 33
　in France, 76, 77

unemployment of immigrants – *continued*
  in Germany, 38, 44
  in Italy, 156, 163
  long-term, 14
  in Netherlands, 97, 99
  in Spain, 178–9
  in Sweden, 196, 206, 207
  in Switzerland,132
  in UK, 54, 55
upward mobility
  France, 76
  Germany, 42, 43
  Switzerland, 140

verbal racism
  France, 87
  Germany, 50–1
vocational mobility/training, Belgium 29
voluntarism, 246–7

welfare states, European, 6
women, marginality of, 109
women migrants, 11, 108ff
  in Germany, 40, 44
  invisibility of, 109

Swedish case-study, 105ff
work as identity reference, 144–5
work permits
  Belgium, 22–3, 24
  France, 80
  Spain, 181–3
worker organisation, 220
workers' rights, limitations on, 1
working conditions, 222, 225
workplace racism
  France, 80–1, 83–7
  Germany, 46
  UK, 64

xenophobia, 17, 219
  Switzerland, 135

young migrants
  in Belgium, 21ff
  Switzerland, 132ff
  UK, 54ff
Yugoslavia, 1
Yugoslavs
  in Sweden, 110, 114, 116–17, 121
  in Switzerland, 135

Name Index

Abou Saada, G., 30
Ålund, A., 109, 110, 111
Alvaraz, F., 187
Anderson, B., 4
Andersson, L., 207
Angel de Prada, M., 9
Aragón, R., 188
Atkin, K., 214

Bachrach, P., 213
Bäck, H., 205, 206, 208, 213
Baker, D., 47, 235
Banton, M., 8, 10, 246
Baratz, M., 213
Bardet-Blochet, A., 139
Barrett, S., 201
Bastenier, A., 26
Beauchesne, M.N., 22
Berghuys, R.E., 99
Biegel, C., 99
Bigo, D., 1
Biller, M., 46
Blocher, C., 133
Bolzmann, C., 140, 144
Booth, T., 206
Borges, G.C., 10
Borkowski, J.L., 74
Bourdieu, P., 29
Bouvier, P., 86
Bouw, C., 99
Bovenkerk, F., 9, 93, 94, 231
Boyd, M., 108
Bracke, S., 25
Brassé, P., 99
Brettell, C., 108
Breunig-Van Leeuwen, E., 93, 94
Bridges, L., 63
Brochmann, G., 196
Burstein, P., 9
Buyse, 233
Büyükbozkoyum, O., 100, 104, 105

Cachón, L., 179
Calvanese, F., 157, 166
Calvaruso, F., 187
Carchedi, F., 157, 166
Carlos, M.L.P., 10
Carter, S., 56
Castles, S., 3, 242

Centlivres, P., 135
Centlivres-Demont, M., 35
Chiapparugi, M., 157
Chozas, J., 188
Connolly, M., 68
Cornioley, C., 137
Costa-Lascoux, J., 33
Crenson, M., 213
Cross, M., 58
Czarniawska-Joerges, B., 212

Dassetto, F., 26
de Certeau, M., 142
De Rham, G., 144
De Rudder, V., 234, 237
De Smedt, J., 225
de Troy, C., 109
Delarue, R., 225
Delors, J., 16–17
Den Uyl, R., 99
Drew, D., 54, 55
Dubar, C., 140, 143
Dummett, A., 246

Ekberg, J., 207
Ekholm, E., 10
Ekmann-Saillant, M., 144
Esmail, A., 56
Essed, Ph., 99, 111, 112
Everington, S., 56
Ezorsky, G., 247

Fagan, C., 222
Fibbi, R., 140
Fijalkowski, J., 40, 45
Fix, M., 100
Fleischer, H., 37
Flückiger, Y., 135
Forbes, I., 12, 229, 241
Freyssinet, J., 158
Fudge, C., 201

Garcia, C., 140, 144
Gillmeister, H., 45, 46
Giraud, M., 86
Goldberg, A., 9
Gould, M., 248
Graham, M., 9, 15, 209, 213, 232
Gras, M., 231

Green, A., 55
Gregory, R., 13, 204, 205
Grell, P., 144
Grillo, R.D., 213
Groenendijk, K., 6
Gunn, L., 200

Haavio-Mannila, E., 115
Hagendoorn, L., 96
Hall, R.H., 60, 197
Ham, C., 200
Hammar, T., 196
Hampsink, R., 6
Hanf, K., 211
Hannerz, U., 111, 112
Harzig., C., 36
Hassan, E., 59
Haugg, S., 236, 237
Heath, A., 71
Heisler, B.S., 6
Hessel, S., 75
Hill, M., 200
Hjarnø, J., 10, 236, 237, 238
Höglund, S., 127
Hood, C.C., 200
Hooghiemstra, E., 99
Hraba, J., 96
Hubbuck, J., 56
Hutton, W., 14

Jacobsson, B., 201
Jenkins, R., 213, 214
Jenkins, W.I., 235
Jensen, T., 10
Jenson, J., 109
Jewson, N., 249
Jonung., Ch., 115

Kartaram, S., 99
Keith, M., 61
Kingdon, J., 198
Kloek, W., 99
Knocke, W., 108, 109, 110, 113, 114, 115,
    119, 122, 123, 126, 128, 129, 130
Köhler, C., 40, 45
Kremer, M., 46
Kurthen, H., 45

Lalive d'Epinay, C., 144
Lapeyronnie, D., 140, 142
Lebon, A., 28
Ledrut, R., 137
Lee, G., 57, 235, 237
Leiniö, T.-L., 121, 128

Lenhardt, G., 47, 235
Lindblom, C., 204
Lippincott, R.C., 204
Lipsky, M., 202
Lochak, D., 83, 88
Lowi, A., 209
Lukes, S., 214
Lyon-Caen, A., 86

MacEwen, M., 12, 229, 240, 241
Macioti, M.I., 158
Mahon, R., 71, 109
Majone, G., 200
Manco, A., 26
Manco, U., 26
Marchand, O., 77
Marie, C.V., 86
Marrodán, M.D., 189
Martens, A., 22, 25, 26, 232, 236
Maurin, E., 78
May, P., 209
Mead, G., 12, 229, 241
Micheletti, M., 212
Michon, F., 160
Miles, R., 4
Mingione, E., 156
Misplon, F., 225
Modood, T., 60, 69, 70, 71
Morokvasic, M., 108
Mottura, G., 161
Mulder, F.E., 231

Nelissen, C., 99
Nozick, R., 246–7
Nys, M., 22

Ouali, N., 30
Owen, D., 55

Parsell, G., 68
Paulson, S., 10, 123, 126, 128, 207
Phizaklea, A., 108, 110, 128
Pitkänen, M., 10
Poglia, F., 149
Preisendörfer, P., 40, 45
Premfors, R., 203
Pugliese, E., 157, 158, 166

Quinn, R.E., 197
Qureshi, T., 59

Ranuzzi, G., 157
Räthzel, N., 3, 235, 236, 238, 239
Rea, A., 7, 30

Ricci, P., 166
Roberts, K., 68
Rodgers, G., 186
Roelandt, Th., 96, 97
Rosvelds, S., 26
Rothstein, B., 210, 212
Rubenstein, M., 248
Rubery, J., 222

Sales, R., 13
Salt, J., 1
Saricca, Ü, 235, 238
Sassen, S., 6
Sayad, A., 148
Scharpf, F., 211
Schaub, G., 10
Schierup, C.U., 111, 126, 128, 207
Seifert, W., 42, 43, 44
Sengenberger, W., 177
Sikking, E., 99
Similä., M., 203
Simon, P., 73, 74, 108
Simpson, A., 56
Soininen, M., 9, 15, 199, 200, 203, 205,
    206, 208, 209, 213, 232
Solomos, J., 57, 133
Spangenberg, H., 46
Stevenson, J., 56

Stoker, R.P., 204
Struyk, R.J., 100

Taylor, P., 238
Thala, L., 159, 160
Toksöz, G., 49
Tribalat, M., 74
Tunevall, C.M., 206

Van Beek, K., 99
Van de Ven, A., 204
van Dijk, T., 234, 235
Van Roost, 233
Vanhoren, I., 25
Veenman, J., 99
Villa, P., 177
Virdee, S., 70

Wadensjö, E., 208
Webb, B., 220
Webb, S., 220
Wildavsky, A., 200
Wrench, J., 3, 57, 58, 59, 229, 232, 235,
    237, 238, 239, 243

Zander, E., 127
Zeger de Beijl, R., 8, 12, 99, 127, 209, 229
Zeroulou, Z., 30